On October 27, a soldier went into the woods to gather logs near a military base ten miles south of Shakhty. He stumbled across the skeletal remains of a woman, covered over with branches. This skeleton also bore the marks of knife wounds, especially to the breasts. Like the one near Shakhty, this skeleton fit none of the missing-persons reports in the files of the local *militsia*, and its identity remained unknown.

And, like the skeleton in Shakhty, and the remains of Lyubov Biryuk in Donskoi, it had traces of knife wounds in its eye sockets.

The skeletons of three females, all found in the woods, all with knife wounds to the eyes, demanded a more energetic response. Early in December, Major Fetisov organized a special work group of ten *syshchiki*, based at headquarters in Rostov, charged with solving the three cases.

Viktor Burakov was the department's best man in fingerprints, ballistics, footprints, and other areas of police science. Kolyesnikov meant to recruit him. . . .

Also by Robert Cullen:

SOVIET SOURCES*
TWILIGHT OF EMPIRE: Inside the Crumbling Soviet Bloc

Published by Ivy Books

THE KILLER DEPARTMENT

Detective Viktor Burakov's
Eight-Year Hunt for the
Most Savage Serial Killer
in Russian History

Robert Cullen

IVY BOOKS • NEW YORK

Ivy Books
Published by Ballantine Books
Copyright © 1993 by Robert Cullen, Webster Stone, and Robert Stone

Library of Congress Catalog Card Number: 92-50776

ISBN 0-8041-1164-2

This edition published by arrangement with Pantheon Books, a division of Random House, Inc.

Manufactured in the United States of America
First Ballantine Books Edition: November 1993

Map by Eric Elias

*To Mary C. Carroll,
with love and gratitude*

Contents

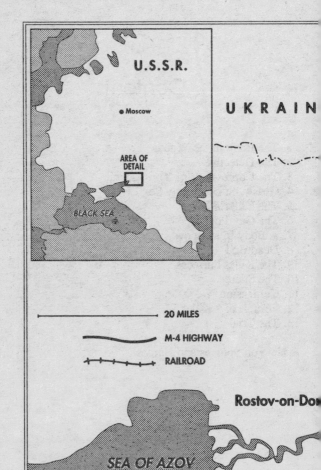

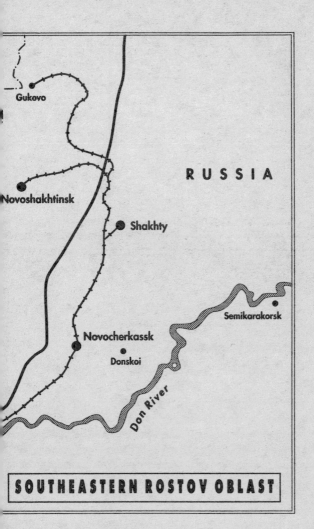

Gukovo

Novoshakhtinsk

Shakhty

RUSSIA

Semikarakorsk

Novocherkassk

Donskoi

Don River

SOUTHEASTERN ROSTOV OBLAST

1

The Body in the Woods

On a sunny Saturday in June 1982, a Russian girl named Lyubov Biryuk left her home in a village called Zaplavskaya to buy cigarettes, bread, and sugar. She did not come back.

Lyubov had just turned thirteen, but she was still a child, short and scrawny. She had light brown hair, cut close and blunt, chubby cheeks, a pug nose, and gray eyes set a little too far apart to be pretty. She was talkative and friendly. One of her uncles thought she was a bit simple, but she got average grades in school. She seemed, in all likelihood, destined to take a place beside her mother among the heavy, tired women who tended the grapes, the cows, the geese, and the pigs at the local sovkhoz, or state-owned farm. She had only one bad habit: though her mother had warned her against it, she liked to hitchhike.

Some of the peasants in the village of Zaplavskaya live in one-story cottages with carved wooden shutters and lintels painted a bright orange or blue, picket fences, tidy vegetable gardens, and perhaps a few plump chickens pecking by the roadside. A few have cars or motorcycles. But Lyubov's family had neither. They lived in a four-family concrete house, owned by the sovkhoz, at the end of a short, dusty path, surrounded by weeds and berry bushes. When Lyubov went on an errand, she walked up the path about seventy-five yards to the paved road, scattering the occasional cluster of sovkhoz geese. There, if she was being obedient to her mother's strictures against hitchhiking, she waited for one of the grimy

1

little buses that occasionally clattered, their sheet-metal panels loose and flapping, down the road to the town of Donskoi.

Donskoi, named for the broad, placid Don River that flows a few miles to the east, has the closest stores to Zaplavskaya. Its population, of about five thousand people, works primarily at the Fiftieth Anniversary of the USSR Electric Power Station, whose triple smokestacks tower over the south end of town. The bus from Zaplavskaya to Donskoi stops at a traffic circle a kilometer or so from the power station, in front of a huge, red billboard with portraits of Marx, Engels, and Lenin. From there, a paved walkway leads to the five-story apartment blocks in the town, past a statue of Lenin and a cultural center with an enormous mural immortalizing the deeds of Soviet soldiers in the Second World War. Opposite the mural stands an unnamed little store that then sold vodka, cheap wine, and cigarettes. Farther down the way, there is a grocery store called the Dawn, which generally displays some canned fish, loaves of bread, a few chickens, and a host of flies caught on a swatch of homemade flypaper. Outside, in the summertime, half a dozen peasant women wearing kerchiefs on their heads usually sit on low stools, their tomatoes and green peppers and carrots spread out on newspapers before them to entice shoppers disappointed with the offerings inside. Donskoi's secondary school is around the corner, behind a weedy soccer field.

When Lyubov's mother, Pelagea, returned from work in the cattle barn that evening and discovered that Lyubov had not come home, she assumed that her daughter had gone to visit relatives, most likely her grandmother in Krivyanka, a village five miles up the road. Pelagea, a stocky woman with a mouth full of gold-crowned teeth, had sisters, brothers, half brothers, aunts, and uncles in many of the neighboring villages. Her own parents had divorced after having two children, and her father had gone on to a second marriage and three more children. She had raised the younger ones. Then she had three children of her own—a girl named Nadezhda, another named Valya, who picked up a germ in a day-care center at the age of five and died, and finally Lyubov. The absence of her youngest child evoked more annoyance than alarm; Lyubov was supposed to let her mother know when she wanted to visit someone. Since Lyubov's grandmother had no telephone, Pelagea would need to make the trip to Krivyanka to confirm her assumption. She decided to wait until morning.

On Sunday, she rode the bus to her mother's cottage. Lyubov was not there. Nor was she with Pelagea's stepmother, nor with her sister, Nadezhda, in Semikarakorsk. Pelagea spent all Sunday fruitlessly calling on relatives. On Monday, increasingly worried, she walked through a driving rain to Lyubov's school, hoping that one of her schoolmates might have seen her. But the children were taking their final examinations, and the principal would not let her talk to them. Finally, on the verge of desperation, she called her half brother Nikolai.

Nikolai Petrov had done well for a peasant boy from Krivyanka. He was a senior lieutenant on the detective squad of the *militsia* in Novocherkassk, the nearest city to Donskoi. In Soviet parlance, the police had always been *militsia,* as if they were just a group of civilians working temporarily until the state withered away. Only bourgeois societies had police. At thirty-one, Nikolai was nine years younger than Pelagea, who had been more a mother than a sister to him. In his youth, he boxed and lifted weights and worked as a construction laborer. He was tough, husky, and handsome, with several distinguishing characteristics. His arms and hands bore a half-dozen tattoos. The knuckles of his right hand bore the letters VALYA, for his wife, and the knuckles of his left had the four suits of cards: spade, heart, diamond, and club. And he had a full, neatly trimmed beard, just starting to turn gray, which he had started to grow a few years earlier, when a skin condition prevented him from shaving. That gave him the nickname by which everyone on the streets and in the bars of Novocherkassk knew him: the Beard.

When he heard that his niece was missing, Petrov got permission to take a *militsia* car and drive the twenty miles to Donskoi to help his sister. Pelagea could tell him very little. Lyubov, she recalled, had been wearing white sandals and a thin, blue summer dress. Her most recent photograph had been taken four years earlier, when the child was nine.

Petrov took the picture and the description of the clothing, and began making the rounds in Donskoi. One of Lyubov's schoolmates, a boy named Yuri Popov, told Petrov he had ridden into Donskoi on the bus with her just after lunchtime on Saturday. They had gotten off in front of the big red billboard and walked together toward the town for about one hundred yards. Then they separated. Popov had gone straight ahead, to see a doctor at the town clinic. Lyubov had turned right, toward the stores. But in the liquor store, where she would have gone to buy the cigarettes, and in the grocery store called the Dawn no one recognized the photograph. It was summer, and a lot of kids were running around, doing errands, flitting in and out of the stores. It was not remarkable that no one remembered seeing Lyubov, particularly since the picture was four years old and she lived not in Donskoi itself but in a village a couple of miles down the road. Petrov learned one more thing. The early-afternoon bus that should have come through Donskoi toward Zaplavskaya had not run that Saturday afternoon. And there the trail ended.

Petrov had his suspicions. They were not pleasant, and he did not share them with his half sister. He imagined that, once Lyubov had learned that the bus was not running, she had decided to ignore Pelagea's warnings and to hitchhike. In Donskoi, on a warm, sunny Saturday in June, a lot of the traffic would be cars from cities like Novocherkassk and Shakhty, passing through on their way to one of the little beaches along the Don. She might have gotten into a car with someone who invited her to go along for a picnic and some swimming. And after that, there was no telling what might have happened to her. The *militsia* focused their search on the roads and fields between Donskoi and the river. They found nothing.

Some two weeks later, on June 27, a middle-aged Donskoi man named S. A. Parukha, looking for fence posts for his garden, walked into a wooded strip between a cornfield and the Zaplavskaya-Donskoi road. Russia has hundreds of thousands of unnamed little woodlands like it, strips left natural by Soviet town and city planners who had decided that, in the workers' state, people should not be jammed together as they had been in the city slums and peasant villages of the old regime. They called such a woodland *lesopolosa*, an amalgamation of the words for forest and strip. But the *lesopolosa*, like so much of the Bolshevik experiment, had not turned out exactly as the planners envisioned it. The strips are everyone's land, and no one's. People use them to dump trash; that summer, there was a big pile of rubbish behind the Marx-Engels-Lenin billboard at the Donskoi bus stop. Even the woodlands without litter are usually untended and scruffy, broken by footpaths worn into the ground by weary Russians plodding from work to store to home. The *lesopolosa* along the Zaplavskaya-Donskoi road is about fifty yards wide and has a dirt path running down its length, like a spine.

Under a tall, spindly oak tree, in the midst of thick green underbrush, Parukha saw bones and flesh beneath a scattered cover of leaves and dirt. Bending over cautiously, he looked more closely. It was the body of a human being, almost completely decomposed, with a hank of black, wet hair hanging from the top of the skull. He left the woods and hurried to the Donskoi *militsia* station, only a quarter of a mile away, and reported what he had found.

The body was naked, on its back, head turned to the left. Its hands were raised to shoulder height, suggesting that the victim had died trying to fend someone off. The knees were splayed about a foot and a half apart. Most of the flesh had already disappeared, but there were patches of dark brown skin on the legs, the skull, and the hands. The length of the hair hanging from the skull and the earring holes in the intact earlobes suggested the victim's sex.

The condition of the corpse left no doubt that this was a murder. Two ribs had been splintered, apparently by a knife, and a closer examination found traces of twenty-two knife wounds, including, most curiously, several serrations on the eye sockets, suggesting that the victim's eyes had been gouged out. The killer's knife had left traces as well in the pelvic area, as if he, or she, had sliced away at the victim's genitals.

The local *militsia* thought immediately of Lyubov Biryuk, and they called Nikolai Petrov in Novocherkassk. He arrived before the body had been moved. For a time, he allowed himself to hope that this was not his sister's child. The hair on the skull was much darker than his niece's, so dark that it looked as if it had been clumsily dyed black. And the process of decomposition had gone so far that it looked, to him, as if the body had been there in the woods for six weeks rather than the two that had passed since Lyubov disappeared.

The Donskoi *militsia* left the remains in place for a few extra hours to allow another visitor, Major Mikhail Fetisov, to inspect the scene. Fetisov had just been named chief of the criminal apprehension section of Rostov oblast. He was, in effect, the chief detective for an area with a population of three million people.

Normally, the discovery of a single body in the woods would not warrant a trip out from *militsia* headquarters in Rostov-on-Don by a person of Fetisov's rank. Murder was an almost daily event in Rostov. Although the statistics were the closely guarded secret of a state that defined crime as an essentially bourgeois phenomenon, the oblast had four hundred or more homicides a year. The chief *syshchik*, or detective, could not take a personal hand in each investigation.

But Fetisov, being new on the job, was making a point of visiting as many local departments as he could, sizing up the men he would be working with and setting an example of diligence. On occasion, he would spend a week at the scene of a murder, sleeping on a table in the local *militsia* headquarters, sharing food and cigarettes with the local *syshchiki*, supervising the first stages of the investigation. Politically, Fetisov hewed to conventional beliefs in discipline and order. But as a law enforcement officer, he was an agent of change, a representative of a generation that could bring a certain professionalism to the *militsia*.

He had no illusions about the abilities of the average Russian *militsioner*. He had been born not far from Donskoi, in the city of Shakhty, the son of a coal miner. (Shakhty means "the mines.") In those days, Nikita Khrushchev had decreed that every Soviet child, no matter how intellectually gifted, should get some practical worker's training, and Fetisov finished high school certified to drive trucks and operate bulldozers. After graduation, he worked for a while in a factory, until the inevitable draft into the Soviet army. Fetisov was stocky, strong, and quick with his hands. He became an army boxer, and won the welterweight championship of the Caucasus military district. One of his army buddies had a sister who worked as a criminal investigator. She would write letters describing the more interesting cases she worked on. Fetisov started to think about becoming a *syshchik*.

When the army discharged him in 1967, Fetisov found that the *militsia* would be delighted to take him on. In the Leonid Brezhnev years, the *militsia* and the Ministry of the Interior, which supervised it, both suffered from a miserable reputation. The minister, Nikolai Shcholokov, was infamously corrupt. When Brezhnev died, in 1982, Shcholokov committed suicide rather than face an investigation into his finances. While Brezhnev had been alive, Shcholokov had enjoyed immunity, in part because he employed Brezhnev's son-in-law, Yuri Churbanov, as his deputy, and Churbanov was also blatantly lining his own pockets. What began at the top extended down through the ranks. Nearly every Russian driver carried a bottle of vodka in his trunk, in case he got stopped for speeding. Handing it over to a traffic *militsioner* beat paying the fine for speeding. People who objected to the high prices charged for produce in the peasant bazaars in the big cities suspected that cartels of Georgian or Azerbaijan "Mafia" were paying off the *militsia* to look the other way when they beat up would-be competitors to maintain their monopoly. The *militsia* pay matched the job's prestige.

As a result, the *militsia* tended to fill its ranks with high-school dropouts from the collective farms. Even Fetisov's own relatives thought that having a *militsioner* in the family would be a step down the social ladder. They felt he would be better off going into the mines.

As a high-school graduate, a boxing champion, and a licensed driver, Fetisov had some leverage with the *militsia* recruiters. He demanded that they take him into the detective ranks immediately, and that he work from the start in civilian clothes. Somewhat grudgingly, the *militsia* agreed.

On a force filled with men of limited education and integrity, Fetisov moved quickly and steadily upward. By 1982 he had been through two academies for advanced training, including the Ministry of the Interior's most prestigious school in Moscow. He had taken courses in economics at a civilian institute in Shakhty so that he could track down white-collar criminals. He had served as chief of a local *militsia* station in Shakhty. He had joined the Party. A spot in the Soviet *nomenklatura* was within his reach, if he succeeded at his new assignment.

To Fetisov, as to Petrov, the corpse looked as if it had been lying there for at least a month. He ordered a check of the missing-persons records to determine whether someone else matching the size and sex of the remains had been reported missing. And he summoned the cadets from the *militsia* training school in Shakhty to the scene to help conduct a thorough search of the area.

The next day, the cadets combing the surrounding under-brush found a white sandal and a yellow bag containing a package of Nasha Marka cigarettes—the brand that Lyubov Biryuk had been instructed to buy. Whatever doubts existed about the identity of the corpse all but vanished. Three days later, the body was officially identified by means of a finger-print taken from a remaining bit of skin and matched with a print taken from a plastic cover on one of Lyubov Biryuk's schoolbooks. The process of decomposition, the medical examiner stated, had probably been accelerated by the heat and heavy rain in Donskoi that June. Not surpris-ingly, the rain had washed away any physical traces the killer might have left. They found no fingerprints, no threads. Nor could they find the girl's dress.

Nikolai Petrov tried to control the rage he felt toward his niece's killer. He was, in fact, known for his short temper; one of his superiors had advised him to stay out of the Biryuk investigation, lest he do something rash. He went to Zaplav-skaya and told Pelagea what had been found. He advised her not to go and see the remains, and she accepted his judg-ment.

The corpse and its location presented Fetisov, Petrov, and the other *syshchiki* with several questions. They could spec-ulate and come up with a reasonable explanation of how the girl had gotten to the scene of her death. It was about ten yards from the path that ran through the wooded strip in the direction of Zaplavskaya, and perhaps five hundred yards from the liquor store, which, judging from the package of cigarettes, she had indeed visited. With the bus not running, she might well have decided to walk the mile and a half back to her village, and been attacked on the way.

But who would attack her, and why? Russian murders gen-erally fell into two categories. Nearly half were committed in fits of rage, most often drunken rage, directed at family members and friends.

In Lyubov's case, as in the murder of any young girl, her father would normally have become an immediate suspect. But she did not know her father, Viktor Maksimovich Biryuk. Around the time of her birth, Viktor Maksimovich had gotten drunk, started to argue with his mother, and stabbed her fifteen times. He was in a prison in Rostov-on-Don, a city forty miles to the south, nearing the end of a fifteen-year sentence.

Pelagea had divorced Lyubov's father and resumed using her maiden name, Petrova. She lived, in 1982, with a man named Nikolai Yeremin, who worked in the sovkhoz warehouse. Lyubov called Yeremin her stepfather. He was the one who smoked Nasha Marka, and he, too, would normally have been a suspect. But he had not left the sovkhoz on the day of her disappearance, and there were witnesses to support his alibi.

Another thirty or forty percent of the murders in Rostov were premeditated; most often, the killer in a premeditated murder dispatched his victim in order to steal something. But the Biryuk murder did not seem to have been premeditated any more than it seemed the work of a relative. The girl had had little money and nothing worth killing her to steal. The fact that the killer left the cigarettes at the scene, in fact, provided one of the few clues about him: he probably did not smoke.

And how had he killed her without being heard or seen? Dozens of people used the path through the woods every day. Even more walked or rode on the paved road, which was about seventy-five yards away, well within earshot. Why had there been no witnesses? Why had the killer been so bold, even reckless? And why were there so many wounds?

Had she been raped? The position of the corpse and the absence of the girl's dress suggested that she had. But any semen that might have confirmed the commission of a rape had washed away in the rains.

The medical examiner's detailed report, a month later, suggested one answer. The decomposition of the body had gone too far to permit a precise identification of the cause of death, but wounds in the skull suggested that the killer had attacked the girl's head from behind with both the blade and the handle of his knife. Most likely, he had first knocked her unconscious with the handle, then stabbed her. That helped explain why no one the *militsia* could find remembered hearing any cries for help. The description of the knife was uselessly vague: a single blade of indeterminate size.

The case was given a file, number 6181 of the Oktyabrsky region, Rostov oblast. Before he returned to Rostov, Fetisov helped Petrov and the local *militsia* do what the book prescribed in cases like this, where neither witnesses nor physical evidence identified the killer. They constructed a list of hypotheses. Basically, the hypotheses amounted to educated guesses about the kind of person who might drag or lure a thirteen-year-old girl into the woods in broad daylight and stab her twenty-two times.

At the top of the list, they put relatives. Though neither the girl's father or stepfather appeared to be involved, grilling the relatives was standard procedure. Even if it did not yield the killer, it could yield information about Lyubov's friends and contacts. Next on the list came people in the Donskoi area previously convicted of sex crimes. Next came friends of the girl, and then anyone in the area suffering from a mental illness with a sexual abnormality. Finally, they decided to check out juvenile delinquents.

A search of the dead girl's possessions yielded a lead. Lyubov's older sister, Nadezhda, had a friend named V. I. Gubenko, who was in prison for theft. He had somehow gotten acquainted with Lyubov, and from prison he had written her a letter, saying he hoped to see her when he got out. He himself could not have committed the crime. But perhaps he had passed her name along to another prisoner, perhaps to a man with violent tendencies and an interest in young girls.

The second item on the list of guesses also turned up a suspect. Vladimir Pecheritsa, thirty-four, had been convicted of raping a woman who taught "Scientific Communism." He had also been accused of assaulting his wife's mother. He lived in the countryside near Donskoi, tending a garden. On the day of the killing, he had been at the clinic in Donskoi, being treated for tuberculosis. More interesting still was the hobby the *syshchiki* discovered when they began to investigate him. He made his own knives.

The written reports on the investigation politely refrained from discussing the length and the style of the Pecheritsa investigation. One report said that Nikolai Petrov had handled the interrogation himself. Petrov, in later years, would deny having done so. But the style of Soviet interrogations had not changed too much since Stalin's time. The *militsia* knew how to put emotional pressure on a suspect. They knew how to apply physical pressure, to beat a man so no marks would show. Suspects had no right to a lawyer's counsel until the case against them had been assembled.

Pecheritsa, who would have learned these things firsthand during the investigation of his earlier crime, could not give his own account of the interrogation he underwent after Lyubov Biryuk's murder. According to the reports filed with *militsia* headquarters in Rostov, he hanged himself after learning that he was a suspect.

"Maybe it was because he was ill. Maybe it was because he didn't get along with his wife," Petrov would say.

Russia was a country sadly accustomed to the idea that, in any major enterprise, there are incidental victims. Peter the Great caused the deaths of hundreds of thousands of his countrymen to build his capital, Saint Petersburg, in the frozen marshes near the Gulf of Finland. Stalin sent millions to their deaths to build Communism. The hunt for the killer of

Lyubov Biryuk would, though Fetisov and Petrov did not then know it, become a major enterprise. Pecheritsa had become its first incidental victim.

After Pecheritsa's death, the Biryuk investigation slowed down. It was not an uncommon problem in Soviet society. In factories, in government ministries, on collective farms, plans were formulated and orders were issued. Very few people dissented, but very few did all they were supposed to do, either. A report on the Biryuk investigation filed in October to Fetisov's office by Rostov homicide *syshchik* A. P. Khrapunov noted this in the wooden, bureaucratic prose so characteristic of the late Brezhnev era. "Active work for the solution of the case is not being done at the present time," the report said. "The organization role of the leadership of the *militsia* station is lacking."

No outside pressure forced the *militsia* to work harder. The local newspapers and radio stations disseminated only the information they were told to disseminate, which amounted to a brief announcement that the authorities were looking for people who might have seen Lyubov Biryuk on the afternoon of June 12. Her neighbors and relatives, of course, knew that someone had murdered her. But they had no influence, and the information did not travel beyond the bounds of Donskoi.

That autumn, though, pressure came from another quarter. On September 20, a railroad worker, walking near the train station for the city of Shakhty, some twenty miles northwest of Donskoi, found skeletal remains in the woods that edged close to the tracks. The medical examiner estimated that the body had been there for six weeks or more. This corpse was also naked, and it lay on its stomach, hands near its head and legs splayed open. The bones showed the striations of multiple knife wounds, including wounds in the eye sockets. But the body could not be identified beyond the fact that it was that of a grown woman, and its size and sex fit no missing-persons reports from the area.

On October 27, a soldier went into the woods to gather logs near a military base called Kazachi Lagerya, ten miles south of Shakhty and fifteen miles west of Donskoi. He stumbled across the skeletal remains of a woman, lying on her stomach, covered over with branches. This skeleton also bore the marks of knife wounds, especially to the breasts. Like the one near Shakhty, this skeleton fit none of the missing-persons reports in the files of the local *militsia*, and its identity remained unknown.

And, like the skeleton in Shakhty, and the remains of Lyu-bov Biryuk in Donskoi, it had traces of knife wounds in its eye sockets.

The skeletons of three females, all found in woods, all with knife wounds to the eyes, demanded a more energetic response. Early in December, Major Fetisov organized a special work group of ten *syshchiki*, based at oblast head-quarters in Rostov, charged with solving all three cases.

2

The Detective

Mikhail Fetisov still had no more than an informed hunch that the skeletons in the woods near Kazachi Lagerya and the Shakhty train station had anything to do with the killing of Lyubov Biryuk. With the investigation in Donskoi going nowhere, he and his deputy, Vladimir Kolyesnikov, decided to recruit some new talent for the *syshchik* squad formed to investigate the three murders.

On a cold day in January, Kolyesnikov waited in the lobby of *militsia* headquarters for a second lieutenant from the criminology laboratory named Viktor Burakov. Burakov was the department's best man in fingerprints, ballistics, footprints, and the other arcana of police science. Kolyesnikov meant to recruit him.

To Kolyesnikov's left, on one wall, hung photographs of the outstanding *militsia* workers of the previous month, looking stern and formal in their gray dress uniforms with the red piping. To the right, the wall was engraved with the names of Rostov *militsia* officers who had fallen in duty. Kolyesnikov could watch Burakov approaching before Burakov could see him. The double doors from Engels Street into the lobby had treated glass, enabling those inside to look out, but preventing the people on the sidewalk from looking in.

Burakov walked in, bundled up against the Russian winter. He looked like an amalgamation of two bodies. He stood about five eight, but he had the torso of a much larger man, with broad shoulders, a deep chest, and thick forearms. Spin-

15

dly, slightly bowed legs gave him a top-heavy look, accentuated by his rapid, rolling walk. He had dark, thinning hair, long sideburns, and a couple of pink warts on his left cheek. The overall impression was of a man more rugged than handsome. He was, Kolyesnikov knew, still active among the martial arts competitors at the Dynamo gym, where the *militsia* and the KGB worked out, even though, at thirty-seven, he was past the age at which most Russian men begin to pursue more sedentary activities.

The two shook hands. Burakov's daily route took him through the lobby and outdoors again, as he walked through an inner courtyard to the rear wing that housed the *militsia* laboratory. Kolyesnikov fell into step with him, and they paused by a fountain, dry in the winter, for a moment of private conversation.

How would Burakov feel, Kolyesnikov asked, about leaving the lab and coming to work as a *syshchik*?

The invitation did not surprise Burakov. He knew Kolyesnikov liked his work. Burakov had perhaps the most complete academic preparation on the Rostov staff. He had studied for four years in the Ministry of the Interior's criminology academy in Volgograd, finishing with certificates of expertise in half a dozen branches of police science. Most Rostov detectives held a certificate in only one area of expertise, if any.

The prospect of leaving the lab piqued Burakov's interest. As a criminologist, he often inspected crime scenes with detectives. But once he had completed his analysis of the bullets fired or the fingerprints left, his work ended. The *syshchiki* went on to track down the criminals. Burakov had long since stopped seeing anything novel in bullets and fingerprints. He needed a new challenge.

There was, he told Kolyesnikov, only one obstacle. He and his wife, after ten years, had finally reached the top of the *militsia* waiting list for an apartment. He needed to know whether switching departments would cost him his seniority on the waiting list. Svetlana Burakova was a patient and cheerful woman, but she had already sacrificed thousands of rubles and years of her husband's company because of his work in the *militsia*. He was not sure she would tolerate the loss of an apartment.

The Burakovs and their two small boys, Andrei and Maksim, lived in half of an old cottage in a section of Rostov formally called the New Settlement. They had three small rooms with a coal stove. Water came from a well a block away, on Twelfth Street, and the outhouse, behind the clothesline where the women dried their laundry, required a walk through a muddy little tomato garden in the courtyard.

The neighborhood bore the informal nickname Nakhalovka, which, loosely translated, means Punkville. It is an area of rutted roads and crumbling pavement, broken sewer mains, rumbling trams, and one-story brick or wood cottages, thrown up without plumbing during Stalin's first five-year plan to house the factory workers of a rapidly industrializing city. Over the years, other, newer sections of Rostov had gotten the bulk of the state's housing investment, sprouting phalanxes of twenty-story white apartment buildings, which, though ugly and poorly built, at least have central heat and indoor plumbing. For years, the city had planned to tear down the cottages in the New Settlement, and for years the influx of people into Rostov had created such a housing shortage that every inhabitable square meter had a claimant.

The city of Rostov-on-Don was a product of imperial Russia's drive to reach warm seas, free of ice. In the eighteenth century, that meant taking land from the Ottoman Empire, with which Russia fought four wars for control of the northern coast of the Black Sea. In 1747, with the Turks still in control of the seacoast, the Russians founded Rostov, on the high, readily defended right bank of the Don, twenty-five miles inland. It was, at that time, as close to a warm-water seaport as Russia had. Over the next century and a half Rostov grew into a cosmopolitan, raffish river port with large minorities of Jews, Armenians, and Greeks and a complement of nineteen brothels, according to a count taken toward the turn of this century.

The Russian Revolution and Stalinism scraped away much of the city's eccentricity and charm. It became a manufacturing center for tractors that plied the southern Russian steppe, a typically Soviet city with nearly a million inhabitants, a single main street, and more monuments than restaurants. A big statue of Lenin stood at one end of Engels Street, and Marx occupied a small square at the other, in a spot once held by Catherine the Great. Outside the tractor factory, which was called Rostselmash, a pedestal held the millionth orange tractor the line had produced.

Viktor Burakov was not, by birth, a city dweller. He came from peasant stock in central Russia, from a collective farm called Bolshevik. He was born just after World War II, a time of famine and hardship in the countryside. He remembered the taste of bread made from potatoes, because, in the wintertime, after the government had requisitioned all the peasants' grain to feed the workers in the cities, his family subsisted on the potatoes they grew in their small private garden next to the cottage. He remembered his father in the fields, cutting wheat with a scythe and pushing a big wheel to break up the ground, because there were no machines and no farm animals. He remembered the day the kolkhoz got a motorized combine and his father gave him a ride. It was a highlight of his childhood. Two of his younger sisters died as girls, one of scarlet fever and another from whooping cough. He came down with both diseases. He survived.

When he was six, his father, Vasily, moved the family to Siberia, to a coal-mining town on frigid Sakhalin Island. Mining was harrowing, life-shortening work. The coal dust was thick inside the shaft and the safety precautions were often forgotten in the rush to fulfill the monthly plan. But mining paid better than the handful of rubles earned by kolkhoz workers under Stalin. The Burakov family lived in Siberia for nearly ten years. Yekaterina Burakova was assigned a job stoking the boiler at the local school, working from morning to evening. As a boy, Viktor Burakov had to cut wood, carry water, and care for his surviving sisters. He prepared their meals, plaited their hair, and ironed their dresses. He played only after he had fed them and washed the floor and waited until his mother trudged home from the boiler room and said, "Good boy, son. Thank you." Years later, the memory of her praise for his dutiful performance could still cause his voice to grow husky.

The wet, frigid Siberian climate damaged his mother's health, and the family returned to the kolkhoz in central Russia when Viktor Burakov was fifteen. He completed the local school and entered the equivalent of high school in a town called Sevsk, fifteen miles away from his village. In the late summer and early autumn, before snow and mud made the road unusable, he rode a bicycle back and forth. In the winter, he lived in a dormitory in town, and his father brought potatoes to the school in exchange for his board. He learned to drive and maintain tractors and combines, which was about as sophisticated an education as the school offered.

He also learned to fight. Russian boys in that time and place needed to know how to take care of themselves. On the eve of Lent, when Mediterranean cultures celebrate Mardi Gras, Russians, though officially atheistic, observed the Russian Orthodox festival of Maslenitsa. The occasion called for feasts of pancakes, called *blini*, and mass fistfights called *stenka na stenku*, or "wall to wall." The boys and men of one village would gather in a field and square off against their counterparts from a neighboring village; the fight lasted until one side gave in. After the battle, the vodka bottles would appear, and the two sides would drink together. Tradition allowed no weapons, so no one was killed, and the *militsia* generally turned their backs. But broken noses and black eyes were common. Fights between villages sometimes arose spontaneously if, for instance, a boy from one village went to a dance in another and stole the affections of a local girl. Viktor Burakov, strengthened by years of farm chores and toughened by Siberian winters, participated in fights of all kinds. He fought well enough that his friends in neighboring villages competed to recruit him for their village sides. Years later, he remembered the *stenka na stenku* brawls with nostalgic affection.

The exigencies of life forced him to continue scrapping. In 1964, when he was eighteen, the state exacted payment for the education it had given him by requiring two years of service in Nikita Khrushchev's scheme to plow up and cultivate the grasslands of the dry Central Asian steppe, known in Russia as the Virgin Lands. For hundreds of years, the nomadic Central Asians managed to subsist by grazing animals on these lands, using them sparingly, not demanding more than the land could give. Khrushchev decided that the steppe could produce much more, that its lands were the key to Soviet agricultural self-sufficiency. The Party sent thousands of young people out to the steppe. It assigned Viktor Burakov to a barrack with sixteen other men, almost all of them older. Food and water had to be trucked in from the nearest settlement, one hundred miles away. When the delivery system failed, the men simply went hungry and thirsty. Burakov plowed all through the hot, dry summer, and spent the cold, windy winters repairing the equipment.

In the barracks, the older recruits demanded that the younger ones do the chores—cleaning, cooking, hauling water. Burakov was prepared to do his share, but his pride prohibited him from acting as a servant to another man. He had to back up his pride with his fists.

The Soviet army drafted Burakov immediately after his two years in the Virgin Lands. The army was more of the same. Soldiers who could drive a tractor were seconded to the collective farms to help with the harvest. And the army had its own hazing system, called *dedovshchina*, in which the older soldiers tried to force the younger ones to shine their shoes and work their shifts in the kitchen and the latrine. Again, Burakov's pride compelled him to fight.

When the army released him, he was twenty-two. He found that the Bolshevik collective farm had no openings for drivers, and he had no desire to work in the fields. He moved to the city of Bryansk and got work as a driver of trucks and bulldozers for a steel factory. He married Svetlana, whom he met at a dance, and moved with her into a tiny rented room, called a three-by-three because each side measured only three yards. It was heated so poorly that, in the wintertime, they could see frost on the floor when they awakened in the morning.

Almost immediately, the Party noticed Burakov's diligence. He won one of the medals the factory occasionally awarded to its best workers, and he became a foreman supervising older men. He was invited to join the Party, which he did in 1971. He studied in the factory's technical school at night. In many ways, he epitomized the ideal that the Party ceaselessly promulgated in the press, on film, and on television—the ideal of the conscientious Soviet blue-collar worker, rising, with the help of the state, from proletarian beginnings, earning the respect of his comrades, and making his contribution to the building of Communism.

In 1972, the local Party headquarters received a directive from the center in Moscow. The Politburo had decided to improve the quality of the *militsia*. Party organizations in every factory and collective farm were to select some of their brightest young men and persuade them to become *militsionery*.

In Bryansk, the Party organization in the steel factory selected Viktor Burakov. They called him into the Party office and told him that the *kollektiv* had entrusted him with this duty.

Burakov resisted. He had no desire to be a policeman. Moreover, the starting salary was only ninety-five rubles a month. Under the Soviet system, skilled blue-collar workers had the highest salaries—higher than those of doctors, teachers, and even, nominally, politicians. (In reality, being in a position of *blat*, or influence, counted for more than money in the acquisition of things like cars and housing.) As a factory foreman, Burakov made as much as four hundred rubles a month if the factory fulfilled its production quotas. As a *militsioner*, he would earn less than a quarter of his factory wage and little *blat*.

But he soon realized that he had no choice in the matter. The Party organization persisted, calling him in every day to remind him that he was a Communist, and a Communist had a duty to serve where the Party needed him. And he perceived a threat. If he resisted the Party's wishes, the commendations and the medals would cease; instead, there would be complaints about his performance. He would find it impossible to continue to work. He gave in.

He got the usual few months of rudimentary training, then walked a beat. He thought, at first, that people respected the uniform. He learned otherwise one night when he had to break up a fight in a restaurant. He grabbed the man who started it and tried to arrest him. In an instant, Burakov found himself on the floor, looking up at the faces of people who showed neither sympathy nor an inclination to help him. The man he was trying to arrest, he would learn later, was a master of sport in a Soviet variant of the martial arts called *Sambo*, from the Russian words for unarmed self-defense.

Burakov had no pistol or club, just a feeling of shame that a criminal had put him on the floor. He got up but, in a few seconds, hit the floor again. He got up a third time, his uniform by now badly torn, with the same result. But he fought on and, after forty minutes, subdued his man.

After that, Burakov was assigned to the new criminology academy in Volgograd, a showpiece within the Soviet bloc that was one of the components in the effort to professionalize the *militsia*. The academy drew students from Cuba,

Eastern Europe, and other Soviet republics, as well as from Russia. Burakov filled his spare time with *Sambo*. He was, by then, twenty-eight—too old to aspire to the title of master of sport and international competition. But he pushed himself through two workouts a day, and he was known for his dogged, stubborn refusal to accept defeat. Once, an opponent inflicted a knee injury that would require surgery. Burakov finished the match in terrible pain rather than pounding the mat and forfeiting.

When he finished the academy, he was assigned to Rostov. His upbringing had produced, in many respects, a typical Russian male, a man who took great pride in his physical strength, a man who enjoyed working on a *kollektiv* with other men, a man capable of both sentimentality and, when he thought it necessary, cruelty. What distinguished him from his peers was the diligence his parents had instilled in him, the desire, bordering on an obsession, to see a job through to the end, the pride that prohibited him from giving up a task short of completion.

In March 1983, Burakov received assurances from the commission that doled out apartments to *militsia* workers that he would get his new apartment regardless of any transfer to the *syshchik* squad. Burakov promptly moved from the forensic laboratory to a dingy room on the third floor of the main wing. It was called the Greek Temple, because it was the largest room in the building. Eight detectives worked at battered desks in the Greek Temple; a portrait of Lenin presided sternly over their labors. They were the mainstays of a sub-unit called, in classically heavy bureaucratese, the Division of Especially Serious Crimes. Burakov went to work on the case that the detectives had begun to refer to as the *lesopolosa* killings.

In the Temple, Burakov first read the files on Lyubov Biryuk and the skeletons, still unidentified, found in the woods. In March, there was one identified victim, Lyubov Biryuk, and three unidentified skeletons. The most recent victim had been found in January, not far from the train station in Shakhty. Like Lyubov Biryuk and the two previous unidentified corpses, the fourth had wounds in the eye sockets, apparently from a knife. The corpse had lain, undiscovered, for about six months, according to the autopsy report. No soft tissue was left, and the determination that the body was a female's rested largely on circumstantial clues. The search of the scene had disclosed some women's clothing nearby, and the skeleton was short, only a couple of inches over five feet. So it was listed as a girl, between the ages of fifteen and nineteen when she died.

Officially, the *militsia* treated the four corpses as murders that might or might not be related. But to Burakov, as well as to others, the wounds around the eye sockets suggested that one person, almost certainly a male, had killed them all. Few killers, in his experience, bothered with the eyes of their victims; they struck at more vital organs. Four corpses, all found within the same general area, all killed within the same year, and all with wounds to the eyes almost had to be the work of a single murderer. There was, he knew, an old Russian superstition that the image of a killer remained in the eyes of his victim. Maybe the killer believed it, and had cut out the eyes to destroy evidence. More likely, Burakov thought, the killer simply could not stand to look his victims in the eyes. That, in turn, suggested that he spent time with each victim before she died. The wounds to Lyubov Biryuk indicated he spent enough time to inflict dozens of knife wounds. Perhaps, Burakov thought, the killer was a teenager, someone not yet hardened enough to look into the eyes of his victims without shame, but someone old enough, and perverse enough, to take pleasure from inflicting pain and watching blood flow.

The four corpses had substantially increased the *militsia*'s interest in reports of missing girls. Fetisov and Kolyesnikov had such a report on their desks. A girl named Olga Stalmachenok, ten years old, had disappeared after her piano lesson on December 11, 1982. The *militsia* in her hometown, Novoshakhtinsk, had failed to find her or witnesses. For Burakov's first assignment, Fetisov and Kolyesnikov decided to send him to supervise the search, letting other members of the team continue to work on the Biryuk murder and the three unidentified corpses.

Novoshakhtinsk (the name means, roughly, New Mining Town) lies some forty miles north of Rostov in the coalfield region of the oblast. Driving to it, Burakov passed mile after mile of rolling collective farm fields, just emerging from the winter snows, waiting to be sown with corn and sunflowers. Outside the town, huge, dirty piles of coal tailings, bigger than Egypt's pyramids, stand like sentinels on patrol. Once in a while, one of them catches fire, sending black, acrid smoke into the skies over the city. Though it has more than one hundred thousand residents, Novoshakhtinsk is really a collection of villages, each clustered around a particular mine. People live in cottages like the one Burakov had in Rostov or in the newer apartment blocks. Nearly all the inhabitants have empty fields and piles of coal tailings within walking distance of their homes.

Burakov checked into Novoshakhtinsk's only hotel, the Zarya, at 52 Lenin Street, around the corner from the local *militsia* station. He got room No. 21, down a dark hallway from a fetid, fly-infested toilet. The shower was downstairs, and there was a miners' cafeteria down the street.

The next morning, Burakov had a local *militsioner* drive him to the Stalmachenoks' home, at the northern edge of the city, on a dirt street named for *Pravda*, the Communist Party's newspaper. Both of the missing girl's parents worked in the mines, Natalia as a machinist and Anton as a fitter. They owned a small house that Anton built himself. It was a simple place, with a kitchen, a bedroom, and a sitting room that contained one luxury—a piano.

Natalia was a hefty woman, with dark hair and gold-capped

teeth, given to walking around the house in a faded cotton dress, her feet bare and dusty. She had premature wrinkles around her eyes, and Burakov guessed her age to be thirty-five, seven years older than in fact she was. She had been eighteen when she married Anton and eighteen when Olga, their first child, was born. She had, by the time Burakov called on her, told what she knew to many *militsionery*, and she had little but contempt for all of them. She answered his questions in a tone of tired disdain.

Olga, she told him, was an ordinary girl. No outstanding talents. No unusual interests. Yes, she got along with her parents. She did reasonably well in school. She liked to read. She wanted to become a music teacher. Yes, her parents had encouraged her in this ambition to find a career outside the mines. Though neither of them played, they bought a piano. Since the age of six, Olga had taken piano lessons twice a week, after school, in the city's music conservatory in the center of town. For the first three years, one of her parents had accompanied her to the conservatory and brought her back. But this trip took more than an hour each way and required changing buses. The Stalmachenoks, in addition to their work underground, had another daughter, four years old. Beginning in the summer of 1982, they let Olga go to her piano lesson alone, although Anton always tried to meet her bus when it arrived at their stop, to take her home in the sidecar of his motorcycle.

They had never taught her to be afraid of strangers. This was understandable. In pre-glasnost Soviet society, the newspapers and television almost never reported crimes against individuals, particularly children. Such crimes, according to the official line, afflicted bourgeois rather than socialist societies. When crime news did appear in the press, it almost always involved economic crimes, committed by people who had succumbed to the capitalist disease, greed. Their captures and punishments were depicted as little morality plays.

Still less would someone like Natalia Stalmachenok know about psychiatric disorders that might impel someone to assault a young girl. The Party, since Stalin's time, had imposed a strict puritanism on the Soviet media. Books and articles available to the general public almost never mentioned sex. Films showed nothing more explicit than a kiss, and a popular entertainment that explicitly portrayed a sexually depraved killer was unthinkable. As far as anyone could learn from the media, Soviet children received only love and sage advice from their elders. The propaganda slogan, hauled out by editors every time they printed pictures of the opening of a new school or swimming pool, was "Children are our only privileged class."

Soviet culture encouraged children to look upon their elders almost as family members. Language itself was suggestive. An accepted way for children to address even unknown adults was to call them uncle, auntie, or grandma. Natalia Stalmachenok had raised her daughter Olga in precisely that spirit.

On the evening when Olga disappeared, Natalia told Burakov, they had expected her home by seven o'clock. When she failed to turn up, they did not panic. Buses often broke down or were delayed, and Olga had occasionally come home from her lesson as late as nine o'clock. Her father thought she might have gone to visit a friend. Although the night was chill and damp, he got back on his motorcycle and began making the rounds of her schoolmates' homes.

But by eleven o'clock, panic had set in. While Anton Stalmachenok continued the search in their neighborhood, Natalia took the bus downtown, to the classical, ocher-colored building of the music conservatory on Lenin Street. At the bus stop in front of the conservatory, she saw two *militsionery*.

"I told the two of them that my daughter was lost," she said. "They just laughed and told me to go down to the station to file a report. So I went to the station and they said she'd probably just gone off to a friend's.'' Natalia Stalmach-enok never got over her feeling that the Novoshakhtinsk *militsia* reacted cavalierly, in the first days, to Olga's disappearance.

Her grudging, monosyllabic responses to his questions disappointed Burakov. He had gone to her in hopes that he could elicit some additional bit of information that might be helpful in finding her daughter. He took her reticence not as an understandable reaction to her experience with the *militsia* but as evidence that she was an indifferent mother or one, perhaps, whose work had worn her body and spirit down. Had one of his own children disappeared, he thought, he would have racked his brain to give the *militsia* any and all details that might help them find him. He had learned nothing from Natalia Stalmachenok that the local *militsia* hadn't known in December. He had nothing new to go on.

He did not tell Natalia Stalmachenok, but he was already convinced the girl was dead. Three days after her disappearance, the Novoshakhtinsk *militsia* had posted fliers around the city with her school picture, showing a pretty young girl in her school pinafore, her hair combed back in bunches and held in place by white bows. The local radio station and newspapers had reported that she was missing, and that the *militsia* were looking for any witnesses who might have seen her on Lenin Street early in the evening of December 11. Despite the fact that the street had been crowded at that hour with people going home from work or shopping, no witnesses came forward. *Militsionery* had gone door to door in the neighborhood around the conservatory, interviewing people who worked nearby or regularly passed through. They found no one who had seen her. They had even used tracking dogs in an effort to find her. They found no scent.

They had one dubious clue to work on. Several weeks after news of Olga Stalmachenok's disappearance began to circulate in Novoshakhtinsk, her parents had received a postcard, mailed from the city. In a shaky, immature hand, someone had written in pencil that if they wanted to find their daughter, they should look in the Daryevsky woods at the southwest end of the city. More ominously, the writer had warned that ''we'' would be taking and killing a total of ten young girls during the next year. Olga was just the first. The writer signed himself ''Sadist–Black Cat.''

By the time Burakov arrived in Novoshakhtinsk, the local *militsionery* had thoroughly combed the Daryevsky woods, finding nothing. Burakov doubted that the Black Cat writer could be the man who had killed four, and possibly five, girls and young women without leaving a trace. The Black Cat's words were ungrammatical, almost incoherent. To Burakov, they suggested the opposite of the cunning he imagined the killer to possess. And, given the fact that nearly everyone in Novoshakhtinsk knew the girl had disappeared, the writer needed to have no inside knowledge of the crime. He could be a psychotic or a warped prankster completely unconnected to the girl's disappearance. But the postcard was all they had to go on, and they began trying to identify the handwriting.

Olga Stalmachenok was found, ultimately, not by *militsionery* or their dogs, nor in the Daryevsky woods, but by a tractor driver at the Sixth Collective Farm, on the northeastern outskirts of Novoshakhtinsk, three miles from the music conservatory. It was April 14, and the driver was plowing a rolling cornfield for spring planting when he noticed that his blades had turned up something small and pale in the wet, black earth.

Viktor Burakov had returned to Rostov that week, and was working at his desk in the Greek Temple. The Novoshakhtinsk *militsia* called him as soon as they got the call from the Sixth Collective Farm, and he rushed north.

In Novoshakhtinsk, riding past the conservatory toward the Sixth Collective Farm, Burakov was struck by the distance the killer had traveled with his victim. If the killer had taken the most direct route from the conservatory to the cornfield, he had covered a couple of miles on Lenin Street, until the countryside began to impinge on the city and weedy fields supplanted the bare, muddy plots of land around the apartment blocks. Then he had turned right, off Lenin Street, and gone through a couple of vacant lots that were bisected by tractor paths. From the vacant lots, he had moved onto a dirt road that ran alongside the cornfield where the body had been found. He had traveled about a quarter mile up this lonely, rutted road on a chilly, damp night. Then, near some pylons that supported heavy electrical lines, he had gone left, through a few yards of woodland that screened the road from the field. Then he had walked perhaps one hundred and fifty yards through the mud to a spot near the crest of a hill, with a view to the east of the farm buildings and to the north of a coal elevator, each perhaps half a mile away. And there he had left the body. By the time Burakov had reached the scene, his shoes were thick with mud.

Burakov had seen hundreds of corpses during his eleven years as a *militsioner*, but he had rarely seen the corpse of a young girl, and he had never seen one with wounds like those visible on the remains of Olga Stalmachenok. The winter snows had preserved much of what had decomposed on the other bodies.

She was, like the others, naked. Her skin was a bluish white, tinged with the blackened remains of blood and spotted and streaked by the dark, damp earth. Her skull, chest, and abdomen had been punctured and shredded dozens of times by a sharp, single-bladed knife. The killer had, at some point in his evident frenzy, ripped open her chest and slashed away at her heart and lungs. The remains of her heart lay in the right side of her chest cavity, and the remains of a lung had been pushed to where her heart should have been. The killer had struck repeatedly around her sexual organs, chopping away at the girl's perineum. More startling, he had completely excised her lower bowel and her uterus. Burakov forced himself to examine the skull. The eyeballs themselves were gone, lost to decomposition. But he could see striations in the eye sockets.

And with that he knew, beyond doubt, that he was looking at the work of a serial killer.

Burakov generally had one of two private reactions to the corpses he encountered in his work. He saw most of them as professional challenges, and he craved challenges. Though he would not admit this to most people, working on a murder case often exhilarated him in a quiet, controlled way. It improved his moods, heightened his awareness, put a purpose in his step when he walked to the office in the morning. Sometimes, though, the sight of a corpse reminded him of someone he knew, perhaps a member of his family, and it would sadden and depress him. This time he felt both reactions welling within himself. The girl could have been a classmate of his younger son, Maksim.

The plowman who had uncovered the body had also uncovered evidence that removed any doubt about its identity. Some fifty yards away, he had turned over some slippers, the kind Russian children wore in school during the winter, a dress, and a music notebook with Olga Stalmachenok's name in it. The murderer had, apparently, stopped and buried them on his way out of the cornfield.

Russian law enforcement had little experience with serial killers. The knowledge that did exist tended to be a tightly held secret, inaccessible even to other *militsionery*. Burakov knew of one other series of bestial murders, near Zaporozhe in Ukraine. They resembled these killings in one respect— the Ukrainian killer had also cut open his victims and slashed at their sexual organs. But that killer had claimed a total of four victims in thirteen years, between 1964 and 1977. Then his activity inexplicably ended. This new killer, if in fact it was not the Ukrainian killer, had taken five within six months.

He had left little or no useful evidence at the scenes of any of his murders. He had lured two normal young girls from places filled with people to isolated spots where he had killed them. More curious still, he had done so without attracting any attention from passersby. Presumably, he had managed something similar with the three unidentified victims. How had he done it? Burakov could only speculate. He might be a man of great charm. He might be a man with an appearance of authority, perhaps with a uniform. Perhaps a *militsioner.*

Most likely, Burakov thought, the killer had a car, either his own or a car belonging to a state agency. A car would enable him to take Olga Stalmachenok all or part of the three miles from the music conservatory to the cornfield at the Sixth Collective Farm. It could have taken him to Donskoi, to Shakhty, and to Kazachi Lagerya.

And, clearly, his superficial charm or authority hid a deranged personality. Burakov had no psychiatric training, and he did not know the difference between a sociopath and a psychopath. But common sense, combined with the wounds inflicted on Olga Stalmachenok, told him that the killer had a serious psychiatric disorder.

The investigators needed to check, then, the whereabouts on December 11 of all the men in the area ever charged with or convicted of rape or molestation, ever confined in a psychiatric hospital, or even treated by a psychiatrist. They needed to recheck all the men who lived or worked around the conservatory. They needed to pay special attention to anyone in those categories who owned a car. It would be, Burakov knew, a long and tedious process, a process that could take much longer than the intervals between the first five murders—unless they got lucky.

Sifting through the first Novoshakhtinsk field reports a short time later, Burakov saw one that intrigued him. In the neighborhood near the music conservatory, the investigators had turned up some interesting gossip about a man named Vladimir Babakov, a man who owned a white sedan.

Babakov was seventy-two years old, though he looked younger. The *syshchiki* had talked with his relatives. His sister told them that throughout his life, her brother had suffered from what she called "a sexual problem." He could never get enough women. Though officially single, he lived with a woman thirty-five years old. He had affairs with numerous other younger women. Most intriguing, the neighborhood gossip suggested that his interests extended to young girls. He had a garage for his car. The gossip had it that Babakov liked to invite girls eight, nine, and ten years old into the garage and there induce them to strip and let him touch their genitals. None of the gossip, though, suggested an inclination to violence.

Burakov and the *syshchiki* in Novoshakhtinsk agreed that Babakov merited further investigation. But the more they investigated, the more contradictory the evidence became. The gossip, in most cases, checked out. He had had sexual relations with dozens of women in Novoshakhtinsk in addition to the one he was living with. But the worst any of them could say about him was that he was excessively tender. The old man loved women's bodies, loved to kiss them, loved to caress them—to a degree that some, though by no means all, of his lovers, used to more perfunctory, pragmatic masculine attention, found hard to take. Most of his women remembered him fondly. There were, apparently, a few instances of untoward attention to girls in his garage. But again, as the gossip had suggested, there had been no violence. And no one could find any evidence that he knew Olga Stalmachenok.

Moreover, Babakov had an alibi for the night of December 11. He had been at home, he insisted, and his car had stayed in the garage all night. His lover and his neighbors all confirmed his story. The *syshchiki* removed the seat covers from the car and sent them off to the laboratory in Rostov to be examined for any fibers, hairs, or other traces of the dead girl.

In the meantime, they decided, they had no choice but to intensify their search for the writer of the Black Cat postcard. In theory, it was possible to obtain a handwriting specimen from each of the more than three million residents of Rostov oblast. Each Soviet citizen had a legal obligation to work; each would therefore have to have filled out documents kept in the personnel files of a Rostov workplace. But there were millions of files and thousands of workplaces. Fetisov called in handwriting specialists from all the surrounding *militsia* departments and set them to work; others were assigned by the KGB. But he and Burakov knew that this job, like the job of checking out all the region's psychiatric patients, could take years before it would yield a clue.

The killer gave them four months. On August 8, a group of boys was walking through a *lesopolosa* near the airport at Rostov-on-Don, on their way to a soccer field. Like the woodland in Donskoi where Lyubov Biryuk died, this one was crossed by several footpaths and was within earshot of a road. In fact, it was near a major highway intersection and the railroad line that ran from Rostov north through Shakhty and eventually to Moscow. A few hundred yards to the north was a village where about a dozen families lived. It had rained heavily in the preceding days, and the boys' path carried them near a small gully that had just dried out. At the bottom, half covered with dirt and leaves, they saw some bones.

Viktor Burakov joined the team that went to investigate, by this time knowing all too well what to expect. A Soviet crime scene investigation involved more than half a dozen people. The local *militsionery* who responded to the first call stayed on the scene. One or two forensic experts, depending on the gravity of the crime, would join them. In cases involving a body, a medical examiner from the forensic lab at the Rostov Institute of Medicine might go to the scene. So would one or more *syshchiki*, like Burakov.

Finally, the procurator's office, the rough equivalent of an

American district attorney's office, would send a lawyer-investigator, known as a *sledovatyel*, to supervise the examination and write the protocol of what the team found. Like many other branches of the Soviet system, law enforcement had overlapping bureaucracies. The *militsia* patrolled the streets and had the responsibility for apprehending criminals. The procurators had the responsibility for supervising cases and questioning suspects after they were brought in by the *militsia*. On paper, the division of labor looked neat enough. In practice, it was blurred. The *militsia* had to plan investigations and question suspects in order to apprehend criminals. On a routine basis, it did. But on a case that was not routine, there were lots of opportunities for the two agencies to get in each other's way. The system worked only when the procurator's office and the *militsia* cooperated.

If it went by the book, a crime scene examination started a fair distance away from the corpse, and the investigators worked inward in ever tighter circles, looking for pieces of evidence, such as the victim's or the killer's clothing. In woods like the strip this body was in, they picked up lots of unrelated garbage—scraps of cloth, pieces of paper, bottles—that people had tossed away as they traveled through. Frequently, the investigators found it difficult or impossible to tell what was related to a crime and what was not. In this case, they found a great deal of trash, but nothing they could determine for certain had belonged to either the victim or the killer.

The corpse itself was little more than a skeleton. The summer heat and heavy rains had, Burakov knew, accelerated the decomposition process. The body could have been in the woods for two weeks or a month. It appeared to be a girl, but the Rostov *militsia* had no missing-persons reports that matched its size. The medical examiner took it in for further analysis.

A few days later the report came back, and it linked the body to the *lesopolosa* killings. Like those of the others, this victim's eye sockets showed signs of knife wounds. The medical examiner noticed something else. The victim's face and teeth showed the assymetries of Down's syndrome. Whoever he or she was, the victim had apparently been severely retarded.

Most Down's syndrome children, Burakov knew, attended special boarding schools, called *internati*. In Soviet society, even more so than in the West, few parents felt capable of coping with the special needs of a Down's syndrome child, and the public schools had no facilities to educate them alongside normal children. Burakov directed the local *militsia* to check out all the *internati* in the region.

Early in September, he got the response he was looking for. A thirteen-year-old girl named Irina Dunenkova had failed to return to an *internat* in Shakhty when classes had resumed on September 1. He sent pictures and dental records of the missing girl, along with pictures of the skull and the teeth, to the Ministry of Interior's laboratory in Moscow. The reply came back very quickly. The body in the woods had been Irina Dunenkova.

She had lived, ostensibly, with a sister in Shakhty. But the family hardly functioned. Irina's sister, Burakov learned, suffered from a milder form of mental retardation and lived on state welfare assistance. She slept, or had sex with, numerous men, who picked her up in stations, in stores, or on the street. A third sister was serving time in jail for violating the statute against spreading venereal disease. Irina, helpless and unsupervised, wandered around the oblast during her vacations from the *internat*, riding the trains and buses. The sister she was living with had not bothered to report her missing.

Only her killer, it seemed, had paid any attention to her. She was the sixth victim in the series.

But at the time her body was identified, Burakov and the other investigators already had a seventh corpse to wonder about. A man disposing of rubbish in a village called Ordzhonikidze, not far from Rostov's airport, found this one on August 28. He had walked from the village, past a wooden kiosk that dispensed beer in the summer, down a clay road toward a thicket. There, in a shallow pit near some brambles, he found the corpse, face up in the dirt. Most of its flesh had decomposed, except for a few patches on the back and legs. After examining the bones, the medical examiner found evidence of nine knife wounds in the chest and two cuts in the left eye socket. The site was about two miles from the wooded strip where the killer had left Irina Dunenkova's body.

But this skeleton was that of a boy. Its size matched the missing-persons report filed August 9 for Igor Gudkov, an eight-year-old from the suburb of Bataisk, across the Don from Rostov.

Burakov, in Novoshakhtinsk when the corpse was found, got involved in the investigation only after the same kind of skull analysis practiced on Dunenkova had confirmed the identity of the remains. The Gudkov family's story reminded him of what he had heard from Natalia Stalmachenok. Igor, off from school for summer vacation, spent his days under the supervision of his grandmother. Occasionally, at lunchtime, he liked to visit his mother, who worked in a store on Engels Street in Rostov. On August 9, the boy had gotten on an express bus from Bataisk to the center of Rostov, a block from the store where Igor's mother worked. He never arrived at the store.

The discovery of Gudkov's body, the second child's body found in the Rostov area in August, prompted the procurator's office and the *militsia* to appoint a new and larger special investigation group—with sixteen members, headquartered in Rostov, under the command of a *sledovatyel* named Aleksandr Ryabko and a *syshchik* named Valery Beklemishchev. And it forced the investigators to reexamine all their theories. In several respects, the facts of the Gudkov case matched those of the previous killings. The victim had used or been near mass transportation. He had suffered multiple knife wounds, including wounds to the eyes. The killer had left the corpse in a woodland.

On the other hand, could the same killer take both boys and girls as his victims? To Burakov's knowledge, scant though it was, serial killers always killed males or females, never both. Could there be two killers, both using knives, both sadists, at large in the oblast?

Before Burakov could answer the question, it became moot. In mid-September, while working again in Novoshakhtinsk, he was called back to Rostov. Valery Beklemishchev, the co-commander of the new special investigation group, had cracked the case. A young man named Yuri Kalenik had confessed to all the killings.

3

The Confessions of Yuri Kalenik

The suspect that Valery Beklemishchev had cracked was a slightly built young man with frizzy brown hair, a missing front tooth, and a wispy mustache. Yuri Kalenik looked, in fact, almost elfin. From the age of twelve, he had lived in an *internat* for retarded children in the town of Gukovo, about eighty miles north of Rostov. In 1981, when he was seventeen and nearing the age limit for *internat* residents, he sent a letter to *Molot*, the Party newspaper in Rostov, declaring that he wanted more education than the rudimentary crafts taught at the *internat*. The state accepted his petition to be deemed trainable and sent him to Vocational-Technical School No. 45 in Gukovo, where he became a floor layer; in the summer of 1983 he began to practice that trade. But Kalenik still spent much of his spare time with his friends among the older boys at the *internat*. They were the only friends he had.

Early in September 1983, one of those friends, Valery Shaburov, suggested to Kalenik that they take a trip on the *elektrichka*. The *elektrichka* rumbles slowly between Gukovo and Rostov four or five times a day. It is the lowest class of Russian rail service, a train that stops at every village along the tracks and takes, if there are no delays, four or five hours to make its one-hundred-twenty-mile run. It has hard wooden benches for seats, and the cars are cold in the winter and stuffy in the summer. Peasants use the *elektrichka* to go to the city markets, and on the weekend, city people use it to seek out a place along the Don with a little fresh air and some room for fishing. For boys like Shaburov and Kalenik, the *elektrichka* had one huge advantage: conductors rarely bothered to check the passengers' tickets. With any luck, they rode for free, killing time and seeing the countryside.

On this particular excursion, they got off the train in Rostov-on-Don, the final stop, and spent the day and early evening wandering around the city. As darkness fell, they decided to spend the night in an empty trolleybus, an electric bus powered by a metal arm attached to cables stretched above the street. The next morning, Valery Shaburov woke up feeling playful. He got into the driver's seat, switched on the lights, turned the wheel, and opened the bus doors. This attracted the attention of the bus driver, who had arrived to start her shift. She clambered into the bus and grabbed Shaburov by the arm, yelling for someone to call a *militsioner*. Kalenik protested that Shaburov hadn't damaged anything. The driver ignored him. Kalenik fled and, later that day, returned to Gukovo on an *elektrichka*.

The *militsia* dragged Shaburov, who was barely coherent, down to the station for the Pervomaisky section of the city and informed him that he could be charged with attempting to steal the trolleybus. Then, because the bodies had been found nearby, they asked him if he knew who had killed Gudkov and Dunenkova.

"Not me," Shaburov said. "Yuri did it."

That afternoon, the *militsia* in Gukovo arrested Kalenik and held him until *syshchiki* from Rostov could come and fetch him. It was his first experience with jail. The men from Rostov arrived at nine o'clock in the evening, handcuffed him, and put him in the car.

"Why are you arresting me?" Kalenik asked them.

"You already know" was all they would reply.

The next day, Valery Beklemishchev began Kalenik's interrogation. If they had had firmer evidence, a *sledovatyel* from the procurator's office might have been summoned to handle the interrogation. But this case was still at the stage where a *syshchik* might work the suspect for a while. Kalenik had no lawyer, and no one read him his rights. According to standard Soviet procedure, the state would provide him with a lawyer after it had completed its investigation and if it decided to charge him. At first, Kalenik denied everything. But after a few days, Beklemishchev secured a confession. Kalenik admitted not only to the seven *lesopolosa* killings but to four others that had been committed in other sections of Rostov and neighboring oblasts.

At that point, the *militsia* began in earnest to collect supporting evidence against Kalenik. This stood what Westerners would think of as normal procedure on its head. The Western idea would be to gather evidence first, then use it either to extract a confession from the suspect or to prove his guilt in spite of his denials.

But in Russia, both under Communism and before it, the confession was the pivotal stage in any investigation. Russians are accustomed to the idea that a guilty man must confess; some Russians, even now, hold the mistaken belief that a defendant who does not confess cannot be convicted. That was why so much of Dostoyevsky's *Crime and Punishment* focused on Raskolnikov's irrepressible urge to admit his crime. It was why Stalin insisted that the victims of his purges be forced to confess in show trials to conspiracies that never existed.

To Viktor Burakov, assigned in late September to work on the corroborating investigation, Yuri Kalenik seemed an eminently likely suspect. Burakov's suspicions had centered from the start on a criminal with a psychiatric disorder. And in Russia, mental retardation was seen not just as a learning handicap but as a form of derangement. In formal terms, a mentally retarded Russian was described as suffering from a disease called oligophrenia. Burakov had little experience with such people. But what he did know suggested to him that they were particularly dangerous in late adolescence, when their libidos were at their peak and they left their child-hood *internati* to live on their own. He did not believe that they could control their desires. He had no reason to doubt Kalenik's confession. But what he saw when he began to work on the case disturbed him.

After extracting a confession, a *syshchik* or a *sledovatyel* next found out whether the suspect could, in effect, verify his admissions. Could he, for instance, show the *militsia* to the scene of the crime? When Burakov joined the team work-ing with Kalenik, the suspect had already led the way to the sites where several of the bodies had been found. He was about to demonstrate that he knew where Igor Gudkov had been killed.

About a dozen *syshchiki*, uniformed *militsionery*, and oth-ers gathered near the village of Ordzhonokidze to see if Ka-lenik could do it. Burakov stayed on the fringes of the operation. According to Kalenik's confession, he had met Gudkov in the center of Rostov, then persuaded him to ride a trolleybus out of the city to Ordzhonokidze. Burakov felt that the investigators should have started their test in the city and required Kalenik to show exactly what he had done from the moment he met Gudkov. Instead, the test started within a quarter mile of the murder site. But it was not Burakov's show; it was Beklemishchev's. Burakov kept quiet.

Even in Ordzhonokidze, Kalenik did not seem to Burakov to be well oriented. In Burakov's experience, an admitted murderer usually walked directly to the scene. Kalenik wan-dered around the village and the beer kiosk for several hours, conversing all the while with Beklemishchev, before finally arriving within a few yards of the site.

A short while later, the troupe moved to Novoshakhtinsk to see whether Kalenik could find the place in the cornfield where the killer had left the body of Olga Stalmachenok. Kalenik pointed out the music conservatory in the middle of the city. Then he led them to the Sixth Collective Farm. But there he wandered aimlessly through its fields for several hours. Finally, the group reached the top of a hillside. Burakov looked down toward the place, under the electrical cables, where the tractor driver had uncovered the body. To his dismay, he saw that the local *militsionery*, curious about the test, had parked a *militsia* car a few yards from the scene. He rushed down the hill to tell them to move it. But by that time, Kalenik and the rest of the group were already heading in that direction. Kalenik pointed to a spot near where the car had been parked. It was close enough for Beklemishchev.

Triumphant, Beklemishchev moved on to another assignment. Fetisov gave Burakov the mop-up duty of completing the *lesopolosa* investigation and the case against Yuri Kalenik.

The more Burakov investigated, the more doubts he had. He began by learning more about Kalenik's past.

He had been born, out of wedlock, to a woman who worked in a mine in Shakhty. When he was two, she had left him atop a warm stove while she went to look for coal. His clothing caught fire, and he suffered severe burns on his back.

His mother thereupon gave him up for adoption, and he lived the next ten years in a foster home. But he did badly in school, when he went at all, and he quarreled frequently with his foster parents. Sometimes, the quarrels turned violent. When he was twelve, Kalenik's foster mother turned him over to the *internat* for retarded children in Gukovo.

Gukovo is a tired, worn little town, growing poorer as the surrounding coalfields play out. The *internat* stands at the end of a dirt lane behind a steel fence, painted blue. Inside the fence, in the summer, the smell of feces and urine wafts through the air. Children roam naked from the waist down or squat on the verandas of their buildings, moaning and rocking in their own private worlds. Seeing a stranger, they may wave and try to say "Daddy."

Inside, they sleep in dim rooms filled with ten, twelve, or more beds, pushed close together. Sometimes two children occupy the same bed, with the bigger one petting the smaller. Their toilets are slits in the floor, and their bathtubs may be filled with yellow water, dead flies floating on the surface. In the rooms for the most severely retarded, the children lie all day in cribs, on dirty sheets, their matchstick arms and legs splayed at odd angles. Flies crawl over their open, vacant eyes and shaven heads. They moan or whimper, but most cannot talk.

Occasionally, one of the attendants, hefty women in dirty white smocks and kerchiefs, rises from a chair and makes an effort to clean or comfort a child. But for hours each day, the *internat* children fend for themselves. One *internat* director has been prosecuted for embezzling money and food meant for the children.

Some of the Gukovo *internat* children would live in institutions in any society, but many others were discarded there by parents or a system that could not cope with them. One of Kalenik's friends was an alert, inquisitive boy named Sasha who hobbled around on crutches. When Sasha was a child, his father, in a drunken rage, threw him off an apartment balcony, crippling his legs. The father wound up in jail, and Sasha wound up at the *internat*. Kalenik himself would probably, in a wealthier society, have been diagnosed with a specific learning disability or behavioral problem, not as retarded. He speaks like any other Russian blue-collar worker, in complete, reasonably grammatical sentences. He reads. He responds to questions. He plays chess.

Burakov, when he visited the *internat*, felt sympathy for Kalenik. But it was no secret that the older *internat* kids engaged in sex in a multitude of ways and with a multitude of partners. Burakov saw the *internat* as a place that, through its neglect, fostered perversions of all kinds: sodomy, statutory rape, even bestiality. He could believe that *internat* graduates might stab and kill girls, slashing at their genitals. They might, he believed, kill both girls and boys.

But he could not believe the written records of Kalenik's

confessions to Beklemishchev. They were, he thought, filled with inconsistencies and inaccuracies. When, in October, Fetisov handed him responsibility for the investigation, Burakov pressed Kalenik hard. What color dress had Lyubov Biryuk been wearing? What had Olga Stalmachenok been carrying? What bus had he taken with Igor Gudkov? Kalenik could not answer.

Gradually, Burakov's initial doubts grew into a belief that Kalenik had not been involved in the seven *lesopolosa* killings. He realized that Kalenik, though he bore the label "retarded," was in many respects a young man of normal intelligence. Yet Beklemishchev and the others had treated him as if he could understand little or nothing. It would not have been difficult for someone like Kalenik to learn a lot about the case from the questions Beklemishchev had asked him. He could have learned the names of the victims, what they looked like, and the way they had been killed. Then, if he had decided to confess, he could have made it sound plausible.

But why would he confess?

Burakov, as it happened, knew firsthand how the experience of arrest and jail could affect someone of Yuri Kalenik's age. He had gone through it himself.

In 1965, Burakov returned from his job plowing up the Virgin Lands for a brief home leave before the army drafted him. On November 7, the forty-eighth anniversary of the Russian Revolution, he took the family dog and gun and spent the holiday alone, hunting rabbits.

Walking home, he passed the cottage of an old schoolmate, Nikolai Kuzmin. The Kuzmins were slaughtering a sow for their holiday meal, and Burakov stopped and ate with them, contributing one of the rabbits he had killed to his hosts' larder. The Kuzmin boys hung a washbasin from the bough of an apple tree and blasted away at it with Burakov's remaining bullets. Nikolai Kuzmin invited Burakov to go to a dance that night.

Burakov declined. He had another social engagement in mind for that evening, a visit to a girl named Tatyana, who lived in the same village. Burakov spent the hours from nine to two with Tatyana. Then he went home.

He awakened the next morning to see a *militsia* car outside his family's cottage. Two *militsionery* came into the house and arrested him. One of them took the hunting rifle down from the wall, opened it, sniffed it, and asked Vasily Burakov for the registration documents. Burakov began to suspect that one of the Kuzmins, during target practice, had shot a neighbor's cow.

But the *militsionery* would not tell him why he was under arrest. They took him to Sevsk and put him in a holding cell with three older men. The men told Burakov he had to sleep on the floor, even though there was a vacant bunk. Burakov refused and, predictably, a fight ensued. The guards broke it up. Burakov did not sleep that night, for fear of what his cell mates might do to him. The next morning, a *syshchik* questioned him about his whereabouts on the night of November 7. Burakov told him he had been with a girl, but, not wanting to embarrass her, he refused to give her name. He went back to the cell.

This went on for three days. Burakov, afraid to sleep, was becoming frightened and disoriented. Finally, the chief of the department in Sevsk, a colonel, told him why he was in jail. His pal, Nikolai Kuzmin, had been found dead after the dance on November 7, stuffed in the bottom of a well. Witnesses had placed Burakov with him before the dance. Burakov had a reputation for fighting. So the police had picked him up, along with other suspects, to see what he might confess. Burakov realized the colonel was trying to do him a favor. He told the *militsioner* what he wanted to know— Tatyana's name. A couple of days later, the Sevsk *militsia* released him, and he entered the army.

He had not confessed to any crimes he had not committed.

But he had an idea of how someone might. Eighteen years later, he pressed Kalenik to tell him.

But Kalenik, in October 1983, refused to say. He was, by then, thoroughly intimidated and thoroughly distrustful of any *militsioner*.

This was due in part to the fact that in the midst of the early investigation, the *militsia* had decided to make sure Kalenik stayed in their grasp, in jail. According to Soviet law, a suspect could be held without charges for three days while the *militsia* gathered evidence against him. After three days, the *militsia* can, if they believe there is sufficient evidence, hold the suspect for another seven days while they prepare the case further. But after this ten-day period, in most cases, the procurator must either formally charge the suspect or let him go.

The *militsia* and the *sledovatyeli* hated to let a suspect go. On the street, they feared, a suspect could learn more about the case against him. He could talk to witnesses, persuade them not to testify, and construct an alibi. The *militsia* much preferred to have him in jail, isolated and afraid. Often, they would plant a *stukach* in the cell with him. Some of the *stukachi* were convicted con men who knew how to lead people on. Sometimes the *stukach*, in the supposed privacy and comradery of the cell, could get the suspect to talk about things he refused to discuss in the interrogation room.

In the case of Kalenik, the Rostov *militsia* charged him with auto theft. According to the charge, he and Shaburov stole an old Moskvich automobile for a joy ride, which ended when they ran the car into a telephone pole. Kalenik vigorously denied the charge. But late in 1983, a court convicted him of auto theft and sentenced him to two and a half years in prison, during which, of course, he would be at the disposal of the investigation.

His growing doubts about Kalenik's guilt placed Burakov in an awkward position. He did not believe that Beklemishchev and the others had purposely fabricated a murder case against Kalenik. In the Soviet judicial system, bringing a case to trial was supposed to be tantamount to obtaining a conviction, and, for the most part, it was. The careers of *sledovatyeli* and *syshchiki* who brought cases that ended in acquittals suffered for it. It would be, Burakov believed, too risky to rig a case against an innocent man for a series of killings. What if the killings continued? Burakov believed that Beklemishchev and the others had seriously misread Kalenik's mental capabilities. They thought that he was severely retarded, and they therefore prompted him as they might have prompted a six-year-old. They would see this not as coercion but as an effort to help a weak mind remember.

But by the autumn of 1983, the entire oblast *militsia* had a great deal at stake in the case against Kalenik. None of them had ever dealt with a series of so many killings. Their yearlong inability to solve the case had begun to attract unfavorable attention from both the local Party leadership and the Ministry of the Interior in Moscow. Up the chain of command from Burakov, everyone wanted desperately to close the case and virtually everyone believed Kalenik was the killer. Before someone of Burakov's middling stature objected and said Kalenik was not the killer, he would have to have his facts lined up. He would have to, in effect, prove that Kalenik was innocent. Otherwise, he could wind up back in the criminology lab or, worse, back breaking up fights in cafés.

The most obvious way to check out Kalenik's confessions was to establish his whereabouts on the days when the killings had occurred. During much of that time, in 1982 and 1983, Kalenik had been a student at the vocational school in Gukovo, learning to be a floor layer. Burakov checked the attendance records. They showed that Kalenik had indeed been in school. But when Burakov checked further, he found a classic Soviet situation. The teachers at Vocational-Technical School No. 45 were in the habit of marking all their students present for every class, regardless of whether they actually showed up. Marking a student absent required that the teacher explain to the school's director why his pupils were not conscientious. It was much easier for all concerned to falsify the attendance records. The same syndrome explained how, every year, the Party announced triumphantly that the country had exceeded its production quotas while, at the same time, the lines in the stores got longer and slower.

When he pressed Kalenik's teachers, Burakov found that they remembered that the boy had missed many classes. Since the records were largely fantasies, it was impossible to know which ones. It might have been easier if Kalenik had led a more settled life. Burakov could have established that he spent certain periods of time in certain places. But as the episode with Shaburov suggested, Kalenik and his friends wandered, spending the night with friends or someone's relatives or in the backs of trolleybuses. Establishing Kalenik's whereabouts on particular days, Burakov realized, was going to require months, if not years, of tedious travel, interviewing witnesses with poor memories.

He might have done all that and still seen Kalenik tried for murder. But more corpses turned up.

The first was found, officially, on October 8, in a wooded area near Novoshakhtinsk. In fact, someone had called the local *militsia* in September and told them there was a body in the woods. The *militsia* had searched and found nothing. They got another report in October, and on their second try, they located the remains.

They were the bones of a young woman, in her late teens or early twenties. She was lying, naked, on her back. Her body had been sliced open from the breastbone down. The killer had amputated both nipples and one entire breast. He had slashed at her left eye.

The remains matched none of the current missing-persons cases around Novoshakhtinsk. The *militsia* could not establish an identity, and without an identity it was hard to investigate. But the medical examiner said the body had been lying in the woods since July or August. Yuri Kalenik had been at large in those months.

On October 30, near Shakhty, the *militsia* found a corpse harder to reconcile with the theory that Yuri Kalenik committed the *lesopolosa* killings. It was another young woman, half covered with dirt. She had been dead only three days, which meant that Kalenik had been in custody for about six weeks when she died. Her wounds seemed to identify her as part of the *lesopolosa* series. Her murderer had bashed her skull in, presumably with the blunt end of his knife. He had strangled her. Then, in a frenzy that was by now becoming familiar to the medical examiners, he had tried to remove virtually all her female physical characteristics. He had cut open her abdomen and removed her uterus, her clitoris, and the labia of her vagina. He had sliced off her nipples. Searchers, combing the woods, found neither the excised organs nor the victim's clothing.

One fact distinguished this case from the *lesopolosa* killings. The victim's eyes had not been touched.

Three weeks later, working with a fingerprint taken from the corpse, the investigators established the victim's identity. She was Vera Shevkun, nineteen years old, a school dropout who lived, officially at least, with an aunt in Shakhty. She had no job and wandered about, frequently riding the *elektrichka*. She drank heavily, and she led what the *militsia* reports described as a "disorderly sex life."

The investigators in Shakhty checked out Shevkun in all the known *pritony* in the city. A *priton* is an apartment whose tenant allows criminals to use it as a hangout. Sometimes the tenant is himself a criminal. Sometimes he simply likes the side benefits: an occasional stolen television set, some illegal drugs, or a woman. Shevkun, it turned out, had been hanging out in a Shakhty *priton* in the days before her death; according to the Shakhty investigators, she had slept with several men in succession there. Most intriguing of all, one of the witnesses said that, on the night before her death, a man rumored to be a *militsioner* in plain clothing had visited the *priton*. The Shakhty investigators, though, had been unable to determine which *militsioner*, if any, the witness had seen.

Burakov, still charged with completing the case against Kalenik, monitored the reports on this new investigation. He had wondered how the *lesopolosa* killer had been able to lure his victims away from their trains and buses without a struggle. One possible explanation was that the killer was someone with an appearance of authority, someone in uniform. He might, Burakov thought, be a *militsioner* or, more likely, someone who had been fired from the *militsia*. Or he might be the man seen in the *priton* the night before Vera Shevkun died. But this case raised other questions. How could the killer, he wondered, know enough about anatomy to remove a woman's uterus? Could he be a physician or someone who worked in a morgue? What kind of sickness motivated him? Was he even the *lesopolosa* killer? And if he was, why had he broken his pattern of attacking eyes?

On November 27, in the woods south of Skakhty, not far from a railroad station called Kirpichnaya, yet another skeleton turned up. This victim had apparently been dead for several months, since summer. Animals had scattered the bones about the site. But there were cuts on the left eye socket. The investigators found some clothing nearby, but the pockets contained only two movie tickets for a theater in Shakhty. The *syshchiki* there could not identify the body.

Still more questions arose. The apparent time of death, in late summer, left open the possibility that Yuri Kalenik had killed her. But if Kalenik had killed her, why had he not mentioned this victim in his confession? And if this was not Kalenik's work, why was the victim's left eye socket cut?

The new year, 1984, entered with at least nine unsolved *lesopolosa* murder cases on the books of the Rostov *militsia*.

Then, on January 4, a hunter walking on a ridge overlooking the Rostov-Shakhty rail line found the body of a boy, covered with pieces of clothing and a wispy coating of snow. Mikhail Fetisov led the *militsia* team that drove out from Rostov to examine the corpse and the site. It was not far from Kazachi Lagerya, the railroad station and military base where the still-unidentified woman's corpse had been found in the autumn of 1982.

Fetisov already had an idea about the new victim's identity. A week earlier, on December 28, the *militsia* had received a report on a boy named Sergei Markov, fourteen years old. Markov lived in Gukovo with his grandfather, and he had a good school record. In accordance with Soviet practice, he had been spending time during the fall semester getting some practical work experience at an agricultural equipment factory called Krasny Aksai, in a small city adjacent to Rostov. On December 27, he had left home, planning to take the *elektrichka* to the factory to collect some belongings he had neglected to bring home. He never came back. The preliminary description of the body fit Markov.

Near Novocherkassk, Fetisov and the other *militsionery* left the paved road and took a dirt road to the ridge where the hunter had found the body. The decomposed remains he had seen in Donskoi and other crime scenes had not prepared him for the body on the ridge. The cold weather and the snow had preserved it like a morgue refrigerator. The killer had perforated the boy's neck dozens, scores of times; the medical examiner would later count seventy wounds there, most of them light and superficial, suggesting how much the killer enjoyed seeing his knife enter his victim. Sergei Markov had suffered dismemberment analogous to that of Vera Shevkun. The killer had excised his testicles, his penis, and most of the scrotum. Turning the body over, they could see signs that his anal sphincter had been stretched and broken. Fetisov shuddered and hoped that the boy had died of his neck wounds before that had happened to him. Nearby, they found his clothes and, curiously, three separate piles of human excrement.

In the valley below, perhaps a mile away, an *elektrichka* rumbled along, slowing for a stop at a rural station called Persyanovka. Most likely, Fetisov thought, the killer—or killers—had met the boy on the train, somehow lured him off at Persyanovka, and then killed and mutilated him. How did the killer lure the boy off the train without being noticed? And why did he kill so sadistically? And how did he do it and walk away without being seen or heard by witnesses? Was the same person dispatching males and females? Or was this a new killer? Fetisov realized that he had wondered about some of the same questions as he examined Lyubov Biryuk's body in Donskoi, eighteen months and perhaps a dozen murders ago. With a sinking feeling, he began to suspect that, despite the arrest of Yuri Kalenik, he might be no closer to the answers than he had been then.

Fetisov began his investigation of Markov's killing in Gukovo, where the boy had boarded the *elektrichka*. It might not, he thought, be coincidental that Markov's last trip began in the same little town that contained the *internat* for retarded children. He stopped at the school and found the conditions as appalling as Burakov had a few months earlier. Stifling his disgust, he asked the director if any of her charges had been out and riding the trains on December 27.

As it happened, a former student, Mikhail Tyapkin, had been at the *internat* that day, and had left to catch the same train Markov had taken. Tyapkin was twenty-three, severely retarded, and massive. He stood almost six feet three inches and weighed over two hundred pounds. He had spent most of his life in *internati*, and it had taken years for him to learn to talk. After he had grown too old for the *internat* in Gukovo, the director said, he had been assigned to an adult home in Shakhty. He had shown up at the *internat* that day to hang out before the director shooed him away.

Fetisov ordered his men to find Tyapkin. He was not at the adult home in Shakhty. He had not shown up at the home of his closest relatives in a village called Gorny. But the relatives suggested that the *militsia* check with Tyapkin's friend, another retarded boy, named Aleksandr Ponomaryev, at yet another *internat*, near Gorny. Ponomaryev was described as short and slender. He was seventeen. Later that night, Fetisov got a telephone call at his hotel. The local *militsia* near Gorny reported triumphantly that Aleksandr Ponomaryev had been found and questioned. He had confessed that he and Tyapkin murdered Sergei Markov.

Fetisov ordered them to stop the interrogation until he could get there. Early the next morning, he conducted his own interrogation of Ponomaryev. Ponomaryev told a plausible story. He and Tyapkin had gone to Persyanovka in hopes of watching an exercise by tanks from nearby Kazachi Lagerya; the tanks, in winter, used the local fields for mock battles. At the station they had met Sergei Markov. They had bought some wine and bread at the station's snack counter. Tyapkin had invited Markov to go for a walk. After walking out of sight of the rail line, he had killed him.

Fetisov tried to check out the story. At the station, the woman behind the snack counter confirmed part of Ponomaryev's story. She had seen him on December 27. He had tried to buy wine, but she had refused to sell it to him because he was under age. Ponomaryev had gone and gotten someone bigger and older, who then bought the wine. Yes, she said, looking at a picture. It was Tyapkin.

"Can you show us where you killed Markov?" Fetisov asked.

"Yes," Ponomaryev replied.

The boy led the group of *militsionery*, along with four citizen witnesses enlisted for the occasion, out along the railroad tracks. For a while, Fetisov thought, he was going in the wrong direction. Then he turned off the tracks and led them up through the muddy field and thorn bushes toward the site of the murder. But he walked past the site and circled around, evidently looking for something.

"What are you looking for, Sasha?" Fetisov asked him.

"For the shit we left here," Ponomaryev answered.

That persuaded Fetisov. The three piles of feces, he knew, had been removed by the investigators. He had written about it in the protocol of the crime scene examination. How could Ponomaryev know about them if he had not participated in Markov's murder?

A short time later, the *militsia* found Mikhail Tyapkin. He was not as bright as Ponomaryev and, to Fetisov, not as useful a witness. At the Persyanovka railroad station, he could not get oriented.

But, yes, Tyapkin said, he had killed someone. He had caught a partisan (a guerrilla fighter during the German occupation) on the train, killed him, and cut off his testicles.

Not only that, Tyapkin's confession went on. He had killed Vera Shevkun. And there was a psychiatrist working at the home he lived in whom he would like to kill. He wanted authorization to drive a tractor, and she refused to give it to him. He wanted to fuck her and cut off her breasts. He had already killed another girl, he said. He had tossed her body into a hole near a gas station and covered the body with branches.

Fetisov ordered a search around the gas station. It yielded nothing. But two weeks later, the *militsia* searched again. They found a woman's body.

Meanwhile, two more bodies were found in different areas of Rostov oblast, one near Salsk and one near Rostov. Ponomaryev confessed that he and Tyapkin had killed both victims.

Very quickly after that, though, the local *militsia* found other suspects, who also confessed. One of them was caught with a victim's jewelry.

* * *

The investigation was beginning to resemble a juggler trying to keep too many eggs in the air as the barrage of bodies, suspects, and confessions got heavier. If Ponomaryev and Tyapkin had confessed to two crimes they had not committed, could their confessions in the Markov case be valid? If they weren't, how had Ponomaryev known about details like the piles of feces and the site of the crime? How had Tyapkin known about the body near the gas station?

Most of the Rostov *militsionery* were ready to ignore the discrepancies and press ahead with the prosecution of what they were now calling the "Kalenik-Tyapkin Gang." Pavel Chernyshev, the deputy chief of the oblast force and Fetisov's boss, held that view. So did Igor Zakshever, Fetisov's deputy in charge of the division of very serious crimes. Fetisov and the procurator, Aleksandr Ryabko, wavered in the middle.

Viktor Burakov stood, more or less alone, on the other side. The reports he was reading about the "gang" failed to persuade him. From what he had seen at the crime scenes, it seemed highly unlikely that more than one person could have taken part in any of the *lesopolosa* killings. Burakov had a difficult time conceiving of the personality that could inflict such wounds. That such a personality could have friends and accomplices struck him as impossible. He had seen enough in the Kalenik investigation to discount Ponomaryev's performance at the crime scene. Ponomaryev might have heard enough during his first interrogation, before Fetisov's arrival, to know that the killing occurred on the ridge above the railroad and that the investigators had found feces near the body. Tyapkin, in his wandering, could have stumbled across the woman's body. The two additional murders that Ponomaryev had admitted to, which were subsequently found to be the work of others, only strengthened Burakov's suspicion that neither Ponomaryev nor Tyapkin had killed anyone.

* * *

Early in 1984, word came from the medical examiner that fundamentally altered the investigation. The examiner had found a small quantity of semen in Markov's anus.

The presence of semen suggested several things. First, it appeared that Markov had been raped before being killed. The previous corpses in the *lesopolosa* series had either decomposed too far or been too brutally mutilated to allow a finding of rape.

But who would rape a boy? Could the killer be a homosexual? Could a homosexual also have killed the female victims?

Equally important, the semen was the first physical evidence that the killer, or killers, had left behind.

The first task was to type it. In those years, in the United States the FBI was developing genetic identification of samples of semen and other secretions, like sweat and saliva, that police encountered at crime scenes. By analyzing the DNA found in a secretion and comparing it to a suspect's, the FBI could make as precise an identification as it could with a fingerprint.

But such tests were years beyond the capability of Rostov's crime lab. In Russia, forensic laboratories tested secretions only for the antigens found in blood. In about eighty percent of a given population, a person with type A blood, for instance, will also have the A antigen in his secretions. (The remaining twenty percent, which show no antigens, are called non-secreters.) In Russian labs, technicians applied standard laboratory antibodies to a blood or sperm sample. Then they examined it under a microscope. They looked to see if the sample cells, which looked like the tiny bubbles in champagne, remained separate or began to lump together in clusters. A sample that reacted to neither the A nor B antibody was type O, the blood type with neither antigen. If it reacted to both, it was type AB, the rarest blood type, possessed by only six percent of the population.

The initial lab report on the semen found in Sergei Markov

confirmed Burakov's doubts that Kalenik or Tyapkin or any of the other boys from Gukovo had been involved. It said the semen was type O, and none of them had type O blood.

But a couple of days later, the lab corrected itself. It had mixed up the sample from Markov with another, the medical examiner's report said. The actual semen sample appeared to be, if nothing had contaminated it, type AB, the type found in only six percent of any given population.

That was Mikhail Tyapkin's blood type.

4

Girls with Disorderly Sex Lives

In 1984, bodies turned up continually, as if silently to mock the pretensions of those who thought they had solved the case. On January 10, someone walking a dog in the woods near the Rostov airport discovered a young woman's remains, naked from the waist down and half hidden in a thicket, on a blanket of snow and dead, rotting leaves. She lay no more than one hundred fifty yards from the spot where, six months previously, someone had killed Irina Dunenkova.

Mikhail Fetisov, when he got word of this discovery from the local *militsia*, ordered them to stay clear of the scene until his staff could arrive. When he got there, he could see that this victim had been dead for only about a day; she had died after both Tyapkin and Kalenik were in custody. In twenty-four hours, time and nature had erased none of the traces of her killer's rage. A knife had ripped her nose and upper lip from her face, then torn open her dress and her body from the neck down. Her breasts, her neck, and belly showed approximately thirty cuts, some shallow and some deep, from the point of the killer's blade. But her wounds differed in two respects from those found earlier in the Rostov woodlands. Her eyes were intact. And the ring finger of her left hand had been cut off. The searchers at the scene found a cheap metal finger ring not far from the body. In the mud near the scene, they found a footprint, a huge one. Whoever left it there had a size thirteen shoe.

The investigators also found traces of semen and blood on

the victim's clothing. They sent them to the laboratory at the Rostov Institute of Medicine for testing.

Fetisov ordered in bloodhounds. They sniffed around the scene and then tugged their handlers north, toward a little village in the woods called Lesnichestvo, a collection of half a dozen buildings that housed workers who harvested the trees in the state forest. *Syshchiki* went door to door in the village. Several residents said they had heard a brief, piercing scream in the woods on the previous afternoon. None of them had thought to call the *militsia* or to investigate. The woods were full of punk kids and tramps, and a lot of strange sounds came out of them.

Then Fetisov's searchers got lucky. If the victim had carried identification, it was gone. But in her clothing, they found a claim ticket for checked baggage at the Rostov bus station, three miles from the scene of the murder. A tag on the victim's luggage identified her: Natalia Shalopinina, eighteen years old, from a hamlet called Zolotaryevka in rural Rostov oblast.

At the bus station, they got another break. The *militsia* had a constant presence at the station, working from a small office furnished with a desk, a telephone, and a sofa with cracked vinyl upholstery, just off the main waiting area. One of the *militsia*'s jobs there was to chase out the people who tried to spend the night in the station. Three times in the evenings before her death, the *militsia* had rousted Natalia Shalopinina. On one of those occasions, she had been with a boy who worked at the nearby tractor factory called Rostselmash.

With this information, the *militsia* quickly assembled a profile of the victim, done in their peculiar, fill-in-the-blanks language. "Work: none. Studies: none. Abused alcohol. Vagrant life-style. Suffered from gonorrhea. Disorderly sex life," the report said. "Disorderly" was the all-purpose Soviet negative. A driver violating traffic rules was disorderly. A factory that failed to meet its quotas was disorderly. A woman who slept around indiscriminately had a disorderly sex life. Conversely, when something was right, it was "in order."

The boy from Rostselmash, it turned out, had known Natalia for several years, since their days together at a school in Semikarakorsk, sixty miles northeast of Rostov. He had, he said, met her for three consecutive nights at the bus station—January 6, 7, and 8. But he lived in a dormitory at the factory. He had no place private to take her. That had not deterred Natalia. On those three nights, she had satisfied him sexually outdoors, almost on the street. They had used alleys and doorways for shelter.

But the boy had an alibi for January 9. He had been at work. Witnesses placed him in the factory or the dormitory from before the last time Natalia had been chased from the bus station to after the discovery of her body.

The medical examiner's autopsy report added three leads. Natalia had been infested with pubic lice; her stomach contained undigested food; there was no semen inside her. Fetisov's men started to work on the hypothesis that someone had met her at the bus station and lured her away with the offer of a free meal. His semen was found on her clothes. And he might well have gone to a doctor or a pharmacy to get treatment for lice, gonorrhea, or both. They began to check out all the local clinics and pharmacies. They showed her picture around the bus station. But no one had seen her go off with anyone. No pharmacist had sold anti-lice ointment to someone who could not account for his whereabouts on January 9. All the people being treated at the Rostov venereal disease clinic also had alibis.

The preliminary investigation established another enticing lead. Natalia had had one close girlfriend, Olga Kuprina. In August 1982, Olga and Natalia had gone together to Semikarakorsk, where Natalia wanted to enroll in a music school. But Olga failed to show up for the bus trip home. Natalia had told a sister at the time that she assumed Olga had gone off somewhere, but she had no idea where. No one in their hometown had seen Olga since 1982.

It took no genius to wonder whether Olga Kuprina might be one of the unidentified bodies. The *militsia* had already obtained an artist's sketches, based on the skulls, of all the unidentified corpses. They were checked against her picture. A resemblance to one sketch was immediately apparent. Then they looked up Kuprina's dental records. They matched the teeth in the skull found near Kazachi Lagerya in October 1982, the second in the *lesopolosa* series.

Kuprina had a biography sadly similar to her friend Natalia's. She had dropped out of school. The neighbors recalled a constant stream of boys and men visiting her. Her relations with her mother were such that the older woman had not bothered to report her daughter's absence to the *militsia*. No one in Olga's family could say how she had come to be near Kazachi Lagerya. Maybe, they ventured, she had been having an affair with a soldier.

The friendship between Natalia Shalopinina and Olga Kuprina was the first link between victims in the case. But the list of unanswered questions only grew. Had someone who knew both Shalopinina and Kuprina killed both of them? Had he also killed Lyubov Biryuk and the others? If he did, why had he stopped slashing at the eyes of his victims? Why had semen begun to show up on their corpses? Was it because the bodies had been found quickly, in cold weather, preserving what had been washed off or had decomposed in the earlier cases, or was this the signature of a new killer? Since Kalenik and Tyapkin were both in jail when Natalia was murdered, was there a third killer at large? Or were they innocent? Could the same person have committed all the *lesopolosa* murders?

Viktor Burakov, still working on the case against Yuri Kalenik, studied the reports on the Natalia Shalopinina investigation. He thought he noticed something, the beginning of a pattern. The victims who had been identified earlier had been boys and girls like Lyubov Biryuk, Olga Stalmachenok, and Igor Gudkov. Each lived with at least one fairly responsible adult, and each had been traveling on innocent missions when they disappeared. But Vera Shevkun and Natalia Shalopinina were, legally, young adult women. Kuprina, though only sixteen when she was killed, was physically mature. All three lived on the verge of prostitution. So, at least theoretically, might have the remaining unidentified victims. Burakov knew their type.

Every *militsioner* who had ever worked a station knew women like them. Russian train and bus stations attract them. In a nation where only a privileged minority own automobiles, tens of millions of ordinary Russians use the transit stations every day. One group, the largest, consists of people passing through on their way to and from work, or to buy and sell in the city markets, or on vacation. These Russians have two things in common: they have money in their pockets, and they will soon be gone. A second group uses the stations as shelters; they are the only warm places in Russia where a person has a plausible pretext for loitering all day and into the night. The third group, thieves and pimps and con men, preys on the first two. They are like sharks, selecting their victims from the constantly changing offerings of the sea, striking and moving on.

On a summer Saturday, at a big train station like Rostov's, perhaps a dozen different gangs run con games. Usually a boy or, preferably, a pretty girl, sets up a folding table with a stack of numbered tickets and six dice. She sells tickets for a few rubles each, then invites someone, from the crowd that always gathers, to throw the dice. The first payoffs are small. But then, when a flush-looking mark shows up, it transpires that two people have the same number, and they must bet against each other for the pot. The second winner, of course, is a gang member, posing as part of the crowd. He may be dressed in rags, or he may be a young man looking too proud and foolish for his own good, whose "wife" begs him not to play because he doesn't have enough money. In this game, a person who cannot match his opponent's bet loses. Miraculously, the poorer-looking player always manages to reach deep into his pocket for enough cash to match and better the mark's cash. Shortly afterward, the girl folds the table and moves on. She will meet with her confederates later on to divide the take. The mark, if he understands he has been conned, will have a choice. He can attempt to find the gang in the swirling throngs at the station and to find a *militsioner* who will arrest and prosecute the gang members. Or he can catch his train to Volgograd and hope no one finds out how stupid he's been. Invariably, he will choose the train.

Russian prostitutes also work the stations, but they are a much lower class of prostitute than the pretty young women who bribe the doormen to get into the tourist hotels of Moscow or Saint Petersburg, looking for customers with dollars, deutsche marks, or yen. The women in the stations have cheaply dyed hair, worn bodies, and tired eyes; they service five to ten customers a night for a few rubles each and consider themselves lucky when a client has a car to give them some temporary shelter.

At the bottom of the station's social order are the Russian homeless. Theoretically, Soviet society had no homelessness and no unemployment. The law required the government to give every citizen a job and a place to live, however menial or miserable. It required every citizen to carry an internal passport and a work booklet, listing his residence and place of employment. If the *militsia* picked up someone with neither document, standard procedure called for turning the individual over to a *priyemnik-raspredyelityel,* a term that means a center of reception and distribution. In fact, these places are all but indistinguishable from jails, complete with *militsionery* serving as guards. An individual served thirty days in the *priyemnik-raspredyelityel,* then received a work assignment, generally on a collective farm looking for field hands. Some people bounced continually in and out of the system, quitting the farms and drifting back to the stations. The men among them might try to get by scavenging bottles and selling them back to liquor kiosks. The women, like Natalia Shalopinina, might take on a man for half a bottle of vodka, or a hot meal, or a warm place to sleep. Sometimes, they became the victims of a shark who was smarter, or stronger, or crueler than they were. Burakov felt a certain sympathy for them. Nearly always, he had found, they came from families unlike his own, families in which the parents drank, or fought, or both. But he also felt an aversion, based on his belief that they were part of an environment that encouraged crime.

Reading the reports on Shalopinina and Kuprina, Burakov found further reason to doubt that the boys from the *internat* in Gukovo had played any role in the *lesopolosa* killings. He could not envision Yuri Kalenik, much less Mikhail Tyapkin, in the role of a shark. Whatever else the two boys might be, they were not guileful. And he thought he saw in the reports an important clue that the other *syshchiki* had overlooked. They had assumed that if Shalopinina was wearing a ring on the finger the killer had cut off, it was the cheap one found near the body, a yellow metal band worth a ruble or two. Burakov wondered whether the killer would have bothered to cut off a finger to steal something so nearly worthless. He thought there might have been a second ring, one more valuable for some reason. Perhaps the killer had given it to her. Perhaps he had put his initials on it.

At that point, early in 1984, Burakov had some time to pursue his suspicions. The investigators had just sent Yuri Kalenik to the Serbsky Institute in Moscow for a psychiatric examination that would determine whether he was legally competent to stand trial for murder, should they decide to charge him. It gave Burakov a break from the constant round of questioning and requestioning Kalenik, trying to determine his whereabouts on the days when the early victims had died, trying to establish which of his friends might be members of the "gang" that some *syshchiki* still believed had gone on killing after Kalenik was jailed.

Burakov requisitioned a car and driver and drove northeast to Zolotaryevka. The village, on a state farm that raises livestock, is a cluster of sagging frame cottages and muddy dirt roads, with geese and chickens pecking in the weeds. It is a place where women age quickly, turning from girls to mothers and from mothers to *babushki* by the time they are forty, becoming square and thick, with metal caps on their teeth, kerchiefs over their graying hair, and muddy rubber boots on their stumpy legs. Burakov could see them as he drove into town, waiting by the war monument for the bread truck to arrive at the village store. When it did, they gathered around it and lined up, gossiping quietly, just as the geese and the chickens would come clucking to them when they brought the bread home.

Natalia Shalopinina's mother, Galina Bondarenko, looked like her neighbors, short and heavy, with a round, weathered face, a kerchief on her head, thick socks in her boots, and dirt under her fingernails. She walked with a slow, rolling gait. Natalia was her first child, born when she herself was only nineteen. Galina's union with Natalia's father was not a happy one, and they divorced when Natalia was three years old.

She snorted when asked why the marriage failed. There was one, pandemic reason for the failure of marriages in rural Russia. Galina flicked her index finger against her neck—the Russian sign for drunkenness. He would drink heavily. They would quarrel. He would beat her. He would drink some more.

Galina remarried when Natalia was five, but her first husband would still show up occasionally, drunk, imploring her to take him back. He always had, Galina recollected, a soft spot for his daughter, and he never beat her. Eventually, he moved to Rostov and he, too, remarried.

Galina thought that her second husband tried to be a good stepfather to Natalia, and for a while she seemed to be growing up normally. She did reasonably well at school, and she learned to play the accordion. But as she reached adolescence, Natalia rebelled. Perhaps it was because of her early memories. Perhaps she simply couldn't stand the idea of becoming one of the women in line at the bread store.

She started to talk back a lot, to do whatever she wanted to do. Mother and daughter would fight. Natalia started going out with boys when she was thirteen. Sometimes, she would stay out all night. Just as she finished the seventh grade, she got pregnant. Her mother persuaded her to get an abortion. What choice did she have? She had to finish the eighth grade. Natalia spoke very little to her mother after that. She refused to say which boy, if she knew, had fathered her aborted child. "If I tell you, they'll kill me," she told her mother.

A year or so later, when she was fifteen, Natalia attracted the attention of an older man, recently divorced. By that time, Galina recalled, Natalia was as attractive as she would ever be. She had a broad face that could charitably be called plain, but she had a woman's figure. She was too young to marry legally, but she dropped out of school, moved into her lover's cottage, and became pregnant again. Again, she got an abortion. Her lover, like her father, drank a lot. Soon, the couple broke up. Natalia spent time at an aunt's in Semikarakorsk, where she worked sporadically in a canning factory. She would occasionally try to live with her father in Rostov, but her father's new wife disliked her and generally threw her out after a few days.

Natalia tried twice to learn a trade. In 1982, when she was sixteen, she announced that she wanted to enroll in a music school in Semikarakorsk and learn to play the accordion professionally. That was when she went to Semikarakorsk with Olga Kuprina. But the director of the school, she said, had been out of town, and she had not enrolled. She never tried again. At the end of 1983, she had decided that she would enroll in a school for trolleybus drivers in Rostov. That was where she was going, or where her mother thought she was going, when she disappeared.

Had she been wearing a ring on her left hand, Burakov asked.

Yes, Galina said. She had noticed it around New Year's. She did not know who gave it to her daughter. She thought it was someone in Rostov.

Who, Burakov asked, were her boyfriends.

There were too many boyfriends to keep track of, Galina replied.

And that proved to be the case. When Burakov and the local *militsia* started checking on men in Zolotaryevka and the neighboring villages, they had difficulty finding someone who had not slept with Natalia Shalopinina, Olga Kuprina, or both. The obvious suspects, like Natalia's ex-lover, had alibis for January 9. No one admitted giving Shalopinina the ring her mother had seen.

Frustrated, Burakov returned to Rostov, leaving the local investigators to complete the work of checking out the alibis of Shalopinina's many partners. So many of the clues in this case, it seemed, led only to endless hours of fruitless checking. In Novoshakhtinsk, the handwriting experts were still trying to match the handwriting on the Black Cat postcard to the employment records in the area. Others were completing the checks on the old satyr Vladimir Babakov. Now more men were painstakingly dissecting the sex life of an unhappy eighteen-year-old who had slept with far too many men for her own good. He himself had months of work ahead of him, trying to pin down the activities of a group of retarded boys. None of it, he sensed, had brought them any closer to the man he felt was out there, a man with a knife and a fearful rage.

* * *

On March 11, railroad workers walking in the woods beside the tracks near Shakhty found another body, just emerging from the winter snows and thoroughly decomposed. It had apparently lain in the woods since the previous summer. The *militsia* could not identify it. But the medical examiner found traces of knife wounds in the eye sockets and on the rib bones. It was the thirteenth body found in the woods since the summer of 1982.

Fetisov ordered a search, with bloodhounds, of all the parks and wooded strips where bodies had been discovered. On April 22, the dogs found a fourteenth body, a woman's remains. They lay in a dense thicket in Aviators' Park in Rostov, near a Mig-21 fighter jet mounted on a plinth as a military monument and about half a mile from the woods where Irina Dunenkova and Natalia Shalopinina were killed. The winter cold and snow had preserved the body well, and its wounds left little doubt about the killer. With a knife, he had extirpated most of her vagina, uterus, and bladder. He had, however, left her eyes alone.

The body was half clothed, and from papers in the coat the *militsia* identified Marta Ryabenko, forty-four, a worker, sometimes, at the Krasny Aksai factory outside Rostov and an inmate, sometimes, of various drunk tanks and alcohol detoxification wards in Rostov. She was a woman born to the Soviet elite. Her grandfather had been a general. But after his death, the family fell into difficulty. The last day anyone had seen her at work was February 22. Under personal traits, the investigators filled in "disorderly sex life."

Her coat and dress bore semen stains, and Fetisov ordered them sent to the lab for identification.

On the theory that the killer might return to the scene, Fetisov also ordered a covert watch of the area near the Mig-21. In short order, the watchers brought in a suspect named Nikolai Byeskorsy.

Byeskorsy lived near the airport, where he worked as a baggage handler. He drank and he showed up for work. Once in a while, he met a woman and persuaded her to share a bottle in the park.

That was what Byeskorsy had been doing when he was caught. He had brought a woman into the area where the Ryabenko corpse had been, opened a bottle, and split it with her. When she was thoroughly drunk, he had stripped her naked, laid her on the cold ground, and had intercourse with her. When it was over, the woman lay where she was, all but insensate. Byeskorsy got up, went to a store, and bought another bottle. When he returned, the watching *militsionery* decided that he was not going to pull out a knife. But to be on the safe side, they took both of them in for questioning. The woman went to a drunk tank and Byeskorsy to a cell. To the embarrassment of the guards in the drunk tank, the woman came to, slipped away, and disappeared. Vladimir Kolyesnikov, Fetisov's deputy in the division of criminal apprehension, participated in Byeskorsy's interrogation and almost immediately returned with triumphant news. Byeskorsy had confessed to the murders of both Ryabenko and Shalopinina.

To Viktor Burakov, it seemed immediately apparent that Byeskorsy's admissions were just another false confession squeezed out of a frightened and disoriented suspect. He was certain that Byeskorsy could not be the *lesopolosa* killer. Byeskorsy's work gave him no opportunity to travel about the oblast; the killer either traveled for his work or had a job that allowed frequent absences. The killer did not, Burakov believed, drink with his victims. He did not have normal sexual intercourse with them. And he certainly did not leave them in the woods while he took off after another bottle.

But Burakov's doubts only fueled the growing rancor within the Rostov oblast *militsia*. Several of the department's leaders, including Fetisov's boss, deputy chief Pavel Chernyshev, had already committed themselves to the case against the "Kalenik-Tyapkin Gang." Chernyshev had not personally witnessed the interrogations of Kalenik, Tyapkin, and

Byeskorsy, nor had be watched the field experiments with them. He had read the reports, and the reports indicated to him that the increasingly embarrassing *lesopolosa* cases could soon be closed. To Chernyshev and others who had supported the theory of Kalenik's and Tyapkin's guilt, Byeskorsy's confession was a welcome event. If he turned out to be the killer of Ryabenko and Shalopinina, it would leave undisturbed the cases against Kalenik and Tyapkin. Just after Ryabenko's body had been found, Tyapkin had been formally charged with Markov's murder. Dropping the charges against him could provoke a major scandal; in the Soviet bureaucracy, it was almost always better to avoid admitting a mistake.

At the initiative of Chernyshev and Kolyesnikov, Byeskorsy was held on a charge of rape, based on the observation that he had incapacited his woman friend with alcohol before their intercourse. But the real goal of the charge was to give the investigators time to build a case against him for the Ryabenko and Shalopinina murders.

Burakov could no longer keep silent about his doubts. When the *militsia* officers working on the *lesopolosa* investigation convened for their regular meeting, he stated openly that he was convinced Kalenik and Tyapkin had nothing to do with the killings. The murderer, he said, was still at large. The deaths of Shalopinina and Ryabenko showed that. So did the flaws in the cases against the boys from Gukovo and the flaws in the case against Byeskorsy.

Burakov's statement provoked a stiff, cold reaction from Chernyshev. It was as if, Burakov thought, he simply did not want to hear a contradictory opinion. Burakov left the room chagrined, all but certain that he would be removed from the case. When he was not, Burakov assumed that Fetisov had interceded on his behalf.

But the division among the *militsia* investigators was open and all but irreparable. One faction believed in Kalenik's and

Tyapkin's guilt in the initial string of murders. The other was convinced that the case against them was a sad mistake.

The forensic laboratory at the Rostov Institute of Medicine had yet to give a definitive analysis of the semen found on the clothing of both Natalia Shalopinina and Marta Ryabenko. Typing semen was almost as much art as science. Much depended on the state of the sample, and in murder cases like the *lesopolosa* killings, the sample might have remained in the woods for months or more. Much depended on the skill of the analyst. Working with only the kind of microscope and test tubes that might be found in an average American high-school chemistry lab, he or she had to make judgments that came down, in the final analysis, to how clearly and convincingly the little bubbles, the magnified antigen cells reacting to an antibody, clustered under the lens.

Dr. Lydia Amelina, the director of the forensic laboratory at the Rostov Institute of Medicine, fell under intense pressure to issue a definitive analysis of the samples the *militsia* had forwarded to her. Finally, the investigators convened a meeting. She could not, she said, tell for certain whether the samples she had were group A or AB. The tests clearly showed a reaction to the A antigen. But there seemed to be a very weak B reaction as well. She delivered a long and frustrating discourse on the possibilities. There might be sweat or saliva from the victim mixed into the sample. There could be more than one criminal involved, and a mixing of secretions.

Amelina's waffling frustrated the investigators. Officials in Moscow had begun to monitor the case with growing impatience. At their suggestion, the Rostov investigators sought help from an outside expert, Dr. Svetlana Gurtovaya, chief of the biology lab in the bureau of forensic medicine of the Ministry of Health in Moscow.

Gurtovaya flew down to Rostov and collected the samples, stopping long enough to criticize the way they had been stored in Rostov. She is a genial, matronly woman, bespectacled, with her light brown hair cropped short. She works in a crumbling old building on the banks of the Moscow River, and her lab's activities range from forensic work to establishing paternity in child-support cases to offering opinions on whether bones dug up near Sverdlovsk could have belonged to members of the family of the late Czar Nicholas II. Gurtovaya shows no uncertainty when she delivers her opinions. She showed none in analyzing the samples she received from Rostov. They were type AB. Nikolai Byeskorsy had type O blood, so the case against him all but collapsed.

The killer was still out there.

5

The Killer's Fever

On the evening of March 24, 1984, the worried parents of a ten-year-old boy named Dmitri Ptashnikov called the *militsia* in Novoshakhtinsk to report that their son was missing. They got a more serious response than the parents of Olga Stalmachenok had received fifteen months previously, when she disappeared from the same street on her way home from her piano lesson. *Syshchiki* from the local station interviewed the parents that same night. They learned that Dima, as he was called, collected stamps. He had saved a few kopecks, and he wanted to buy some stamps at a kiosk on Lenin Street, the main thoroughfare in Novoshakhtinsk. He had gone out to get them and hadn't returned.

The *militsia* mounted a search and notified headquarters in Rostov that another child was missing. But their efforts led to no more success than in the search for Olga Stalmachenok. Three days later, it was a group of boys, playing in the woods about a mile from the site of Stalmachenok's murder, that found the body.

Viktor Burakov left Rostov immediately to supervise the examination of the scene. The body lay on a low, wooded hillside that overlooked a dirt road and a drainage pond that served the Sixth Collective Farm.

Ptashnikov was on his side, loosely covered by some of his own clothing. From the position of the arms and the marks on the wrists, it was clear that his hands had been tied behind his back. His body bore the evidence of numerous

74

knife wounds. The killer had cut off the boy's penis and the end of his tongue. His anus showed traces of penetration, and there were splotches of semen on his T-shirt. The investigators sent the shirt to the forensic laboratory in Rostov; the semen was found to be type AB.

Burakov expanded the search to the other side of the dirt road, and there his men found one of the boy's shoes. They also found a footprint of roughly the same size as the one found near Shalopinina's body. But the ground was too muddy to give more than a rough gauge of the shoe's size.

Burakov directed a house-to-house interrogation of everyone in the central quarter of Novoshakhtinsk and everyone in the general area where the bodies had been found. He had higher hopes for this operation than he had harbored for the interrogations after Olga Stalmachenok disappeared. Only three days, instead of three months, had passed since the boy disappeared. And Ptashnikov, unlike Stalmachenok, lived in the neighborhood around Lenin Street. People knew him.

This time, the inquiries produced some witnesses. Four people recalled that they had seen Dima Ptashnikov walking along Lenin Street on the evening of March 24. They all said that he had seemed to be following a tall man who strode along a step ahead, not speaking to the boy. All of them had noticed the man's gait: he walked with stiff knees, almost goose-stepping. A couple of people recalled that he had unusually large feet. But their descriptions of the man's clothing varied. One said he had on an old, brown fur hat. Another said he had a cloth hat. One said the man wore dark glasses. Another said the man had glasses with clear lenses. None of them had recognized him and none had gotten a particularly good look at him. It had been dark, and he had walked past them in profile.

The *militsia* working the Sixth Collective Farm also found witnesses. They reported seeing a white Volga sedan, the type supplied to mid-level Soviet government workers, parked on the dirt road as night fell on March 24. They remembered that the car's radio had been playing. They had not thought much about it. Couples from Novoshakhtinsk who were lucky enough to have cars frequently used the more remote places on the farm. The town had, after all, no motels. The witnesses had not noticed the car's license plate. They could add only that the driver had glued a strip of blue, translucent plastic to the top of the windshield. But so did a lot of drivers, since tinted glass was not an option on Soviet cars.

The questioning of Ptashnikov's parents produced a third lead. On the day before he disappeared, Dima had visited a middle-aged bachelor, a fellow stamp collector named Malyshev, who lived with his mother. Malyshev, however, said he knew nothing about Ptashnikov's disappearance. And he did not own a car.

Burakov tried to sort out the useful information from the useless. It seemed clearer than ever to him that the killer had a car, quite possibly the white Volga with the blue plastic strip. How else to explain how he got his victims to remote locations before killing them? How else to explain how he left the scenes of his murders, his clothes presumably spattered with blood, and yet avoided being seen by anyone?

He was not sure what to make of the man seen walking ahead of Dima Ptashnikov. The size of the man's foot suggested that he might well be the killer. But none of the witnesses had seen him exchange so much as a word with Ptashnikov, let alone grab him or drag him. He could have been someone just coincidentally walking ahead of the boy. And if he used a car, why was he walking? Nevertheless, Burakov ordered an artist's sketch done, based on the witnesses' recollections—a glowering man with hollow cheeks, a cleft chin, glasses, and a hat pulled down over his face. The *militsionery* began carrying it with them as they made their rounds from door to door. But no one recognized the picture. And they could not pin down which white Volga, of all the thousands in the oblast, had been parked on the Sixth Collective Farm on March 24.

Even before the investigators could finish their first round of inquiries in the Ptashnikov case, a new victim turned up in June in the countryside near Aksai, the industrial suburb on the rail line northwest of Rostov. It was a woman, naked. Someone had stabbed her dozens of times—in the back, in the neck, in the area of the genitals—and left her lying in a cluster of reeds near the Don.

It took a week for the investigative group from Rostov to identify the body. She was Tatyana Polyakova, age seventeen, and she was, like Shalopinina and Kuprina, a young woman with a disorderly sex life. But she differed from Shalopinina and Kuprina in one important respect. They had abused alcohol. According to friends whom the interrogators questioned, Tatyana was part of a circle that also smoked marijuana.

Drug use, in the Soviet Union of 1984, was a distinctly underground phenomenon. The news media almost never acknowledged its existence within the country, hewing to the line that narcotics were a capitalist plague. In a certain sense, this was true. Since the Soviet ruble was worthless outside the country, there was no incentive for foreign sources to try to smuggle drugs past the extremely vigilant Soviet border guards. The drugs that did exist inside the country were almost all home grown, and since private property was forbidden, growing marijuana plants or opium poppies in any quantity meant running the risk of using collective farm or forest land that anyone could walk through. But a limited amount of drug use occurred. Cynics among the users calculated, with good reason, that the *militsia* and the KGB tolerated it for political reasons: when they caught a drug user or seller, it was rather easy to turn him into an informer.

Once Burakov and the investigators discovered that Tatyana Polyakova had smoked marijuana, it was simple to establish a number of her friends and contacts among Aksai's drug users. None of them, however, immediately looked like a murder suspect. Then the team got a break from another source.

Thinking that Polyakova and her killer had perhaps used the *elektrichka* to ride out into the countryside, Fetisov stationed *syshchiki* at the closest station to her home and began questioning everyone who used that platform. Had they seen her? When? Whom was she with?

After a couple of days, they turned up a young man, a couple of years younger than Tatyana, who had attended her secondary school. Early on the morning of the day she disappeared, he had seen her with a man she introduced as Artur. They had talked for a while about old school friends, then got on the train in separate cars. He did not know Artur's last name, where they were going, or why.

But Artur is not a common Russian name, and it was not hard for the *syshchiki* to find his name among the lists of drug users they had compiled. Artur Korshenko was twenty-three, married, and the father of a child. He worked as a laborer in the local farm equipment factory, Krasny Aksai. He had blue eyes and light brown hair; he was a good-looking man. For a hobby, he practiced karate.

The *militsia* placed a tail on him for a week, waiting to see if he would exhibit behavior that would link him more closely to the *lesopolosa* killings. He did not. They decided to take him in for questioning.

Stealthily, the *militsionery* surrounded the house where Korshenko lived with his parents, wife, and child in Aksai. Several of them went to knock on the door. When Korshenko heard the knock and the words "*Militsia*, open the door!" he tried to bolt through a rear window. The men waiting outside caught him.

His arrest excited Burakov. For the first time, they had a suspect who fit his idea of what the killer would be like. Korshenko's drug use, he thought, might explain the perverse rage reflected in the victims' bodies. Karate might explain how he had subdued them all so quickly and quietly. Certainly his flight suggested guilt.

For the preliminary interrogation, they took Korshenko to Burakov's new office, Room 24 in the main *militsia* building on Engels Street. This suspect was too hot to be left entirely to the *syshchiki*. Aleksandr Ryabenko, the procurator in charge of the *lesopolosa* killings, hurried over from his office to ask the questions. Within fifteen minutes, Korshenko began to talk.

Yes, he said. He had murdered Tatyana Polyakova. They had attended the same school, some years apart, and he had known her for more than ten years. He knew she used drugs, and he had suggested that they go out to the country to a place he knew where poppies grew. Korshenko knew how to gather poppies, process them, and produce homemade heroin for the syringe he kept hidden at home. He had brought along a few bottles of vodka for their outing. They found an isolated place in the reeds, and drained two of the bottles. Drunk, he tried to initiate intercourse. She was not in the mood. She pushed him away, and they quarreled. He lost his temper. She struck him, he said, and tried to run away. He ran after her, knife in hand. He caught up to her and plunged the knife into her back. Then he spun her around, and kept thrusting the knife into her, penetrating her neck, her abdomen, her genitals. Stabbing her became a surrogate for the sex she had denied him. When it was over, he left the body in the reeds, picked up the bottles, and went home.

But Korshenko insisted that she was the only person he had killed. His blood, the tests said, was type A.

Burakov could not give up on Korshenko easily, regardless of what the lab results showed. But just as the investigators began the tedious process of establishing Korshenko's whereabouts on the days of previous murders, a report came in of yet another body.

Farm workers, spraying insecticide on trees near the village of Kirpichnaya, just south of Shakhty, had found the remains of a young girl in a densely wooded area not far from the railroad. It was early July, and the heat had accelerated the process of decomposition. The body lay, naked, on its stomach. When the investigators turned it over, they had no doubt that the *lesopolosa* killer had struck again. The victim had apparently been about ten years old. The remains fit none of the active missing-persons files in the area, but Burakov was getting used to the idea that the killer in the woods often picked victims whom no one would miss.

This time, however, Burakov sensed something else. He thought he could smell something in the woods. For days, he and his men tramped through the trees and thickets in widening circles. They found some of the girl's clothes, rent by a knife, strewn in a trail a quarter of a mile from the body. They found the carcasses of some dead animals. And after three weeks, they found another body, a half mile from the first.

This was the body of a grown woman. Her murderer had bashed in her skull with something blunt, perhaps the handle of a knife. But when the medical examiner's preliminary report came in, it stated that this victim's wounds differed from those of the girl discovered on July 5. Her killer had not stabbed her.

But the medical examiner had the makings of an explanation for that. As closely as he could determine, the two victims had died at the same time, toward the end of May.

Burakov tried to maintain his grip on reality. In an ordinary time, he would have had no doubt that these two bodies were related. The odds against unrelated victims being killed separately by different killers in the same woodland, at roughly the same time, were too high for him to bother trying to calculate. This was, obviously, no ordinary time. Bodies had been turning up at an extraordinary rate—these were, by his calculation, the sixteenth and seventeenth in the *lesopo-*

losa series. Still, he could not imagine that one killer, or even two killers, could have taken unrelated victims in roughly the same area at roughly the same time. He would operate on the assumption that these victims knew each other. They could have been sisters. They could have been a mother and a daughter.

He could envision some particulars of the crime. Maybe one of the victims—the younger one?—had surprised the killer and the older one. He might have smashed the older one's skull, then turned and chased the younger one through the woods. Burakov could almost feel the terror the girl must have felt as she ran, futilely, for her life. It seemed to hang from the leaves in the woods.

Or could the killer have lured both victims into the woods at the same time? Had he wanted the girl to watch what he did with the woman? And if he had, what power did he possess that caused people to take leave of their senses and follow him?

The summer of 1984 was a time of disorientation in Russia. In Moscow, it seemed as if no one was in charge. One aging and infirm leader, Yuri Andropov, had died after a long illness, only to be succeeded by Konstantin Chernenko, a wheezing Party hack who was incapable of reading a speech without losing his place. The Politburo had announced that Soviet athletes and their socialist allies would boycott the Los Angeles Olympics. NATO was deploying new classes of nuclear missiles in West Germany, missiles that everyone in the Soviet Union had been told would cut the warning time against a nuclear attack in half, to a matter of ten minutes or less. Sober Soviet scientists published articles about the possibility of a war being started by computers, kept primed to return a nuclear salvo without requiring the intervention of a human mind. It seemed that the world might soon spin apart into chaos.

And in Rostov that summer, the *lesopolosa* killer kept

pace with the feverish events. Bodies accumulated faster than the *militsia* could even identify them. On July 25, railroad workers near Shakhty found the naked corpse of a woman, lying in the woods on her stomach about half a mile from the station. She had been dead for about a week, and her body bore the mutilating signature of the *lesopolosa* killer. He had cut away her nipples, her vaginal area, and her uterus. He had slashed at her eyes. She was identified as Anna Lemesheva, twenty, a student who had disappeared six days previously, on her way to visit a dentist.

On August 3, the police found the body of a sixteen-year-old girl, Natalia Golosovskaya, in a grove of trees in Aviators' Park in Rostov, not far from where Marta Ryabenko and several other bodies had been discovered. Her killer had mutilated her as terribly as he had Anna Lemesheva, but she was lying on her back, with leaves stuffed into her mouth.

A week later, on August 10, they found the body of Lyudmilla Alekseyeva, seventeen, in a grove of trees on the left bank of the Don, near Rostov's city beach. Unlike many of the others, she was a studious young woman with no known bad habits. She had been returning from a visit to her brother, who worked on a barge upstream from Rostov.

Two days passed, and workers in a cornfield on a state farm called Niva, outside Rostov-on-Don, found the body of a boy, Dmitri Illaryonov, thirteen. He had disappeared on July 10, apparently while on his way to school to get a health certificate he needed for summer camp. His killer had broken the boy's skull, probably with the butt end of a knife, perhaps with a hammer. Then he had castrated him.

On August 26, a woman gathering mushrooms near a camping area thirty miles east of Rostov found the decomposed remains of a young woman, partially covered by leaves and branches. She had been dead for about two months, and the *militsia* could not identify the remains. But the wounds in the breast area suggested that her killer had stabbed her to death.

On August 28, a boy named Aleksandr Chepel, eleven years old, disappeared from the middle of Rostov. A man getting set to mow a meadow on the left bank of the Don, not far from where Lyudmilla Alekseyeva had been found, discovered his mutilated body on September 2.

Five days later, on September 7, the *militsia* discovered yet another body in Aviators' Park, near the Rostov airport. This victim, a woman, had been dead for only a day, and the body showed the signature mutilations. It was identified as that of Irina Luchinskaya, twenty-four years old, who had worked at a day-care center. But she had a history of mental illness and alcohol abuse, and her personal activities qualified for the designation "disorderly sex life." She was, by Burakov's count, the twenty-fourth victim in the *lesopolosa* series.

The killer, or killers, left little evidence. On five of the bodies—those of Lemesheva, Golosovskaya, Alekseyeva, Chepel, and Luchinskaya—the medical examiners found traces of semen, and in all five cases they identified it as type AB. On Chepel's body, the investigators had found a single graying hair, which the examiners said probably came from a man. Chepel's body also bore a burn mark, as if someone had tortured him with a cigarette. And near the body, the investigators found some scraps of cloth that did not match the boy's clothing.

But the investigators found no witnesses, and they still had only the vaguest idea of who the killer might be. One frightening fact stood out. In 1982, the *lesopolosa* murderer had taken five lives. In 1983, he had taken six. But in 1984, there were thirteen bodies on Burakov's list. In the five months since Dima Ptashnikov's death, the killer, or killers, had been striking at a rate of once every two weeks. Whatever impelled the man, or men, to seek out victims and mutilate them was getting harder to control.

By the summer of 1984, the work load involved in the case was overwhelming the resources of Rostov's *militsia* and pro-

curators. Eleven of the twenty-four victims remained un-
identified. Checking out and eliminating suspects required
hundreds of hours of work, and the backlog only grew.
For instance, by the time the *syshchiki* had finally crossed
Vladimir Babakov, the old man in Novoshakhtinsk, off
their list, they still had to complete the investigations of
Yuri Kalenik, Mikhail Tyapkin, Nikolai Byeskorsy, and
Artur Korshenko.

The dissension among the various players in the investigation grew as rapidly as the number of victims. The chief
of the Rostov procurator's office, Aleksandr Ryabko, had begun in the spring to move toward Burakov's view that the
retarded suspects from the *internat* in Shakhty had nothing
to do with the killings. In April, he had decided to drop the
charge filed against Mikhail Tyapkin for the murder of Sergei
Markov.

This infuriated the faction within the *militsia*, led by deputy chief Pavel Chernyshev, that still believed that Tyapkin
and Kalenik were involved, at least in the early murders.
Even though more than a dozen victims had been found since
Kalenik's arrest, the members of this faction theorized that
a gang of boys from the *internat* was responsible and that
the other, unknown members had gone on killing after Kalenik and Tyapkin were in custody.

The faction insisted that if only the procurator's office
would provide enough competent *sledovatyeli*, the case could
be solved by aggressively investigating all the friends and
contacts of Kalenik and Tyapkin. Although in practice the
procurators often delegated the task of planning investigations and questioning suspects to the *militsia*, the growing
pressure to solve the *lesopolosa* case made the procurators
loath to expose themselves to any criticism that they had been
lax in their work. So they had begun to insist more often on
questioning suspects themselves, and there were often not
enough of them to handle the interrogations the *syshchiki*
thought necessary.

Complicating matters even more, Vladimir I. Kazakov, a veteran *sledovatyel* from the central Russian procuracy in Moscow, arrived in Rostov in June 1984 to review the investigation. Kazakov's arrival reopened all the questions in the case, including the involvement of the suspects from Gukovo. Everything had to be rehashed and decided anew.

The disagreement became an open rift, with both sides accusing each other of fouling up the investigation. Meetings called to coordinate the investigation became tense and hostile. Despite Burakov's opinion, the *militsia* leadership sent a letter to Vitaly Fedorchuk, the Minister of the Interior, asking his help in organizing a team of experienced procurators to be sent into Rostov from jurisdictions all over the country. Within a few months, the team, numbering about a dozen men, arrived and began to work.

Fetisov and Chernyshev allotted more than two hundred men and women to the case. Within Fetisov's department of criminal apprehension, they created a special sub-unit assigned to deal with serious crimes of a sexual nature. It was a killer department aimed exclusively at catching the man, or men, responsible for the *lesopolosa* murders. Fetisov prevailed on Chernyshev to allow him to appoint Viktor Burakov to head the new team. From then on, Burakov, though still subject to orders from officers farther up the ladder, would have the direct responsibility for the *militsia* end of the investigation. He would be the one to make the first evaluation of new leads, to analyze the conflicting streams of information. He would be the one required to come up with a plan to bring the killer to justice.

Fetisov and Burakov deployed some of the new forces to work under cover at bus and train stations, looking for men who approached boys, girls, and young women. A dozen men were assigned to wear sports clothes and ride bicycles through Aviators' Park in Rostov in the hope that they would spot the killer. They assigned the largest contingent to an operation called *Poisk*, or Search, designed to round up and check out anyone in Rostov oblast who fit their general idea of what the killer might be like.

But they had only a general idea. Burakov and one of the new procurators, Yuri Moiseyev, jointly wrote a paper giving their best estimate of the killer's characteristics. He was, they wrote, a man between the ages of twenty-five and thirty; that seemed the most likely age for a man capable of luring young women in their teens and twenties into the woods. He had type AB blood. He was tall and well built, probably an athlete. Far from being retarded, he was probably of at least average intelligence, observant, and careful. He could argue persuasively. He might work as a driver or in some capacity that required him to travel. He probably lived in Novocherkassk, thirty miles north of Rostov-on-Don; it seemed to be the geographic epicenter of the murders. He might or might not be married. If single, he might live with his mother, as the housing shortage required most bachelors to do.

That only narrowed the list, Burakov knew, to five or ten thousand people. He had to try to narrow the circle further. He directed the men in *Poisk* to start by compiling and checking out lists of all former psychiatric patients, all men previously convicted of sex crimes, and drug addicts. Perhaps, he thought, drugs were at the root of the killer's murderous rage. He directed the force to check out former and present *militsionery*, on the theory that the killer might be using a badge or a uniform to win the trust of the victims, and workers in the medical profession, on the theory that the killer's skill with a knife and apparent knowledge of anatomy suggested professional training. Once these lists were compiled, he directed, the first thing to do was to check the suspects' blood types.

By September 1984, the *militsia* could no longer ignore public opinion. The newspapers and television remained compliant instruments of the state, and there were no headlines proclaiming that the killer was still at large. The papers had printed only what the investigators had told them to print, and this had amounted to short, obscure notices announcing that the *syshchiki* were seeking witnesses who had seen a particular victim on the day he or she disappeared. These notices circulated only in local newspapers.

But with so many bodies, and so many people being questioned, the news of the killings leached into the public domain. Rumors filled the vacuum created by the official silence. One rumor had it that a gang of cannibals had descended on the oblast, making Aviators' Park its headquarters for killing, dismembering, and eating its victims. Another had it that a gang of Rostov criminals had lost a card game to a gang from another city, and that the stakes were fifty children's lives. Another rumor said that a group disguised as photographers had arrived at a Rostov school, shown some kind of credentials, and taken all the children away to a studio to be photographed. None had returned. Some of the rumors had it that the gang had medical training and killed its victims with surgical precision. Yet another said the gang came from the trans-Caucasus republics of Armenia, Georgia, and Azerbaijan. Many Russians, already disposed to regard the peoples of these republics as congenital criminals, found that rumor particularly attractive. But the rumor most disturbing to the authorities had it that the killer rode around in a black Volga sedan, the type supplied to Party officials, with a special license plate that began with the letters DSC—for Death to Soviet Children.

A silent and partial panic gripped Rostov. Some mothers began to keep their children at home or escort them around the city. But not everyone knew, and not everyone took precautions. Many people discounted the rumors, and many simply had not heard them. Prostitutes continued to work the stations, and children continued to ride the trains and buses.

The murder of Aleksandr "Sasha" Chepel, in particular, exacerbated the situation. Unlike so many of the other victims, he came from the kind of family that Soviet propagandists liked to show as typical of socialist society. His father, Nikolai, was an engineer, and one of the small number of people in Soviet society entrusted by the state to work abroad. When Sasha disappeared, Nikolai was in Tehran working on a coal-enrichment plant that was part of Soviet efforts to woo the revolutionary government of Iran irrevocably out of the American sphere of influence. His mother, also an engineer, worked in an institute that drafted plans for coal mines. Sasha, a soccer player and a good student, normally stayed at home under the care of his grandmother. But on that day, he had gone downtown to see his mother. He had general permission to travel by himself. He had to, to get to soccer practice.

Chepel's parents had many friends, and the news of his disappearance, then of his death and the wounds on his body, spread rapidly. The authorities reacted cruelly and clumsily. General A. N. Konovalov, then the head of the oblast *militsia,* invited Nikolai Chepel to meet with him. Then he all but blamed the grieving father for his son's death. Why, Konovalov asked, was the boy riding alone on public transportation? Local politicians tried the same line when they addressed a meeting of concerned parents who lived in the Chepels' neighborhood. The boy was not properly supervised, one of them said.

It was, Nikolai Chepel thought, a damnable slander. He had not set up a system where the schools were overburdened and children had to attend in shifts, meaning that they were at liberty for half the day. He had not set up a system that demanded that both parents work. He had not set up a system that required a boy like Sasha, who wanted to play soccer, to get on a bus and ride halfway across town. The Chepels' friends agreed with him.

The oblast Party leadership decided that something had to be done to soothe the population. General Konovalov was ordered to prepare a speech, to be given on local television, and an ''interview,'' to be printed in the local newspapers.

He delegated the writing to Viktor Burakov, who prepared a brief and straightforward account of the crimes. But that was not what Konovalov delivered.

"Please comment on the fact that there is a lot of talk in the city about extraordinary occurrences," the Party paper, *Molot*, asked delicately.

"There is absolutely no basis for such rumors, to say nothing of panic," Konovalov replied. "These rumors are unhealthy, even provocative.

"Objectively, the situation is that many people have been excited by the death of an eleven-year-old boy, Sasha C. [Konovalov, following Soviet practice, kept the boy's surname out of the news.] But this is a lone occurrence," he lied.

"We have all good reason now to state firmly that the criminal who committed this murder will be taken into custody," Konovalov said.

That was also a lie, but it was the least of Viktor Burakov's concerns. The word "glasnost" had yet to pass the lips of a Soviet leader, and the concept of the public's right to know had never occurred to Burakov. He had a strictly utilitarian view of the news. If giving information to the public would help him solve the case, fine. If it would not, then information should be withheld. That was a decision for his superiors to make.

Militsia workers had begun to visit schools and factories, delivering lectures about safety, about keeping an eye on children, about not going off with strangers. That, he thought, should be sufficient to warn conscientious parents.

Meanwhile, he had an overflow of work. In addition to handling the new cases, he was still trying to pin down all the details that would put a close to the Kalenik case. He had more work to do with Korshenko and Byeskorsy. And almost every week, the *militsia* assigned to Operation *Piosk* were turning up new suspects.

Toward the end of August 1984, Major Aleksandr Zana-sovsky, one of the men assigned to Operation *Poisk*, was on duty in plain clothes at the Rostov bus station. Zanasovsky, a stout, pug-nosed *militsioner* with curly black hair, led a detachment of four men who worked the bus station from eight in the morning to eleven at night, the hours during which *lesopolosa* victims had disappeared. Generally, the detachment hung around the main waiting room, a big, dingy hall with rows of plastic benches.

At around eight in the evening, standing in the waiting room, Zanasovsky noticed a man talking to a young woman, about seventeen or eighteen years old. The man could have been her father. He had gray hair, wore a tie and eyeglasses, and carried a briefcase; he looked, Zanasovsky thought, like a cultured man. But then the girl smiled, got up, and went to catch a bus. The man did not go with her. Instead, he stood up, circled the room slowly for a while, and then sat down near another young woman and started to talk to her.

Who is this guy, Zanasovsky thought.

He walked up to the man and broke his cover, producing an identification badge. He asked the man to come with him, and led him to the little *militsia* office off the waiting room.

The man's documents were in order. His name was Andrei Chikatilo, and he worked as the manager of the supply department at a Rostov-based machinery enterprise called Spetzenergoavtomatika. His passport said he was the father of two children. He had a document attesting to the fact that he was in Rostov on a business trip. He was about to return to Shakhty, where he lived. He had once been a teacher, Chikatilo explained. He liked talking to kids, he was bored, and so he had struck up conversations with a couple of young people.

Zanasovsky shrugged and let him go. Then he talked to the girl in the waiting room. Had Chikatilo, he asked, suggested that she go anywhere with him.

No, the girl said. He had asked where she was studying, and what. That was all.

A couple of weeks later, on the evening of September 13, Zanasovsky saw the same man in the Rostov bus station, dressed as he had been in August, wearing a tie and carrying an attaché case. Chikatilo could hardly have forgotten him, but Zanasovsky prided himself on his skills as an undercover observer. He knew how to watch without being seen.

Chikatilo got on a bus. Zanasovsky and a colleague, a plainclothesman named Akhmatyanov, got on after him. They rode for two and a half hours, switching buses at apparently random places around the city. Eight or ten times, Zanasovsky observed Chikatilo strike up a conversation with a young woman. Nothing untoward happened.

Finally, Chikatilo got off a bus in the center of the city and walked into a restaurant. He sat down and started to talk with a woman whose body listed to one side, an evident drunk. Then he left her, and walked across the street to a café, where he chatted up more women. Then, still alone, he sat on a bench for a while in Maksim Gorky Park, the public garden in downtown Rostov. From there, Zanasovsky and Akhmatyanov followed him down Engels Street to the railroad station.

It was by then past midnight, but Chikatilo's wandering continued. He went to the bus station again, chatting up women, all of whom talked for a while, then caught their buses. At about three o'clock, Chikatilo saw a young woman, perhaps nineteen, lie down on a bench. He walked over and sat down beside her.

Zanasovsky could watch, but he could not get close enough to hear. He saw Chikatilo running his hand through the woman's hair. Then, suddenly, she stood up, and Zanasovsky thought she might be accusing him of trying to unbutton her blouse. But she had a flirtatious look on her face, and soon she lay down on the bench again. This time, Chikatilo took off his jacket and covered her head with it. Zanasovsky could see movement under the jacket, and he assumed her head was bobbing up and down as she fellated him in the nearly empty station.

Then Chikatilo and the woman got up and walked, separately, to the toilets. Chikatilo, the first out, walked around impatiently for a moment. Then, suddenly, he walked rapidly out of the station and got on a streetcar. Zanasovsky had seen such behavior in people he was tailing. It usually meant that they had spotted the surveillance.

He cursed silently. Akhmatyanov had worn a yellow shirt to work that night, which offended Zanasovsky's sense of proper dress. To him, plain clothes should be just that. He never wore bright colors on the job. He told Akhmatyanov to look for the woman, then got on the streetcar and stayed on Chikatilo's trail.

It ended, a mile or so away, near the empty stalls of the Central Bazaar. Chikatilo got off the streetcar, and Zanasovsky decided to take him in. He could always charge him with committing a perverted act in a public place.

He walked up behind Chikatilo. "Have you gotten where you were going?" he said.

Chikatilo turned and recognized him. It was nearly dawn, and in the gray light Zanasovsky could see beads of sweat on the man's forehead. Chikatilo told him he had missed his bus to Shakhty and was just killing time until the next one left. But he offered no resistance when Zanasovsky told him he would have to go to the nearest *militsia* station.

Before he went home, Zanasovsky helped open and catalog the contents of Chikatilo's briefcase. They found a jar of Vaseline, a dirty towel, some rope, and a kitchen knife about ten inches long. Zanasovsky left the station convinced that he had found and arrested the *lesopolosa* killer. Why else would the man be carrying a knife and trying so hard to pick up women?

Yuri Moiseyev, the procurator who had been sent in as part of the team from outside Rostov, drew the duty of questioning Chikatilo. He reported the next day that Chikatilo was sticking by the story he had told Zanasovsky. He had missed his bus. He was killing time. He carried the knife because he often needed to cut things, like sausage, when he was traveling.

Shortly afterward, the forensic laboratory reported the results of Chikatilo's blood test. He was type A. According to the analysis of the semen samples found at the scenes of nine murders, the killer had blood type AB.

Chikatilo also, it turned out, was a member in good standing of the Communist Party. The investigators checked with the Party secretary at his workplace. The Party gave him a standard character reference—there was nothing unfavorable on him in its files. Being a Party member did not offer immunity against prosecution, but it added weight to a suspect's denial. Moiseyev was prepared to let Chikatilo go.

But the background check turned up something else. Chikatilo had worked, until two months before his arrest, as a *tolkach* in an enterprise called Rostovnerud in Shakhty. The *tolkach*—a word that means "pusher"—is a key man in Russian industry. Because the state-run supply system worked so badly, every sizable factory had a staff of *tolkachi*. Their job was the reverse of a salesman's. They traveled around to the factory's suppliers, glad-handing and passing out gifts, to persuade the supplier to sell what the factory needed to buy, when it needed to buy it. Chikatilo, some months previously, had gone off on a mission to buy automobile batteries for Rostovnerud. He had managed to get sixteen of them, and he had allegedly kept one for himself.

On the scale of theft and pilferage in the Soviet Union, this was almost too small to be noticed. And in fact, the case had never been prosecuted. Chikatilo had, however, changed jobs in July, going to work as a *tolkach* at Spetzenergoavtomatika. If one read between the lines, it was possible to see that he had left voluntarily in return for Rostovnerud's dropping the charges.

The *militsia* in Novoshakhtinsk, still looking for a suspect in the Dmitri Ptashnikov case, asked to revive the theft charge and keep Chikatilo in their jail for a while. Along with their Rostov colleagues, they believed firmly in the persuasive powers of a jail cell, and they thought that time in jail, perhaps with a *stukach* as a cell mate, might get Chikatilo to reveal things he had not said to Moiseyev. Moiseyev agreed to their request.

Once charges had been filed, the *militsia* had a legal right to search Chikatilo's apartment. Viktor Burakov was asked to supervise the search. He knew vaguely that Chikatilo had been detained in a station and that he had type A blood. He had not, however, questioned the suspect himself. Burakov regarded the assignment as an unwelcome interruption of the work he was doing, finally to put an end to the Kalenik case. Moiseyev had already decided not to charge Chikatilo.

But Burakov drove to Shakhty, to an apartment on a street named for the fiftieth anniversary of the Communist Youth League. Chikatilo lived in an apartment on the ground floor of a student dormitory; he had formerly been a teacher. Their search turned up nothing of interest—a fur hat, an overcoat, and a pair of large boots Burakov found under the stove. He turned the evidence over to Moiseyev and went back to work on the Kalenik case.

Chikatilo, in jail, continued to deny any involvement in the *lesopolosa* killings. He got a six-month sentence for the battery theft, and he was stripped of his membership in the Communist Party.

Burakov found himself pondering more and more the character of the man he was seeking. Thanks to the muzzling effect of official censorship, the criminological literature available told him little or nothing about serial killers. In September, he took a major risk. Without permission from his superiors, he breached the secrecy that still surrounded the case by asking members of the psychiatric profession for advice. He sent information on the killings to psychiatric experts in Moscow. And he asked the rector at the Rostov Institute of Medicine to convene his psychiatrists and sexual pathologists so that he could tell them about the case.

Burakov gave them a cautious, sketchy overview. Someone, he said, was killing girls, women, and boys. In a general way, he described the pattern of mutilation. Then he posed his questions. Could the same killer be interested in both sexes? Could a group of some kind be responsible? What kind of illness drove such people, and how might it affect other aspects of their behavior?

The response disappointed him. Most of the psychiatrists, he thought angrily, could not have cared less about catching the killer. (Given the history of repression in the Soviet Union, they perhaps had reason to be cautious with a *militsioner* who came around asking provocative questions.) Some of them appeared to pay little attention. What the others said was vague and contradictory. One thought the killer was a lone individual. Another said it might be a group.

But after the lecture, one of the psychiatrists, Dr. Aleksandr Bukhanovsky, approached Burakov and invited him for a further talk in his office. Burakov had already heard about Bukhanovsky. A plump, swarthy man with a wavy black pompadour and long sideburns, Bukhanovsky stood out sharply against the low, gray ranks of Russian psychiatrists.

Of all the sciences, psychiatry and genetics had suffered the most under Communism. Genetics, under Stalin, had been forbidden as a bourgeois fiction because it conflicted with the Party's dogmatic insistence that a new, socialist environment could change the very nature of man. The Communists repressed whole branches of psychiatry for similar reasons. They could not tolerate a view of man that stipulated the primacy of the individual and the motive power of his quest for personal pleasure. They could not tolerate a view of society that stressed the importance of childhood relationships, rather than economic class, in the formation of character. So they virtually banned Freud. Soviet psychiatrists practiced in intellectual and often physical isolation from their counterparts in the West. Their research emphasized things like the optimal conditions for increasing productivity in the workplace.

Aleksandr Bukhanovsky, by origin and inclination, was different. He was born in 1944, the child of a wartime marriage between an Armenian woman and a Polish Jew who had been sent to Russia to fight the Germans. His father, as the war ended, made his way back to Poland and, eventually, to America. But the Iron Curtain closed on Bukhanovsky and his mother before his father could send for them. Eventually, his mother remarried and resigned herself to life as a Soviet citizen.

Bukhanovsky became a Red Diploma student in the Rostov schools, meaning that he earned straight A's. He entered the Rostov Medical Institute and chose to study psychiatry because he had an aversion to blood and an inclination to chat with people.

He received the standard Soviet psychiatric education, but then he broadened it. During his obligatory two years of army duty in the late 1960s, Bukhanovsky lived in Murmansk, near the Arctic Circle. There was little to do, especially during the long, dark winters when the sun never rose above the horizon and the mercury never rose to zero. The army tried to compensate by arranging for soldiers with an inclination to read to borrow books from the best Moscow libraries.

Bukhanovsky read voluminously and unsystematically. He read about genetics, which had just been legalized by the Central Committee. He read the works of the Soviet psychiatrists of the 1920s, who wrote before Stalin completed the corruption of their discipline. He found that what he was reading not only contradicted much of what his textbooks had said. It made more sense.

When he returned to Rostov and the institute, he started

to study schizophrenia and sexual pathologies, an area that constantly bumped up against the puritan streak in Soviet ideology. The problem of transsexualism, men who wanted to become women, seized his interest. He became one of a handful of Russian psychiatrists who developed a program, in conjunction with institute surgeons, to guide patients through the process. In the early 1980s, he began a research program on homosexuality. At the age of forty, when Burakov met him, he was a maverick within his profession.

Burakov followed Bukhanovsky and a few of his colleagues into Bukhanovsky's office and berated them for their indifference. He showed them a picture of one of the victims and let them see, rather than hear about, the wounds inflicted by the killer. If they failed to help him catch the criminal, he warned, there was no assurance that the next victim wouldn't be one of their own children. Bukhanovsky had a daughter, Olga, who was fifteen. He agreed to help.

Two weeks later, he produced a seven-page report for Burakov. It cast aspersions on some of the theories the investigators were working with. The crimes, he said, were almost certainly caused by a sexual personality disorder. The killer was a sadist who could obtain sexual satisfaction only by causing another to suffer. There were, he reported to Burakov, instances in the psychiatric literature where sadists liked to use a knife or needle to inflict numerous superficial wounds.

The killer was compulsive, Bukhanovsky wrote. When the need to kill arose, he could no more decide not to kill than a normal man could decide not to eat when he was hungry or not to drink when he was thirsty. He could make and follow a plan to find a victim, even a subtle and convoluted plan. But until he obtained the release that killing offered, he would be depressed and irritable; he might suffer from headaches or insomnia. His compulsion to kill could be triggered by periodic events like the phases of the moon or weather conditions.

Most likely, Bukhanovsky wrote, the killer suffered from impotence when it came to normal sex. He needed to see suffering to arouse himself. He probably could not sustain a heterosexual relationship, although he might, occasionally, have sexual intercourse with women. He might, Bukhanovsky suggested, have seen a doctor about his sexual problems or tried to check out special literature from a medical library.

Although the killer suffered from a mental illness, most likely schizophrenia, he was not crazy or retarded. He had an intellect sufficient to work out plans and avoid being caught. He probably lived in an internal world, with little social activity. If he ever had had close friends, he had probably lost them. It was extremely unlikely, Bukhanovsky concluded, that a group was involved. The chance that two or more such personalities could find each other and cooperate was extremely remote.

The National Scientific Center for the Study of Sexual Pathology in Moscow weighed in with a somewhat different report, based on the information Burakov had provided. Its report, written by G. S. Vasilenko and I. L. Botneva, theorized that the killer might have a hormonal surge of some kind that occurred once or twice a month. Almost unconsciously, he would begin a period of passive searching for a victim. He would start by hanging out in train stations, bus stations, parks. Girls, women, or boys all might attract his attention. He would become garrulous with them.

He had a knack, the report said, for sizing up victims. With adults, he could pick out the ones who needed food, or money, or a place to stay. He invited such people to have a drink or spend the night; he might just offer to show a woman the way to the next stage in her journey. With children, he was more impulsive. Something in a particular child's appearance might trigger his compulsion. When it did, he had the wits to make up a story to lure the child away.

Once he had his victim in the woods, the killer's personality changed, and his rage burst from him. Like Bukhanovsky, the Moscow specialists believed that the killer could not get or maintain an erection during normal sexual intercourse. He aroused himself by stabbing and seeing blood. Then he ejaculated, either through masturbation or spontaneously. That explained why the semen turned up on the victims, rather than inside them. His need for sexual gratification was so intense, they suggested, that he might not even notice exactly when his victims died.

The killer, they noted, had developed a ritual of mutilation. This probably occurred either after the victim's death or after his own sexual climax. If he had not achieved an orgasm by the time the victim died, they said, cutting off the sex organs might increase his excitement and permit him to do so.

Afterward, they concluded, he might calmly clean himself up, wash the traces of blood from his clothes, and check to make sure he had left no fingerprints or other evidence at the scene of the crime. He might either throw away the body parts he had cut off or take them with him. But he would emerge from the woods calm and genial, capable of chatting casually with people he encountered or of driving a car.

Like Bukhanovsky, they thought it highly unlikely that a group was involved. And they believed that the same individual was killing both males and females.

But Burakov got a third opinion, and it conflicted with the first two. A research specialist at the Serbsky Institute in Moscow, V. E. Pelipas, said there were probably two killers involved. The first, a man between the ages of thirty-five and forty, killed boys. This murderer, Pelipas wrote, might work in a school or *internat*. He had experience with children. He probably lived alone or with relatives. He had no relations with women and few, if any, friends. He probably had secret interests in pornography and fetishes, including the sexual organs removed from his victims. The second killer, Pelipas said, was responsible for the women and girls. He was probably younger than the first, between the ages of twenty-five and thirty. He was no doubt stronger and more attractive than the boys' killer. He worked, perhaps, as a driver.

Reading the reports, Burakov pondered. They confirmed some of his own opinions. They seemed to discount Kalenik and Tyapkin, for instance. They ruled out the notion of a gang. And they offered an explanation for the wounds inflicted on the victims. He could believe the descriptions of the killer's impotence and sadism.

But as a practical matter, did they bring him closer to the killer? The psychiatrists could not even agree on whether there was one killer or two. Their vague descriptions of the killer's personality could fit any of thousands of men in Rostov oblast. If it was a single individual, Burakov could imagine him biding his time somewhere, laughing quietly at the people who were trying to catch him, and waiting for his hormones to rise.

6

The Gay Pogrom

By the autumn of 1984, the twenty-four victims in the *leso-polosa* series included five boys, ranging in age from eight to fourteen: Igor Gudkov, Sergei Markov, Dmitri Ptashnikov, Dmitri Illaryonov, and Sasha Chepel. They had all been killed within the preceding year. With the accumulation of male victims, and the discovery of semen on or in their bodies, the investigators began to look harder at the two theories that explained the addition of a second sex to the killer's targets. One was the idea, supported by Dr. Pelipas of the Serbsky Institute, of two unrelated murderers, one killing girls and women, the other boys. The second theory postulated a single killer, but one whose basic orientation was homosexual. Viktor Burakov began to investigate both.

Like most Russians, he knew little about homosexuality. Most Russians, in fact, knew little about sex in general. The official mores of the country were still, by and large, the mores of Stalinism. Like Mao and Hitler, Stalin saw sex solely as a means of creating new revolutionaries, new servants of the state. He saw any form of licentiousness as a threat to the discipline he demanded.

Stalinism reinforced a conservative Russian sexual tradition. Laws against sodomy that the Bolsheviks had repealed in 1918 were reinstated in 1934. Boys and girls were separated in school classes. Their curriculum included no sex education. A strict puritanism held sway in films and novels. People had to live in communal apartments where privacy did not exist, making their sexual relations stealthy and hurried. They lived with the fear that an extramarital affair, to say nothing of a homosexual liaison, might be discovered and reported anonymously to the secret police. The state's controls gradually loosened in the decades after Stalin's death. Public school classes, for one, became coeducational again in the mid-1950s. But Russia remained one of the most sexually intolerant countries in the developed world.

Social attitudes and the socialist system combined to create particular difficulties for gay men and Lesbians in the Soviet Union. The general attitude toward homosexuality hovered between revulsion and derision. And socialism gave gay men and women no opportunities to create a more hospitable subculture. They could not, for example, open a small business and become economically independent. They had to work for state enterprises, and they knew that their bosses would be likely to fire them if their sexual orientation became known. They could not, for the most part, rent their own apartments, to say nothing of clustering in neighborhoods with other homosexuals. The state assigned housing, and single adults generally had to share cramped quarters with their parents until they married. They had a hard time simply finding places to meet other homosexuals. The few bars and restaurants that the state provided were uniformly dingy and closely watched.

In 1984, one of Aleksandr Bukhanovsky's students at the Rostov Institute of Medicine, a young psychiatrist named Aleksei Andreev, began the first systematic effort to study the homosexual population of Rostov. Bukhanovsky and Andreev held progressive views, by Soviet standards, about the nature of homosexuality. They believed that a certain, small percentage of men are born with a hormonal abnormality that defines them irremediably as homosexuals. Bukhanovsky sympathized with this group and abhorred society's hostility toward it. Society, he felt, taught gay men to loathe themselves, and this self-loathing drove them into behavior that was destructive toward themselves and others.

But Bukhanovsky's concept in some respects reinforced the legal hostility toward homosexuals. Bukhanovsky believed that, beyond the core group of congenital homosexuals, there were many other boys and men who, to one degree or another, were uncertain of their sexual orientation. They might, under certain circumstances, be heterosexual. They might, under other circumstances, be "recruited" by homosexuals. This raised the specter of pedophilia, of gay men seducing straight boys.

Andreev's research, conducted largely through contacts he made treating patients at the city's psychiatric clinic, filled out this theoretical structure. He found a secretive, multilayered gay subculture that involved about one percent of the Rostov population of a million people. At the top of the subculture, he found two elite groups. One consisted largely of artists, many of whom worked at the city's operetta theater. Behind closed doors and within this circle, men might wear jewelry, women's clothing, and cosmetics. Some of them had long-term relations with other men.

The second elite group consisted of men with high-ranking positions in the Soviet *nomenklatura*. These men lived deeply closeted lives. Often, for the sake of appearance, they married and had families. Their wives remained ignorant of their sexual orientation. Sometimes, they carried on long-term, furtive relationships with other men in similar circumstances. Sometimes they had a series of one-night stands with boys or men who passed through their lives on vacations or business trips. Some of them, Andreev found, occupied posts not far below the apex of Party and government power in the oblast.

At a much lower level in Soviet society, Andreev found men whose lives were defined by their homosexuality. These men could afford to be careless about secrecy. They lived on the fringes of society, either unemployed or working in marginal jobs, perhaps waiting on tables in restaurants. Many of them engaged in prostitution. They hung out, in Rostov, at a spot in Maksim Gorky Park, not far from the public toilets.

Andreev believed that the "recruiters" came from within this group. In his view, many Rostov gays prized nothing more than an uninitiated young boy. Recruiters worked the stations and parks, looking for those lonely, confused teen-agers who, perhaps, had run away from an abusive home, searching for some tenderness and understanding, needing something to eat and a warm place to sleep. The recruiters, he found, derived their own satisfaction and sometimes their livelihood from finding such boys and either seducing them or introducing them to friends.

Men who dropped below this layer of the gay subculture had truly bottomed out in Rostov society. Many of them drank heavily. They lived as best they could in parks, sta-tions, and *priyemniki* for the homeless. Their more fortunate gay counterparts had a word for them—"dirt."

Andreev, like Bukhanovsky, believed that the repressive attitudes of Russian society bore some of the responsibility for the aggressive pedophilia he found in some strata of Ros-tov's gay subculture. Soviet society did not tolerate or pro-vide conditions for open, stable relationships between gay adults. It taught gay men that they were soiled and loath-some. This encouraged, he believed, quick, furtive cou-plings and a desire for partners who were undefiled.

Rostov's gay population had, of course, a different view. Adult gay men often acknowledged having their first homo-sexual experience when they were teenagers, quite often with an older man. But they tended to believe that their gay incli-nations had firmly developed by the time they had their first encounter and that the adults only provided what they had left home to seek.

In any case, the law against sodomy had a second section, providing longer sentences for men convicted of sodomy with a minor.

* * *

Viktor Burakov had barely met Bukhanovsky and had yet to receive his profile of the killer when he began to work on the homosexual theory. Burakov had occasionally heard of cases in which a gay adult killed or injured a boy, although never a series of boys. However, he thought of homosexuality as a sexual disorder, and he believed that the *lesopolosa* killer suffered from a sexual disorder. He had no qualms about working on the theory that the killer, or one of the killers, might be gay.

His problem was identifying gay suspects to check out. Prior to 1984, the *militsia* had not aggressively prosecuted homosexual activity. There was not much need to. The social and economic structure of society, combined with Russian homophobia, was repressive enough. The *militsia* generally confined their attention to a few cases they ran across each year, usually in the course of searching for a runaway boy, in which gay men were accused of sodomy with a minor. The *militsia* files had few leads for Burakov to start on.

One of them was a bulging dossier on a man named Valery Ivanenko. Six times, over the course of about twenty years, he had been convicted of violations of Soviet statutes against sodomy and perversion. The sixth time, in 1982, he had convinced the psychiatrists at the Serbsky Institute that he was insane. He was sent to a psychiatric hospital in Koval-evka, a village north of Rostov. In 1983, the files showed, Dr. Bukhanovsky had taken custody of Ivanenko and brought him to Rostov, to a bed in the hospital at the Rostov Institute of Medicine. He wanted Ivanenko to serve as a subject in the study he and Dr. Andreev were beginning on the city's gay population. But shortly after arriving at the Rostov Institute of Medicine, Ivanenko escaped. In the summer of 1984, he was still at large.

Ivanenko's background intrigued Burakov. Ivanenko was a cultivated man. He spoke English and German, and he had graduated from a theatrical institute in Leningrad. He had worked as a teacher prior to his first sodomy conviction. He had, according to the files, a winning manner: he was affable, amusing, and quick to make contacts with people. And his physical features fit the vague description of the man seen walking ahead of Dmitri Ptashnikov: Ivanenko was six feet tall, forty-six years old, and gray haired, had a cleft chin, and was nearsighted and bespectacled.

Ivanenko's mother still lived in Rostov, in an apartment on Maksim Gorky Street in Nakhalovka, the neighborhood where Burakov had lived in his first years in Rostov. Burakov went to see her. The building resembled a lot of other slum housing in Rostov. It was four stories high, made of crumbling brick. It framed a courtyard in which people had, over the years, built shacks and lean-tos to add to their living space. Burakov found Ivanenko's mother in No. 46, a two-room hut on the courtyard level.

The old woman was paralyzed, as a result of a stroke. Who fed her, Burakov asked. Who changed her linens? She had, he could see, no money to pay someone to look after her. Did her son Valery come to help out?

No, the old woman insisted. She had not seen him since the court had sent him to the psychiatric hospital in Kovalevka.

She was, Burakov felt certain, lying to him. So he began to stake out the Ivanenko hut at night, taking up a position on the second floor, on a fire escape that offered a clear view of the courtyard. A few nights later, at two o'clock on a Saturday morning, a tall, gray-haired man entered the courtyard and slipped into No. 46. Burakov descended silently and arrested the man. He offered no resistance.

The details of Ivanenko's activities soon emerged from the interrogation, which Burakov conducted himself. Since escaping from Bukhanovsky's custody, Ivanenko had been living illegally in Donetsk, a Ukrainian city just over the border from Rostov oblast, making his living as a photographer.

Twice a week, he risked taking the train into Rostov, late at night, to bring food to his mother.

A blood test and a further background check quickly eliminated Ivanenko from suspicion in the *lesopolosa* killings. His blood was type A. And he had been at the Serbsky Institute on the day Lyubov Biryuk was killed. The blood test disappointed Burakov keenly. He asked Ivanenko to produce a semen sample for testing, just to double-check. Ivanenko agreed. The semen sample, too, came back type A.

But that did not mean Burakov had to let Ivanenko go. Ivanenko feared terribly being sent back to the psychiatric hospital. Burakov made him an offer. He could arrange for Ivanenko to live freely in Rostov and have the opportunity to help his mother openly—if Ivanenko helped him identify and investigate the gay population of Rostov.

Ivanenko agreed. He had, as Burakov had calculated, no other choice.

But Burakov had not calculated on the extent of the help he would get from his new informant. Ivanenko had a habit of keeping records, and one of the first things he turned over to Burakov was an index-card file containing the names, addresses, and sexual proclivities of more than two hundred fifty Rostov gays, ninety percent of whom were trying to keep their sexual orientation secret. Burakov stashed the card file in his office safe, and next to it he placed a secret informant's file, with a flap of white paper pasted like a curtain over Ivanenko's photograph. He revealed his new informant's identity only to Fetisov.

Ivanenko soon began to fill this file with more information. After eliminating Ivanenko as a suspect in the killings, Burakov took him slightly into his confidence. He told him that someone in Rostov oblast had been killing girls, women, and young boys. He told him a few particulars of the killer's signature. Ivanenko said he wanted to help Burakov find the man. Normally, Burakov was as cynical as the next *syshchik* in evaluating human motivation, and a normal *syshchik* would assume that a man like Ivanenko cooperated with the *militsia* solely from self-interest. But Burakov, in this case, chose not to believe that Ivanenko was betraying his friends and acquaintances to protect his own freedom. He believed he sensed an altruism in the man, an interest in finally being of service to society.

Whatever his motives, Ivanenko turned out to be a gifted undercover investigator. He was particularly useful in cases where a potential suspect displayed no criminal behavior and thus gave the *militsia* no leverage to use in interrogating him. Burakov, for instance, wanted to check a man named Ivan Fyodorov, living alone, quietly, in a cottage in the country. He had been convicted ten years earlier of molesting a neighbor's daughter. Burakov feared that a *syshchik*, particularly a heavy-handed one, might prompt Fyodorov only to clam up. So he sent Ivanenko.

Ivanenko approached his task by finding a way to befriend the suspect. In Fyodorov's case, the key was his hobby. Fyodorov raised rabbits, whose pelts were used for the ubiquitous Russian winter hat, the *shyopka*. Ivanenko went to the library and studied the art and problems of raising rabbits until he could pass as a fellow hobbyist. Then he went out to the country and dropped in on Fyodorov to ask him questions about rabbit husbandry.

Ivanenko hit it off with the suspect immediately, and spent a week as his guest, studying rabbits and chatting. Then he returned to Rostov and sent a detailed, handwritten report for the secret file in Burakov's safe.

Fyodorov, Ivanenko reported, had once had a compulsive attraction to young girls. But his conviction for molestation had destroyed his marriage and cost him his family, leaving him a sad and lonely old man. That was why, Ivanenko said, he lavished so much attention on his rabbits. He no longer had much of a sex drive and showed no signs of attraction to girls, women, or boys. He was physically fragile. He could not be, Ivanenko concluded, the *lesopolosa* killer.

Burakov did not immediately trust Ivanenko's judgment. But, over time, he realized that Ivanenko was an accurate reporter and an astute judge of character. His reports checked out. A peculiar relationship gradually developed between the two men. It remained that of policeman and informant, but overtones of friendship and respect tinged the edges of their conversations.

Meanwhile, Burakov was using Ivanenko's card file to tear down the closet walls of hundreds of gay men in Rostov. These men did not require a furtive undercover evaluation like the one Ivanenko prepared on Fyodorov. It was enough to find them in the card file, watch them surreptitiously, catch them in the act of violating the sodomy law, and bring them in. Then, faced with jail time, they would talk about their friends, their contacts, and any particularly perverse, violent types they might know.

That was how, for instance, Burakov came to prosecute Boris Panfilov. He was a name on one of Ivanenko's cards, a bachelor in his early twenties who worked as a sound and lighting technician at the operetta theater. He lived in a single room in a building designated for demolition by the city's urban renewal program. Panfilov, according to Ivanenko, particularly liked teenaged boys, but boasted of having a female lover as well. He had a collection of pornography. Once in a while, he traveled to Moscow or Leningrad for a sexual spree with gay friends in those cities. There was no evidence that he had violent tendencies.

Panifilov had, in fact, a personal history not unlike those of Natalia Shalopinina, Yuri Kalenik, and so many others involved in the *lesopolosa* case. He had an alcoholic father and a mother who handed him over to an *internat*, Children's Home No. 7, in the city of Taganrog, when he was a toddler. This *internat* was primarily an orphanage for children of normal intelligence. But the conditions were not much better than those at the retarded-children's *internat* in Gukovo. Panfilov remembered as rare pleasures the times the *internat* staff passed out candy and the time they took him to see his first film, a Russian fairy tale called *Zolushka*. He started to think of himself as a future actor.

When he was eleven, his mother took him out of the *internat* because of a new policy requiring her to pay for his room and board. But his mother lived in a single room, and she had a lover. Panfilov spent his time on the streets, and he often slept in a space behind the screen at a Rostov movie theater. One night, he fell off his perch back there and broke his leg, which left him with a slight limp. He returned to the *internat*.

At fifteen, he left both the *internat* and his mother for good. He enrolled in a vocational school for the film industry, supporting himself on a student stipend of thirty rubles a month. Panfilov had become a handsome man, though small and slightly built; he had a delicate bone structure, fair hair, and blue eyes that suggested he might photograph well. He tried out for acting courses. But his limp and a slight lisp eliminated him. He studied lighting and film projection.

Since puberty at the *internat*, he had known that boys and men attracted him more than girls. He had his first sexual experience at sixteen with a girl. But it was at her initiative, and he found the encounter emotionally sterile. At seventeen, he started hanging out in Maksim Gorky Park, and that year he had his first gay experience, with a man of twenty-two.

Thereafter, Panfilov sought work close to one of Rostov's furtive gay milieux. At first he worked as a projectionist in the Rossiya Theater, adjacent to the gay gathering spot in Maksim Gorky Park. After eighteen months, he got a job at the operetta theater. For the first time in his life, he had the company of colleagues with whom he could be open about his sexual preferences.

After four years, Panfilov quit in a dispute with the theater's management. While on tour, he and other technicians had to sleep four to a hotel room; he thought he deserved more privacy and threatened to quit if he did not get it. The theater management took him up on his offer. Unemployed, Panfilov tried to get into a Moscow institute for cinematography, but failed. He trained as a bartender, but didn't like it. He was at loose ends when four of Burakov's men broke down the door of his room, catching him with a boy eight months shy of eighteen.

The procurator's office, reviewing the evidence of the raid and subsequent investigation, charged Panfilov with sodomy, sodomy with a minor, and possession of pornography, found when they searched his apartment. The search also turned up a couple of 7.62-mm bullets, so he was charged as well with violating the law against possession of unregistered weapons.

Burakov and a procurator named Igor Ananyev handled the interrogation. To Panfilov, it seemed as if they were playing the good cop–bad cop game with him. Burakov was the calm, rational interrogator. He told the prisoner that his blood test had eliminated him as a murder suspect. Burakov merely wanted his cooperation in identifying other possible suspects. They had his address book, so most of his contacts were already known. If he helped the *militsia*, Burakov offered, he might get a reduced sentence. Otherwise, he was looking at a long time in jail.

Ananyev, the attorney who handled nearly all the cases against gay men during the *lesopolosa* investigation, did not bother to be civil. Most of the gay men who encountered him during the investigation deemed him extremely hostile . One of them, a man named Sasha Sivolobov, recalled how Ananyev badgered him to describe the taste of semen. Panfilov noticed Ananyev's round, red face, close-cropped brown hair, and light mustache and thought him piggish. Ananyev cursed him freely and demanded the same information Burakov wanted. He, too, offered a reduced sentence—perhaps only a year or two in jail.

Panfilov tried to resist. He faked a nervous disorder that deprived him of the ability to speak, and sat mute through a couple of interrogations. They sent him to a psychiatric hospital, where a doctor put a mask over his mouth and nose and dropped ether on it until Panfilov cried out. He got injections, which he believed to be psychotropic drugs designed to weaken his will. Then they returned him to jail. His cell mates beat him; they told him they did it at the guards' behest, with a pack of cigarettes as their reward. Finally, Panfilov talked.

By then, his resistance had cost him any leniency Burakov and Ananyev might have tried to arrange. He was sentenced to five years in prison.

He served his time in a special section of the oblast penitentiary in Novocherkassk, a section reserved for men convicted of sexual crimes. One of the people he met there was Yuri Kalenik. Kalenik had finished his auto theft sentence in March 1985. But there were *militsionery*, led by deputy chief Pavel Chernyshev, still determined to prove that Kalenik had committed at least some of the *lesopolosa* murders and determined, therefore, to keep him in jail, where he could be watched and worked on. So before Kalenik could get out, these *militsionery* found a young man, also a former inmate of the *internat* in Gukovo, who testified that Kalenik had sodomized him during the time they both lived there. Kalenik bitterly denied the charge, but the judge believed the witness and the *militsia*. Kalenik got another two and a half years.

Passing the time, Kalenik told Panfilov how the *lesopolosa* investigation had careened into his life and virtually destroyed it in the rush to find the serial killer. Panfilov, not surprisingly, found the story entirely credible.

Viktor Burakov, by that time, had concluded that the theory that a gay man was committing some or all of the *lesopolosa* murders was another false trail. He had begun to discuss the case more often with Aleksandr Bukhanovsky, dropping by the psychiatrist's apartment late at night, drinking tea, and listening to Bukhanovsky's theory of a schizophrenic sadist who was most likely heterosexual. Burakov had also spent more time discussing the case with his gay informant, Valery Ivanenko. Ivanenko, though he lacked Bukhanovsky's erudition, pressed a similar theory on Burakov. Finally, there was the experience of questioning the gay suspects. None of them struck Burakov as the type of person who could stalk more than twenty victims, lure them into the woods, bash their skulls in, and dismember their sexual organs.

In a memo to his colleagues at the end of 1985, Burakov wrote down his own best guess about the identity of the killer. He put nothing in the memo about Bukhanovsky's contribution to his thinking about the case. It seemed best, for the time being, to keep quiet about his growing rapport with the psychiatrist and the information he was disclosing to him.

They were probably looking, Burakov wrote, for a man between thirty and fifty, either a sadist or a necrosadist. He could attain sexual satisfaction only by stabbing and mutilating his victims. He might take the excised body parts home for use in a masturbatory sexual ritual. For that reason, Burakov could not conceive of the killer's having a family. He lived alone or in some circumstances that permitted him to leave whenever the urge to kill struck him and to return without being seen.

The killer had the ability to hide his mental disease from co-workers or other people around him, which suggested average or above-average intelligence. He no doubt had a job, one that required him to travel a lot. But he probably did not, Burakov wrote, use a car in the commission of his crimes. If he did, why would he go to the trouble of hiding the clothing of most of his female victims? He had, for instance buried Olga Stalmachenok's clothes in the cornfield near her body. If he had a car, he could have stashed the clothes in the trunk until it was safe to discard them.

Although the killer might have had some sexual experience with males, his basic orientation was heterosexual. "Could this be a homosexual?" Burakov wrote. "From my experience with homosexuals of various ages, I don't think he can be, at least not of the pure sort."

But by that time, the investigation of Rostov's gay community had acquired a momentum of its own. Interrogations begot suspects, who begot more interrogations and more suspects. By the time it was over, the *lesopolosa* investigation had identified and investigated four hundred forty gay men in Rostov. One hundred five of those were convicted under the Soviet anti-sodomy statute and sent to jail.

The investigation terrorized nearly all of Rostov's gay men, not just those directly swept up in it. The gay meeting place moved from park to park in the gay men's effort to stay away from the *militsia*. Many of them found ways to leave the city and move elsewhere. Others put their sex lives in abeyance.

Some did not survive. Viktor Chernyayev, a waiter, was called in by the *militsia* during the *lesopolosa* investigation and threatened with prosecution under the sodomy statute. He slashed his wrists and died. Yevgeny Voluyev, a bisexual telephone engineer, was harassed by the *militsia* continually after his name showed up on a list of gay men being treated for syphilis at a city clinic. He poisoned himself. Anatoly Otryeznov, a carpenter in a café, opened his wrists and died a day after he told friends that the *militsia* wanted to question him about pedophilia.

7

A Body in Moscow

The progress of the *lesopolosa* investigation did not satisfy the authorities in Moscow. Public opinion counted for little in the Soviet system, and the system's rulers had no fear of a popular outcry that might turn them out at the next election. But the system did generate reams of plans and reports and lots of meetings and conferences. Inevitably, some of that talk and some of that paper made its way to the top of the law enforcement system.

Minister of the Interior Vitaly Fedorchuk summoned Mikhail Fetisov and Pavel Chernyshev to Moscow late in 1984 to demand an accounting. Fedorchuk enjoyed a fearsome reputation. He had risen through the ranks of the Ukrainian KGB, suppressing political dissent with a ruthlessness that distinguished him even among his Russian colleagues. When Yuri Andropov became general secretary in 1982, Fedorchuk filled his spot at the head of the Soviet KGB in Moscow. But Andropov died after only fifteen months in power. The new leadership shuffled Fedorchuk off to the Ministry of the Interior, calculating, perhaps, that it would do the country no harm to have someone of his temperament turned loose on common, rather than political, criminals.

When Fetisov and Chernyshev arrived at the ministry building on Ogaryeva Street in Moscow, they dropped in first on some of Fetisov's friends from his days at the ministry academy. When Fetisov told them of Fedorchuk's summons, they responded with harsh sympathy. One of them made the

Orthodox sign of the cross over Fetisov's head, like a priest at a funeral.

"You're already dead," the friend said.

Precisely at five o'clock, an aide ushered them into Fedorchuk's office. Fetisov understood at once that Fedorchuk was not going to fire them, at least not that day: he was in civilian clothes, with his jacket draped over the back of his chair. For a formal firing, Fetisov figured, Fedorchuk would have worn his uniform and kept the jacket on.

Fedorchuk was quietly hospitable. He ordered an aide to bring tea. He listened for an hour to their report. At the end of the hour, he said simply, "We'll get back to you in six months."

Fetisov understood that this was a time limit. If he had not captured the killer by the middle of 1985, he might be looking at the career in the coal mines his family had long ago advised him to seek.

As winter gave way to spring in 1985, Fetisov and Burakov waited nervously for the next summons to view a body. By their calculations, the killer struck most often in warm weather. Bodies left in the woods in late autumn or winter were frequently not found until the snows receded in March and April. But those months passed, and no bodies turned up.

In addition to working on gay suspects, they cleaned up a few of the many loose ends left from the rash of killings the previous summer. In January, an old woman in Donskoi reported that her daughter and granddaughter were missing; she had not seen them for six months. The daughter, Tatyana Petrosyan, was thirty. The granddaughter, Svetlana, was ten. A few months later, the medical examiner reported that the mother and daughter's dental records and physical characteristics matched the pair of bodies found in the woods near the railroad tracks south of Shakhty the previous July.

Tatyana's personal life matched those of the previously

identified adult females. She had no husband, no work, no permanent place of residence. She had spent time in a mental hospital. She abused alcohol and she had a disorderly sex life. She was said to occasionally entertain men in her daughter's presence.

Because Tatyana's life was so erratic, her mother had not thought her absence unusual until six months had passed. Tatyana would often disappear for months, staying with other relatives or who knew where. The old woman knew few, if any, of the men in her daughter's life. She recalled one person who came by her apartment for fifteen minutes in April 1984. Tatyana said he was a teacher, but her mother could not remember the man's name.

By July 1985, ten months had gone by since the discovery of the body of Irina Luchinskaya, the last victim bearing the signature of the *lesopolosa* killer. The deadline imposed by Vitaly Fedorchuk had passed as well.

But political events had given Fetisov a reprieve of sorts. In March of that year Konstantin Chernenko had died, and Mikhail Gorbachev succeeded him as general secretary. One of the first personnel moves of the Gorbachev era was Fedorchuk's retirement. It would probably take a while, Fetisov knew, for the paperwork about the unsolved murders in Rostov to rise to the level of the new minister's agenda.

Burakov and Fetisov had three theories to explain the absence of victims in the first half of 1985. The killer, they thought, might have committed suicide, no longer able to cope with the demons within himself. He might have moved out of Rostov oblast. Or he might have been confined in a jail or psychiatric hospital for another crime. They began to check out the lists of suicides and the lists of imprisoned criminals.

If the killer had moved out of Rostov oblast, Burakov reasoned, that did not mean he would stop killing. He sent a circular to all the *militsia* units in the Soviet Union, briefly describing the signature of the *lesopolosa* killer. The Soviets lacked a centralized, computerized clearinghouse for crime information. But Burakov hoped to be notified if anyone else encountered a murder like the ones in the *lesopolosa* series.

Early in August, he received word about a murder in Moscow. The body of a young woman named Natalia Pokhlistova had been found, naked, in a thicket of woods near Domodedovo Airport, about one hundred fifty yards from the nearest paved road. From the school portrait photograph sent with the bulletin, Burakov could see that she had been a pretty girl, with short, black hair and brown eyes. The next photograph in the packet showed her as she had been found. Her face was smudged with dirt and her mouth was frozen open in a silent scream that had become all too familiar to Burakov. Her murderer had left puncture wounds in her neck and between her breasts. Then he had cut off the tips of her nipples.

Her parents had told the Moscow investigators a story that was also familiar to Burakov. Natalia had been mildly retarded and hard to control as she grew older. She smoked and drank, and she tended to wander.

Domodedovo Airport, Burakov knew, normally served flights between Moscow and the southeast Soviet Union. Flights to and from Rostov normally landed at another of Moscow's airports, Vnukovo. But in the summer of 1985, Vnukovo was closed for repairs. Flights on the Moscow-Rostov route were using Domodedovo.

Burakov felt, by this time, only a slight twinge of regret that someone else had died. He was seized with a belief that his quarry had surfaced again, and surfaced in such a way that it might be possible, finally, to close in and catch him. A finite number of people flew between Rostov and Moscow. They could all be checked out. Burakov grabbed a couple of files with pictures from the Rostov killings and caught the first train he could get to Moscow.

Once in the capital, he went directly to a meeting of the

Lieutenant Colonel Viktor V. Burakov in his dress uniform. As head of a special investigative unit, Burakov struggled against a decaying Soviet system, archaic attitudes toward sex crimes, and false confessions, as his determination to hunt down the real serial killer became an obsession.

Major General Mikhail Fetisov, chief of the Rostov oblast *militsia*, who recognized Viktor Burakov's investigative skills by appointing him to head the team that finally identified and trapped the most savage serial killer in Russian history: Andrei Chikatilo.

Vladimir Kolyesnikov. Now head of the Criminal Apprehension Bureau of the Russian Ministry of the Interior, he was Fetisov's deputy during much of the eight-year-long investigation of the serial murders and drew the assignment of placing Chikatilo under formal arrest.

Pelagea Petrova, mother of thirteen-year-old Lyubov Biryuk, who never returned from a trip to buy bread. The discovery of Lyubov's body in a wooded strip, in 1982, first suggested to Fetisov that a killer of unusual savagery was at large.

The bus station in Donskoi, where the killer spotted and stalked Lyubov Biryuk.

Some of Chikatilo's victims. At first he killed girls and young women. Later, young boys also became his prey. Top row, left to right: Lyubov Biryuk, Yelena Bakulina, Irina Luchinskaya, Lyudmilla Alekseyeva, Irina Karabelnikova; second row, left to right: Irina Pogoryelova, Lyubov Kutsyuba, Vera Shevkun, Olga Stalmachenok, Ivan Fomin; third row, left to right: Inessa Gulyaeva, Igor Gudkov, Sergei Markov, Svetlana Petrosyan, Tatyana Petrosyan; fourth row, left to right: Viktor Petrov, Yelena Varga, Dmitri Illaryonov, Yaroslav Makarov, Natalia Golosovskaya; fifth row, left to right: Viktor Tishchenko, Natalia Shalopinina, Aleksei Khobotov, Olga Kuprina, Aleksadr Chepel.

Yuri Kalenik. As a result of a coerced confession in 1983, Kalenik became the prime suspect in the killings and spent five years in jail.

A *militsia* artist's sketch of the man seen walking with Dmitri Ptashnikov on the night he disappeared.

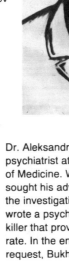

Dr. Aleksandr Bukhanovsky, a psychiatrist at the Rostov Institute of Medicine. When Burakov sought his advice in the midst of the investigation, Bukhanovsky wrote a psychological profile of the killer that proved remarkably accurate. In the end, at Burakov's request, Bukhanovsky was called in to the stalemated interrogation of Andrei Chikatilo, and convinced him to confess.

Andrei Chikatilo on the night of his second, and final, arrest, November 20, 1990.

Burakov (center) questioning Chikatilo (right) during a visit to a murder scene, where Chikatilo showed the location of the body and described how he had killed the victim.

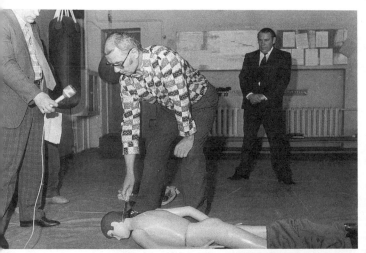

Chikatilo using a mannequin to show Burakov (background) and other detectives how he killed one of his victims.

The Rostov courtroom, where the five-month-long trial of Andrei Chikatilo began in April 1992. Judge Leonid Akubzhanov presided, flanked by the two official jurors.

Andrei Chikatilo at his trial. He sat in a cage designed for murder defendants, ostensibly to protect him from vengeful relatives of the victims.

syshchiki working on the Pokhlistova case. Burakov placed his own pictures, which happened to show the corpse of Lyudmilla Alekseyeva, on the table, not far from the Moscow investigators' pictures of Natalia Pokhlistova's corpse. The Moscow detective, as he made his presentation on the Pokhlistova case, accidentally picked up the pictures of Alekseyeva and used them to talk about Pokhlistova's wounds and the site where she had been found. In fact, there was one slight change in the killer's signature on the two victims. Pokhlistova's killer had stuffed her mouth with leaves and dirt; Alekseyeva's mouth was empty. This nuance did not shake Burakov's conviction that the *lesopolosa* killer had slain both of them. He attributed it to a twitch in the killer's state of mind. Once Burakov pointed out the similarities in the crime scene photographs, no one in the room doubted that Rostov's killer had struck in Moscow.

They began working with the hypothesis that the killer was on a visit to Moscow and had flown back to Rostov shortly after Pokhlistova's death, which the Moscow investigators had calculated occurred either on July 31 or August 1. A mixed group of Rostov and Moscow *syshchiki* went to Domodedovo Airport, to the offices of Aeroflot, the Soviet Union's state airline. They collected all the ticket records for Moscow-Rostov flights in the first week of August.

Reading them was a daunting task. Aeroflot lacked a computerized reservation system, and its tickets were handwritten. The *syshchiki* had to work with carbon copies of tickets that had often been written in a hasty, nearly illegible scrawl. Even when the *syshchiki* deciphered the handwriting, they had only initials and a surname. The ticket might say "I. V. Petrov," but it gave no further indication of who Petrov was or where he lived. Since Soviet consumers paid cash for everything, there were no credit card records to help in identifying passengers. Nevertheless, over a month's time, the investigators had slowly compiled a list of names for the *syshchiki* in Rostov to check out.

Burakov had other ideas to check out. Pokhlistova's murder had coincided with the World Youth Festival in Moscow, the first big international event of Gorbachev's tenure as general secretary. Two types of people had traveled from Rostov to attend. There were local officials of the Communist Youth League who made a profession of organizing and attending Party-approved events for young people. And there were *militsionery*, recruited to help the Moscow *militsia* with the tight traffic and security arrangements that the Party demanded to make sure that the festival made a proper impression on all the foreigners invited into Russia for the occasion. And there were carpenters, plumbers, and electricians sent to the festival as well.

The Moscow region, although not known for resorts, had dozens of sanitoria and vacation homes maintained by various Soviet trade unions for their workers. Summer was their peak time. Burakov wanted them checked out.

Finally, there was the chance that the killer had nothing to do with either the festival or the sanitoria. He might simply have gone to Moscow on orders from his enterprise. The investigators checked with the Rostov oblast government. There were three hundred forty-two enterprises in the oblast that traded with Moscow enterprises. They all had to be checked to find out whom they had sent to Moscow at the end of July.

This investigative net had some sizable holes, Burakov knew. The killer might have relocated permanently to Moscow. He might have traveled to Moscow by overnight train, for which there were no passenger lists. But Burakov suspected they were finally getting close to their man. He set virtually the entire *lesopolosa* task force to work checking out the new leads.

The Moscow *syshchiki* came up with a lead of their own. Beginning in the autumn of 1984, when the *lesopolosa* killings abruptly stopped in Rostov, three boys, all ten or eleven years old, had died at the hands of a brutal killer in Moscow.

This killer had raped all three boys and decapitated one of them. The Moscow *militsia* theorized that the same killer had committed the murders in Rostov and had then either moved to Moscow or had begun a job that required regular trips to the capital. And they had a lead on a suspect. One of the Moscow victims had disappeared from a summer camp. Among the victim's camp friends, the Moscow *syshchiki* found a boy who told them that he had met a man named Fischer with the victim just before he disappeared.

Burakov received orders to check out anyone named Fischer in Rostov oblast. It was a major undertaking. Centuries ago, Empress Catherine II, born a German princess, had invited thousands of German farmers to settle in the lower Volga area. Some of them were named Fischer, and many of their descendants lived in Rostov oblast.

All the Fischers that the investigators found proved to have alibis that eliminated them as suspects. They found an intriguing non-Fischer in the person of a powerfully built man named Nikolai Popov, a man with a long criminal record. Popov had a tattoo on his left shoulder that said "Fischer," which he claimed honored the American chess grand master. But Popov had been in jail until July 1985.

As if to confuse the issue, the killer struck again at the end of August 1985, back in Shakhty in a grove of trees not far from the bus station. The victim this time was an eighteen-year-old named Inessa Gulyaeva, another girl with no home, no job, and a weakness for vodka and worthless men. Her mother had raised her without a father. She had dropped out of school after the eighth grade. Her mother had not seen her, she told the *syshchiki*, since early April.

The examination of Gulyaeva's body turned up several details that particularly piqued Burakov's interest. She had been dead only a day or so when her corpse was found on August 28. Her mouth, like the mouth of Natalia Pokhlistova in Moscow, had been stuffed with leaves. Apparently, the killer had now added this to his ritual. The examiners found sweat mixed with the blood coming from the wounds in her neck. They typed the sweat AB; her blood type was O. And Gulyaeva had two threads, one red and one blue, under her fingernails. Presumably, they came from the clothing of the man who had killed her. They also found a single gray hair between her fingers.

The Shakhty *militsia*, it turned out, already knew a fair amount about Inessa Gulyaeva. A couple of days before she died, the *militsia* chief in the village of Konstantinovka, a river town about forty miles east of Shakhty, had arrested her as he walked to work. Her crime was lying drunk on the Don embankment at eight o'clock in the morning. When she sobered up enough to talk, she told the Konstantinovka *militsia* that she had no home they could send her to, that she was, in the Soviet parlance, a *bomzhe*—an acronym from the Russian words *byez opredyelyennogo myesta zhityelstva*, or "without a defined place of residence." The nearest place where the state dealt with such people was in Shakhty, and the *militsia* sent her there.

Only a law enforcement bureaucrat could distinguish the Shakhty shelter for *bomzhe* from a jail. It is a two-story concrete building with a steel gate and bars on the windows. The guards are *militsionery*. The *bomzhe* live in large, dark rooms, crowded with iron bunks and scraps of bedding, and secured by cell doors with ancient steel padlocks.

Soon after she arrived, Inessa Gulyaeva decided that she wanted to wash the dress in which she had been lying on the ground, so she went to the laundry room and took it off. She had no other clothes except for her panties, and no one offered her something to cover herself. She was a homely girl, with a broad, flat face, a wide nose—and enormous breasts. Word of what she was doing spread instantly through the building, and the guards and those male inmates who were out of their cells to do chores soon gathered in the laundry room to gawk at her.

While the men stared, the procurator in Shakhty was reviewing her case. As it happened, she still had her passport, the internal identification document that every Soviet citizen had to carry. And the passport showed that she was registered to live with her mother in Krasnodar, a city several hundred miles south of Shakhty. She was not, therefore, technically a *bomzhe*, and she was not, the procurator ruled, entitled to a month of free food and lodging at the expense of the Soviet people. He directed the guards at the shelter to let her go, and they did so on the afternoon of August 27. The next day, her body was found.

The investigators could not immediately establish her identity. The body was, as usual, naked; they found neither clothing nor documents. The investigators showed a photograph of the corpse to, among others, the guards at the shelter, but all the guards said they had never seen the woman before. It took a week to identify the body from fingerprints and retrace her path to the shelter.

The early investigation in Shakhty filled Burakov and Fetisov with both fear and eager anticipation. Rarely had the *militsia* managed to discover a *lesopolosa* victim so soon after his or her death. Rarely had the militsia been able to establish a victim's whereabouts before the murder so precisely. The strange inability of the shelter guards to identify the corpse's picture aroused suspicion, particularly in the context of the two threads, one red and one blue, found under the victim's fingernails. Both colors could be found in the summer uniform of the *militsia*, which included a blue cotton shirt and trousers with a red stripe. And that was the source of their fear.

The investigators had already entertained the idea that a *militsioner* might be the killer. It explained how so many victims would trustingly follow him into the woods. It explained the killer's evident ability to leave little or no evidence at the murder scenes. But they hated the thought that this hypothesis might be the one that finally proved out.

They had no choice but to press ahead with it. Once they had established Gulyaeva's presence at the shelter, they had little trouble finding witnesses who remembered the incident in the laundry room. Several of them mentioned that a *militsioner* named Sergei Kolchin had paid particular attention to Gulyaeva. They remembered seeing him talking to her.

Kolchin had come to the attention of the *lesopolosa* investigation once before. He vaguely fit the description of the *militsioner* who had supposedly visited the *priton* where Vera Shevkun hung out on the night before she died in 1983. But he had denied any knowledge of the *priton*, and he never became a suspect.

The more Burakov learned of Kolchin's personal life, the more it seemed that clearing him in 1983 had been a grave mistake. Kolchin worked as a chauffeur at the shelter, driving a *militsia* car on various errands, including trips to Rostov. That kind of work gave him unsupervised access to a car and lots of occasions when he could disappear from work without attracting attention. Kolchin was in his mid-twenties, strong, tall, with dark hair and eyes. He had been married, but his wife had divorced him after discovering that he had had an extramarital affair. Like so many of the *lesopolosa* victims, he had a disorderly sex life. But that was not all he had. He was asked to give a semen sample, and he complied. He had type AB blood and secretions.

Both Burakov and Fetisov worked on Kolchin's interrogation. Over the course of ten days, they battered Kolchin for six to eight hours a day with the facts that were coming to light, particularly the type of secretion found on the body.

Kolchin dug the hole he was in a little deeper. Naively, he sent a note to his mother, asking her to wash a particular shirt. The note was, of course, intercepted and read. The shirt was found. It had a bloodstain. The bloodstain was analyzed, and it proved to be type AB. That meant that it might be Kolchin's blood. It might have been someone else's blood, mixed with Kolchin's sweat. Why, they demanded, had he wanted his mother to wash it?

On the tenth day, Kolchin broke down.

He had arranged to meet Gulyaeva after she left the shelter. He had taken her into the woods. He had tried to have intercourse with her. She was willing, but for some reason, he could not get an erection. She had laughed at him. He had struck her on the head. He had killed her.

Something about his answers did not ring true with Burakov. Like Yuri Kalenik, Kolchin did not know details he should have known, such as the type of wounds the killer had inflicted. And when they asked Kolchin to show them the place where he had killed her, he took them to a wooded spot several miles from the grove near the bus station where Gulyaeva's body had in fact been found. He had taken her there, tried to have sex with her, and hit her, he said. Then, when he was formally presented with the indictment the procurator was planning to present to the court, accusing him of Gulyaeva's murder, he partially recanted. He had not, he insisted, killed her.

Burakov talked for hours with Kolchin, trying to figure the man out. Was he just a weak-willed man who broke down once under pressure and confessed to something he didn't do? Or had he really killed Gulyaeva, then shown them the wrong spot to confuse them? Burakov didn't know.

He had ordered the investigative staff in Rostov to find out as much as possible about Kolchin's whereabouts on the days of the other murders. The first results were inconclusive. No records existed to show exactly where Kolchin had been on the dates in question. During the days, the investigators established, he could well have been in Rostov and in the other places where murders had occurred. But at night, the car remained at the shelter. He could hardly, for instance, have used it to drive Olga Stalmachenok into the cornfield on the Sixth Collective Farm on the evening she died. Of course, they didn't know for certain that she had been driven there.

Burakov and Fetisov made a quick decision, in conjunction with the procurators. They held off on formally charging Kolchin with murder. But they did, in October, accuse and convict him of something virtually all state-employed Soviet drivers were guilty of: siphoning state-owned gasoline out of the shelter's car and selling it on the black market. He got eighteen months. That would give them time to investigate further.

By the autumn of 1985, the investigation had become badly mired down. There were still unidentified victims. Periodically, Chernyshev or Fetisov would call a meeting of the officers supervising work on the case and demand to know the progress of one or another line of inquiry. They seldom got a satisfactory response. The work on the list of Aeroflot passengers to Moscow in July 1985 threatened to drag out indefinitely. The *syschiki* in the field had barely made a dent in their assignment to check out all the enterprises and come up with a list of names of people sent to Moscow at that time on business trips. The records in the various factories were often a mess—scattered over many offices or incomplete. But it was also true that too many *syshchiki* went through the motions of checking the records, just as many of the laborers at Rostselmash went through the motions of assembling tractors, and just as many kolkhoz workers went through the motions of growing food. The problem was endemic in Soviet society.

The pressure from Moscow to solve the murders intensified in November with the appointment, by the chief procurator of the Russian Republic, of a special procurator named Isa Kostoyev to supervise the investigation. Kostoyev, though he worked in Moscow, was not a Russian. His roots were in the Chechen-Ingush Autonomous Soviet Socialist Republic, in the Caucasus Mountains to the south of Rostov. His people, who were originally Muslims, had been added forcibly to the Russian Empire in the nineteenth century. They had suffered terribly under Stalin's persecutions in World War II, when he accused them of collaborating with the Germans.

Kostoyev was a man of less than average height, stocky and swarthy, with a brushy mustache and a receding hairline. He had risen through the ranks of Russian procurators and had participated in the solution of a serial killer case, involving far fewer victims, in Smolensk, a city in western Russia.

Burakov and Fetisov reacted ambivalently to Kostoyev's appointment. They had expected the appointment of a procurator from Moscow, especially after the Pokhlistova killing made it clear that the *lesopolosa* case spanned more than one jurisdiction. They were disappointed to learn that Kostoyev did not plan to take up residence in Rostov. He would make periodic visits, staying for a week or a month, holding meetings, then heading off to other work. Burakov felt that as long as Moscow was going to send a special procurator, he ought to devote full time to the case.

Burakov and Fetisov were not free of the standard Russian prejudice against Caucasians. Though the Soviet Union was officially a land of tolerant and friendly relations among its numerous nationalities, ethnic tensions were never far from the surface in southern Russia. The region had more than a dozen minority nationalities from the Caucasus—Armenian, Ossetian, Georgian, Chechen, Ingush, Kabardinian, and others. Though these Caucasian people had lived under Russian rule for centuries, they had long memories. They still saw the Russians as imperialists who would, if they let down their guards, impose the Russian language and culture on them.

The Russians, for their part, knew the Caucasian people largely from the bazaars, or farmers' markets, where they brought the produce they grew on their small plots of personal land to sell at free prices. Many Russians felt that the Caucasians were altogether too clannish, greedy, and criminal, and that they conspired to inflate prices. The word "Mafia" fell easily from their lips when they talked of one or another Caucasian nationality—as in "Georgian Mafia" or "Chechen Mafia."

Burakov felt that Caucasians were excessively self-aggrandizing, that they would do anything to advance their own careers. He had heard disconcerting rumors to the effect that Kostoyev had tried to claim all the credit for cases in which he was just part of a collective effort. But Burakov was a Communist. That implied a willingness to go along, formally, at least, with the Party line that ethnic differences counted for nothing in relations among Soviet citizens. It certainly meant that he accepted discipline and commands from the center. So he set out to work with Kostoyev as amiably as possible.

The *lesopolosa* working group by then had become huge. It included fifteen procurators and twenty-nine *syshchiki*. They had at their disposal as many automobiles and regular *militsionery* as they needed to watch the train and bus stations and the parks where they thought the killer might strike next. On some days, that meant as many as two hundred fifty people. They had an undercover team of men and women called Project Decoy, which worked in the evenings at the stations. The women hung around until a man approached them. Then the man was questioned. If he did not satisfy his questioners, his blood was checked.

Kostoyev, after reviewing the case files, upbraided the group for its slow work. Why, he demanded, had they not finished working through the lists of gay men, mental patients, and taxi drivers? Why had they identified and checked out only eighty-one people from Rostov who had been in Moscow in July 1985, when there must have been hundreds in the capital at that time? He was certain, he said, that the killer had at some point already been in their hands, and they had erroneously let him go. That had happened in his previous serial murder case in Smolensk. The killer's inactivity from September 1984 to July 1985 suggested that something had stopped or frightened him. Had they checked out all the people who had been in jail since August 1984? Why hadn't they finished collecting handwriting samples from Novoshakhtinsk that might match the handwriting on the Black Cat postcard?

But, like many inspectors sent out from Moscow to check on factories and farms, Kostoyev had a much easier time telling the locals what they were doing wrong than how to do it right. He presented no novel ideas for the investigation. His main contribution was to approve a plan first proposed by Moscow's 1984 emissary, Vladimir I. Kazakov. It was a scheme based on the theory that the killer was using a car. The *militsia*, Kostoyev said, needed to check the blood type of every automobile driver in the area of the killings—some one hundred sixty thousand people. From that group, they were to investigate thoroughly all those with blood type AB. Statistically, that could be expected to amount to seven thousand people.

All Soviet drivers were, according to a seldom-enforced law, supposed to have a document indicating their blood type, in case they were involved in an accident and needed a transfusion. The operation Kostoyev ordered involved a campaign to enforce this law. Drivers who were stopped and did not have their blood type in their documents would have to be tested. It promised to be a long and costly process, but it got under way.

Kostoyev de-emphasized, but did not terminate, the investigation of Yuri Kalenik and the other boys from Gukovo. It dragged on, but with fewer men.

The Serbsky Institute's opinion that a homosexual could have committed at least some of the *lesopolosa* killings appealed to Kostoyev. He ordered the campaign in Rostov's gay community to continue, and he tried to expand it. He dropped in one morning on Irina Nikolayevna Stadnichenko at the Rostov venereal disease clinic.

Irina Nikolayevna was then in her late forties, with a chunky, short body, hennaed hair cropped close to her head, and flat shoes. She looked like a villainess in an early James Bond movie, but she was in fact an attorney and a former procurator. She worked in a cluttered office off the clinic's main entrance, a room made even more cluttered by the presence of a huge Afghan hound, whom she periodically fed raw meat and nuzzled between the legs. Her job was to advise clinic patients that they would be violating the law if they knowingly transmitted venereal disease and to persuade them to help bring their sexual partners in for treatment. As a result of her work, she knew as much about the gay community of Rostov as anyone in the city, with the possible exception of Drs. Bukhanovsky and Andreev. But unlike Dr. Andreev, who did not conceal a personal distaste for gays, she liked and tried to protect them. She called herself Mama Golubykh, ''Mother of the Gays.''

Kostoyev gave Irina Nikolayevna some material from the case files and asked her if she would be interested in joining the team of procurators and helping them unmask gay suspects. She replied that a gay man could not be the killer. The pursuit of gay suspects, she said, would waste time and ruin a lot of lives. It would be the kind of Soviet make-work that looked impressive in a report bumped up the bureaucratic chain of command but that produced no real results. She refused to help him.

Viktor Burakov did not have that option. He could, when Kostoyev was back in Moscow, try to shift the emphasis of the team's work, pursuing leads that he thought more productive. But he could not avoid entirely giving gay suspects to the procurator.

Shortly after Kostoyev's appointment, one of the many tangents off the Yuri Kalenik investigation produced a suspect named Nikolai Arkadyev. *Syshchiki* were constantly interrogating Kalenik in his cell, pressing him for the names of his friends. They were still trying to prove the existence of a ''Kalenik-Tyapkin gang,'' with some members still at large, to explain how the murders continued after Kalenik's incarceration.

One day, Kalenik mentioned Arkadyev. He turned out to

be a dental technician from Gukovo, twenty-seven years old, living then in Ukraine. As soon as Burakov met him, he could tell that Arkadyev was psychologically unstable. The man quickly apprised his interrogators that he was gay.

It was pitifully easy for the *syshchiki* to get Arkadyev to confess to murder. As soon as they did, and Kostoyev heard about it, the procurator from Moscow took over the investigation. He questioned Arkadyev without a break for an entire day.

Reading the written record of the interrogation, Burakov grimaced. Arkadyev had confessed to murdering Lyudmilla Alekseyeva, Yelena Bakulina, and Natalia Golosovskaya, three of the victims from the summer of 1984. But it was obvious that he knew nothing about the crimes. He described cutting off the ears of the victims—when the victims' ears were in fact intact. He described how the "gang" took blood from the victims and used it to make a drug that they then injected into their veins.

At the end of the day, Kostoyev gave up in disgust. He turned Arkadyev back to the *syshchiki* for more checking. To keep him handy, they arranged for him to be convicted of a charge that could be applied to virtually any Soviet health worker—that of appropriating state materials for work with private patients.

It was, by Burakov's count, the fifth time the *lesopolosa* investigation had obtained a false confession. Meanwhile, the work he considered more vital, like identifying and checking out the people who had been in Moscow when Natalia Pokhlistova was murdered, was not getting done.

8

Dead End

Increasingly frustrated by the failure to solve the case, Viktor Burakov began turning more frequently to Dr. Aleksandr Bukhanovsky for advice. They made an unlikely pair of collaborators. Apart from the vast differences in their education, they looked at Soviet society from opposite ends of the social spectrum.

Bukhanovsky could never forget that he was not a Russian, but had a mixture of Armenian and Jewish blood. Worse, from the authorities' point of view, he had a father living in America. He saw men whom he considered lesser psychiatrists, but men with more acceptable ethnic and political affiliations, getting promotions that were denied him. He chafed constantly under the pressure to abide by Party dicta about psychiatry, rather than by his own ideas and the ideas of other psychiatrists, both Russian and foreign, whom he respected. He sensed, all too acutely, that in a free society he would be leading a more creative, prosperous life.

Burakov, on the other hand, rarely, if ever, entertained doubts about the system. He had seen enormous hardships during his lifetime. But his ancestors had all been peasants— too poor, even, to merit repression during Stalin's collectivization drive. Life had been still harder for them.

Burakov had gone along with what the system asked of him, had joined the Party, and gradually had begun to see some rewards for it. In 1983, he and Svetlana had finally gotten their apartment, in a new brick building on Cosmonauts' Street in the north end of Rostov. The builders had done shabby work, and it had taken the Burakovs two years of part-time work to get the doors hung right, the joints all sealed, and the plumbing corrected. But they finally had a decent home. Their older son, Andrei, was about to graduate from high school and had expressed an interest in joining the army for officer training, an idea that made his father proud. Burakov was moving close to the top of the *militsia* waiting list for a chance to buy a car. And there was talk that the *militsia* might take title to a piece of collective farmland just outside Rostov and divide it up for dacha plots. He could count on a quarter acre.

Burakov would normally have had little or nothing to do with someone like Bukhanovsky—an intellectual, a maverick. But as the hunt for the *lesopolosa* killer entered its fifth year, he was desperate to find a way to narrow the list of suspects. Bukhanovsky might help him do that. As their late-night meetings continued, Burakov began increasingly to respect the psychiatrist's insights. He began to add words like necrosadism to his own vocabulary.

Bukhanovsky perceived in Burakov something he had not seen in many representatives of the Soviet law enforcement establishment. He sensed a man eager to learn and willing to expose his own ignorance to do it. And he sensed as well that he might never have a more fascinating ''patient'' than the unknown killer who was leaving evidence of his afflictions on the bodies of so many victims.

The two men reached an understanding. Burakov would open virtually all the files to Bukhanovsky, letting him examine crime scene reports, medical examiners' reports, and any other pertinent data. Bukhanovsky would, in return, write for Burakov a much more detailed profile of the killer.

It was, as far as they knew, a unique enterprise in the annals of Soviet crime. In the United States, police departments and the Federal Bureau of Investigation had a long history of working with psychiatrists. The FBI school in

Quantico had an office of experts on serial killers and their mental quirks. Bukhanovsky and Burakov would be working virtually alone.

For months, without pay, Bukhanovsky labored over his profile of the killer, which had grown to sixty-five pages by the time he finished it. He called the killer X.

X was not a madman in the conventional sense of one with no control over his actions, Bukhanovsky wrote. "X controls the situation and its development in the direction he needs. He exercises care and farsightedness in the selection of his victims/partners. His desires are accompanied by a strong sense of self-preservation. He probably feels a sense of superiority to the investigators, a sense of his own giftedness, a conviction that he is supremely farsighted."

In fact, the psychiatrist deemed X a man of average, not excessive, intelligence. He had devised a fundamentally sound plan for murdering people and getting away with it, but he had not displayed the kind of improvisations and variations on the plan that Bukhanovsky would have expected from a man of superior intelligence.

X was not a homosexual. "Women predominate among the victims, suggesting that the real object of desire for X is a woman, and the attacks on boys are connected not to his desire but to modifying factors of a practical nature. Boys are probably a vicarious surrogate. On the days that he killed them, he probably had contact with a woman that was broken off for some reason."

As in 1984, when Burakov first sought his advice, Bukhanovsky excluded the possibility that a group of people was responsible for the murders. The killings were the work of a uniquely twisted individual, not the type to coordinate his activities and proclivities with others.

X was not simply a sadist, but a necrosadist. He needed to see his victims die to achieve sexual satisfaction, and his killings were an analogue to sexual intercourse. After he lured his victims into the woods, he began his ritual by rendering them helpless with blows to the skull, either with his hands or the handle of his knife. Then he stripped them naked and either squatted beside or sat astride them. His knife became a surrogate for a penis that failed to function normally. He would begin with light, shallow knife thrusts that created the superficial wounds found in the victims' necks and breasts; they corresponded to foreplay. He would go on to deep, penetrating thrusts in the abdomen; they corresponded to the final thrusts of a man reaching orgasm.

But X's actual penis remained in his other hand, or, perhaps, hidden in his clothes. He might on some occasions get enough stimulation from the sight of the victim's blood and death throes to climax without masturbation. He might on other occasions need to open his pants and masturbate with his free hand. That explained why the *militsia* found semen on some victims and not on others.

Bukhanovsky offered four possible explanations for the blinding of some of the victims. X might find the eyes a sexually exciting fetish. Eyes might appeal to him as a symbol of his power and control. Or he might be unable to bear the gaze of his victims, even if those victims were helpless or unconscious. Finally, he might believe the old Russian superstition that the image of the murderer is left on the eyes of the victim.

X cut out the sexual organs of his female victims to symbolize to himself his power over them. He might then smear his own body with the bloody organs, achieving further excitement. He might take them away and later eat them; Bukhanovsky had read of a nineteenth-century case in which a man made soup from his victims' organs and had an immediate erection and orgasm as he consumed the soup. And he knew of primitive tribes in which warriors believed that eating certain organs from the bodies of slain enemies endowed them with the characteristics of those organs. Hearts gave courage, testicles gave potency, and so on.

In the case of boys, X probably cut off their sexual organs because the sight of them blocked his sexual arousal.

Bukhanovsky gathered weather data for the days when killings had occurred. He noted that on most of those days, barometric pressure was falling; in eleven cases, it rained on the days of killings. The barometer also tended to drop one to two days before a killing and five to seven days before. To Bukhanovsky, this suggested that X's rage was triggered not by a feverish rush of hormones, as the Institute of Sexual Pathology in Moscow had contended, but by "changes in the physical condition of the surrounding environment . . . [and] changes in the psychological climate in his family or at work." In other words, if X was having a hard time with the people around him, and the atmospheric pressure dropped, something happened inside his brain to set him off. The weather, Bukhanovsky pointed out, had been particularly unstable in the summer of 1984.

Bukhanovsky made a pie graph showing the days of the week when the killer struck. Most of the crimes had occurred on a Tuesday or a Thursday. There were no killings on Wednesdays or Fridays and only one on a Sunday; he apparently had other things to occupy his time on those days. Saturdays and Mondays were somewhere in between. Most likely this suggested that X was tied to a production schedule. He might work in a factory supply department or in a job where he was required regularly to check goods into or out of a warehouse.

Unfortunately, some of Bukhanovsky's opinions were quite vague. X, he predicted, was perhaps six inches taller than the average victim, making him about five feet seven. That contradicted the evidence of the large footprints and the tall man seen walking with Dmitri Ptashnikov. But Bukhanovsky hedged his estimate by saying the man's true height could vary by as much as six inches.

He hedged his opinion on X's occupation as well. He wrote that X might have sought a career that didn't require him to mix with people, such as being a mathematician or a physicist. Then again, he might be in an area that allowed him to vent his need to dominate people, such as being a teacher or a prison guard.

X was probably between forty-five and fifty years old, because the psychiatric literature suggested that sexual perversions were sharpest at that age. He had suffered through a painful and isolated childhood, characterized by cruel discipline. He might have had to watch his parents have sex because the family lived in one room.

The conflicts within him probably made X a taciturn and careful individual, Bukhanovsky wrote. Socially, he could be well adapted in a superficial way, and he might be competent at his job. But his defense against life's difficulties would be a retreat into an internal world filled with fantasies. He had probably never been adept at making friends, and he would probably have had to put up with a certain amount of ridicule from his co-workers because of his personal peculiarities. But he would flare up only if someone infringed on that inner fantasy world where he spent much of his time.

X was incapable of a normal sexual relationship, flirting, or courtship. His sexual activity consisted of masturbation, and he probably could not achieve, or sustain, an erection during normal sexual intercourse. But, again, Bukhanovsky backed away from an unambiguous prediction. He could not exclude the possibility that X had fathered a family at some time in his life or that he was still married. He could, Bukhanovsky said, have a wife who demanded little of him sexually, perhaps because she was indifferent or frigid. His wife, if he had one, would be happy to let him keep his own hours.

And whoever he was, X was not likely to stop killing of his own volition. He would be capable of stopping temporarily if he sensed an increased danger of capture. He might even be hiding the bodies of his victims more carefully at this stage, which would explain the sudden decrease in the number of bodies found after the summer of 1984. But only his own death or capture could contain the perverse fires within X that drove him to kill.

Burakov found Bukhanovsky's report fascinating and persuasive, but also frustrating. It supported his belief that neither the persecution of gay men nor chasing after a supposed gang of retarded boys would lead to the *lesopolosa* killer. It explained, as much as such a thing could be explained, the awful wounds inflicted on victim after victim.

But Burakov longed for more practical information. If Bukhanovsky had said X's perversion was caused by the lack of the left testicle, the *militsia* could have organized the physical examination of every man in Rostov. If he had said that the killer was definitely a prison guard or definitely a bachelor who lived alone, that would have narrowed the search. But Bukhanovsky's report, boiled down, said that they were looking for a middle-aged man capable of hiding his perversion from all, or nearly all, the people around him—a man who might even be married and a father. That description could fit hundreds of thousands of men.

Chance soon gave the Rostov investigators another window into the mind of a serial killer. In Stavropol, a city a couple of hundred miles south of Rostov (where Mikhail Gorbachev spent his formative political years in the local Communist Party organization), the *militsia* in 1985 captured a man named Anatoly Slivko. Over the course of twenty-one years, beginning in 1964, Slivko had killed seven young boys. The court in Stavropol sentenced him to death. In that part of southern Russia, death sentences were carried out at the prison in Novocherkassk, the city thirty miles north of Rostov that was the geographic epicenter of the *lesopolosa* killings. Slivko was, in the final days before his execution, at the disposal of the Rostov *militsia*, who ran the prison in Novocherkassk.

Burakov, Fetisov, and Kostoyev agreed that it was worth studying Slivko to glean whatever insights they could into the mind of a serial killer. They knew that Slivko had no role in the *lesopolosa* killings. The Stavropol police had already accounted for his whereabouts on many of the days when people were murdered in Rostov oblast. And, he had type B blood. Burakov requested copies of the investigative files from Stavropol and began reading them, looking for patterns of behavior or personal quirks that might help in the search for the man Bukhanovsky called X.

Anatoly Slivko, Burakov learned, had been such a respected member of the community in Stavropol that he had been awarded one of the honorary titles that the Soviet Union bestowed in lieu of higher salaries. He was a Meritorious Cultural Worker; for many years he had headed a children's club called Chegid, organizing youth trips and activities. His hobby was photography. He was married, and the father of two boys.

But Slivko had a hidden sexual problem. He had been born in a village in southern Russia, the child of a stormy marriage. At one point in his childhood, his father left his mother, although they later reunited and still lived together. Slivko had told the investigators that his family had a history of schizophrenia.

Anatoly Slivko had little or no interest in girls as a boy and young man. He married at twenty-nine after a chaste courtship. His wife-to-be had taken his lack of physical interest in her for a becoming modesty. He was, at first, unable to consummate his marriage. He told his mother about the problem, and she persuaded him to consult a sex pathologist. The doctor had only laughed, prescribed a tonic, and told him everything would be fine if he relaxed. Eventually, he did occasionally manage a weak erection and quick, humiliating intercourse with his wife. But it had happened, he estimated, no more than ten times in seventeen years of marriage, and never after the birth of their second son.

By that time, Slivko had already discovered what did arouse him sexually. In 1961, when he was twenty-three, he had happened to see a grisly traffic accident in which a boy of thirteen or fourteen had died. The victim had been wearing the standard Soviet schoolboy uniform: a white shirt, a red neckerchief, blue trousers, and black shoes. Slivko saw flames and smelled gasoline. There was blood all over the asphalt. And for reasons that he himself could not explain, this scene sexually excited Anatoly Slivko. He began to dream about it, to think about having such a boy himself, making the boy feel pain, and getting that feeling of sexual arousal again.

Unfortunately, his work gave him a chance to do so. He developed a pattern. Once or twice a year, he would make friends with a boy of the right age, a boy who wore the requisite red neckerchief and black shoes. He would be a boy who had not yet begun his growth spurt and was worried that he would forever be shorter than his peers. After gaining the boy's trust, Slivko would tell him that he knew of an experimental way to accelerate growth. It involved a controlled hanging—to stretch the spine—while the boy was anesthetized with ether. Slivko would then take the boy into the woods and fashion a noose. The boy, wearing the neckerchief and shoes, would inhale the ether, put his head in the noose, and hang, like a man being executed. During this time, Slivko would take photographs or make a film and masturbate. Then, most often, he would revive the victims.

It seemed incredible that he could persuade boys to do this, but over the course of twenty-one years, he had done so forty-three times. In thirty-six cases, he had revived the boys. They, cautioned by Slivko not to talk about the experiment, had gone on with their lives. It was a testament to the way Soviet society reared young people never to question authority figures.

But seven times, Slivko's lust demanded more. In those instances, Slivko's behavior turned bloody. He dismembered and decapitated the bodies, taking photographs of the raw stumps where limbs had been. Then he poured gasoline on the remains and set them afire, reminding himself of the sights and smells from the auto accident that had first triggered his sadistic perversion. Then he buried the remains, took his film home, and developed it. The pictures and movies served as stimuli for his masturbation fantasies for months or years, until he needed fresher stimuli and killed again.

Because of the long periods of time that elapsed between murder victims and the burial of their bodies, the Stavropol police had apparently never mounted the kind of intense investigation that could have captured Slivko earlier. The victims who disappeared were dismissed as runaways.

Burakov asked Slivko to write him a letter, trying to explain the way serial killers thought and behaved. Slivko, facing death and eager to show that he felt remorse, complied.

He wrote that many people had asked him how society could cope with killers like himself. He had given the matter much thought and reached several conclusions. People like him, Slivko said, all had difficulties engaging in normal sex. They were sadists, aroused by the blood and suffering of their "partners." They were prone to incessant fantasies and savored the act of planning their crimes. They had a nature that craved rules and discipline, so they created rules for themselves. They had rules for the kind of equipment they could use in committing their murders. They had rules for the kinds of victims they could select. Slivko, for instance, never selected a boy older than seventeen.

Slivko suggested that Soviet schools, which studiously ignored all but the basic biological facts of reproduction, had to provide children with more knowledge about sexuality. "If I had had it," he wrote, "I might have gone to a doctor as soon as the first abnormal symptoms appeared." He suggested a vague kind of social campaign against perversion and homosexuality in the army, in the prisons, and other places where young men gathered. But he knew nothing about the murders in Rostov, and he offered no practical tips for catching the murderer.

Burakov, Fetisov, and Kostoyev agreed that it could be worthwhile to drive to Novocherkassk and interview Slivko personally before his sentence was carried out. They met him in an interrogation room. He was a gaunt, haggard man with eyes that looked haunted by guilt, a shaggy dark pompadour, and a wispy mustache.

How did his attraction toward boys arise, they asked him.

"Without my wishing for it," Slivko replied. "I hadn't read anything about it, I hadn't seen or heard about such an attraction. It just came of its own volition." Then he told them about the automobile accident he witnessed when he was twenty-three.

He had tried, he said plaintively, to control himself. But the desire had become an arbitrary and dictatorial tormentor that seemed to exist as a force outside himself. "It persecuted me constantly," he said.

They asked him detailed questions about his murder ritual. Had he ever sodomized his victims? Had he ever massaged their sexual organs?

Slivko seemed to pull back in disgust at the idea. He had had no such desire. He had simply used the tableaux he created, especially the boys' shoes, as masturbatory stimuli.

They reminded him that the medical examinations of some of the exhumed bodies suggested that he had cut off their penises.

"I don't remember that," he said. "If I did it, I can't explain it."

Was he covered with blood after he dismembered the bodies?

"Never," he said. "Because after the person was dead, the blood flowed very lightly."

This was important. The Rostov investigators had often wondered why no one had ever come forward after a *lesopolosa* killing to report seeing a man spattered with blood leaving the area of a murder. This might explain it. Slivko was suggesting that an experienced killer would know how to kill without causing excessive bloodshed. He would know that once the heart had stopped, the blood flow ebbed to a trickle. And he would tailor his killing ritual accordingly.

One of the more innocuous questions elicited the most remarkable answer. Had he ever used tobacco or alcohol?

Slivko reacted slightly indignantly. He had never smoked. Once, he had tried to get drunk, thinking that it would help him feel attracted toward women. It did not.

More importantly, he said, he took his duties as a youth worker very seriously. "I was always working with children, and I felt a responsibility toward them," said the man who had killed seven boys. "It was a matter of morality, a matter of principle, that I could not appear before them smelling of alcohol."

That comment, as much as anything else Slivko said, gave the investigators a glimpse into the mind of the type of man they were seeking. Slivko was a man whose psyche was so compartmentalized that he could kill a series of children and still think it immoral to appear before children with liquor on his breath. The *lesopolosa* killer could be equally compartmentalized. He could be living an altogether normal existence—except for the times when the sadistic lust that seemed to live outside him compelled him to kill.

Something, however, had banked that lust. The melting snows of the spring of 1986 revealed no new bodies. Since the horrible summer of 1984, only one, in fact, had turned up in Rostov oblast—Inessa Gulyaeva in the summer of 1985. The public mood in Rostov reverted to its normal cynical apathy. The investigation rolled along like a great, suspect-producing machine, testing drivers and spitting out the names of those with type AB blood, and turning up occasional gay men, psychiatric patients, or sex criminals. But the near absence of new victims perversely increased Burakov's frustration, by adding to the questions he could not answer. Had the original *lesopolosa* killer left Rostov or just stopped killing in Rostov? Was he in jail, or had they come so close to catching him that they had frightened him into curtailing his killing? Could Inessa Gulyaeva be the victim of a different killer? He didn't know.

Then, on July 23, the *militsia* in Chaltyr, a farming town south of Rostov, reported the discovery of the body of Lyubov Golovakha, thirty-three, a collective farm worker. She had been stripped naked by her killer, then stabbed twenty-two times. Near the body, the *militsia* found a scrap of cloth that looked as if it might have come off a man's shirt. They tested it and found traces of semen—type AB.

Burakov had his doubts whether this killing belonged to the *lesopolosa* series. The victim had last been seen at a wedding feast, which she left at one o'clock in the morning to walk home. And her killer had not cut her breasts or her sexual organs. After what he had heard from Bukhanovsky and Slivko, he had an enhanced appreciation for the importance of ritual and rules in the mind of the *lesopolosa* killer. He had always selected his victims in the daytime or evening, and always near or on public transport. And he had always, in the cases where enough of the body remained to make a determination, turned his frenzy on the victim's sexual organs.

The Golovakha investigation turned into frustrating work over a long, hot summer. Nearly all Golovakha's neighbors were Armenian peasants, descendants of the Armenians invited into the Rostov area by Empress Catherine II in the 1750s. They did not talk readily to outsiders, particularly Russian *syshchiki*. The investigation produced no witnesses and no leads. Burakov kept the murder on the *lesopolosa* list, though he suspected Golovakha had been killed by someone she knew, due to something that happened at the wedding feast.

Then, on August 18, the *militsia* in Bataisk, one of Rostov's industrial suburbs, reported the discovery of the body of a young woman named Irina Pogoryelova on the grounds of a collective farm. This time, the *lesopolosa* killer appeared to have left an unmistakable signature. Her body had been slit open from her neck to her genital area. One breast had been hacked off, there were numerous shallow knife wounds, and her eyes had been cut out.

But there was an intriguing new quirk in the crime scene. Pogoryelova's body had been left in a natural depression, almost a pit, in the earth. Then the killer had apparently gone to a greenhouse about three hundred yards away and stolen a shovel. He had used it to make a serious effort to bury the body. Previously, his attempts to cover his female victims had seemed to Burakov largely symbolic; he had used leaves or branches. This time, the killer had apparently wanted to really conceal the body; only a hand had been visible above the ground. The medical examiners estimated that Pogoryelova had been dead for a week before dogs happened to sniff out her remains. Could this explain the relative dearth of new victims since 1984? Were there more bodies out there, buried deeper?

Pogoryelova, it turned out, held a responsible job as a secretary in the local criminal court. But she also, the *syshchiki* soon established, led an extremely active and varied sex life. Some of her partners were men she met at the courthouse, and not all of them had come there on the right side of the law. Burakov's team quickly assembled a thick file of potential suspects whose whereabouts on the day she disappeared had to be checked out.

But he suspected, even as he ordered the work, that all her prior sexual contacts would prove to be false leads. The killer would turn out to be a man just passing through Bataisk, a man she hadn't known until she met him, perhaps at a bus stop or on a train, when she agreed to go somewhere with him. They knew only that the man had type AB blood and at least twenty-six prior victims.

* * *

So many of the investigators' leads and plans frittered away after enormous expenditures of money and manpower.

Shortly after the initiation, in early 1986, of the operation to check all drivers and investigate the ones with type AB blood, Burakov got some disturbing news. Thieves had broken into the city hospital in Aksai and stolen the rubber stamps used to denote blood types A and O on official documents.

He could guess why. It would not take long for criminals in the Rostov region to figure out that the *militsia* were looking for people with type AB blood. The way for a criminal to avoid a potentially damaging investigation was to have a stamp on his driver's license or in his passport certifying his blood as any type other than AB. Now there were people ready to sell such a stamp. All that their checks of drivers had accomplished, Burakov thought, was the creation of a new black market enterprise. The operation went on nevertheless.

A year into the investigation of all the Fischers in Rostov oblast, in the autumn of 1986, the investigators got new word from Moscow. The boy who had originally reported seeing the man had recanted. Now he said he had made the whole story up.

At about the same time, the team of handwriting experts in Novoshakhtinsk gave up. After three years of effort, they had been unable to find any documents with writing that matched the style of the Black Cat postcard.

The advent of glasnost made it possible for the *militsia* to publish, in coordination with the editors of the Rostov newspapers, a few cautious stories that suggested the existence of a serial killer and grouped some of the victims' photographs. They asked the public to respond with information.

In response, they got a steady stream of telephone calls and letters attesting to the miserable state of many Rostov marriages. Women complained that their husbands asked them for perverted sex, or beat them, or stayed out all night for no good reason. The *militsia* checked all these "leads" out. In many instances, they found that the couple was divorcing, and the woman had decided that she would rather see the man in jail then split up the communal property with him.

In some cases, the receipt of such a tip would devastate a man's life. The *militsia* investigated one respected, married university instructor after receiving a tip that he drove around the city at night, trying to pick up girls. They found no connection to the *lesopolosa* case, but they did find that the man had a pornography collection and a string of liaisons with students. He lost his job.

By the autumn of 1986, the men in Burakov's special department had decided they had to work harder on the possibility that the killer had relocated, to another part of the Soviet Union. Since the summer of 1984, there had been only two—or three, depending on how Lyubov Golovakha was classified—victims found in Rostov. Natalia Pokhlistova's murder in Moscow in the summer of 1985 established the fact that the *lesopolosa* killer could travel outside his original home territory. It was entirely possible that he had moved to another city and that the *militsia* in his new home had encountered a couple of bodies and not yet realized they were part of a series begun in Rostov. He could be returning for summer vacation visits to Rostov, which would account for the fact that the three post-1984 victims found in Rostov were all killed in the summer months.

Burakov and his crew began to work on a booklet about the case, to be sent to *militsia* departments throughout the Soviet Union. Burakov found writing it a useful exercise, for it forced him to collect and classify all the data about the murders. He made a chart showing all the victims. In a row running to the right of each name, he placed notations indicating the presence or absence of the clues found until that time: eyes cut out, semen samples, disfigurement of the corpse, and so on. He listed the sex, age, and characteristics of the victims. Thirteen of the twenty-seven victims were homeless or tended to wander. Twelve had promiscuous sex lives. Five had psychiatric problems.

He boiled down the killer's modus operandi. Only two common threads ran through all the cases. All the bodies had been found near a road, and all had been killed with a knife. There were many disparities. Seventeen of the victims were women over sixteen. Four were girls under fifteen. Five were boys, all under fifteen. Most came from Shakhty and Rostov, but there were three from Novoshakhtinsk and others from scattered rural areas. Some had had their sexual organs completely removed and some had not. Some had had their eyes removed but others, particularly among the more recent victims, had not. The killings for which they could establish the exact time of death had occurred on every day of the week except Wednesday and Friday, although the killer seemed to prefer Tuesdays and Thursdays.

Compiling the list of suspects was the most embarrassing part of the exercise. The investigators culled from the files a list of twenty-two prime suspects and forty-four lesser suspects; then Burakov ranked them in the order of likely culpability.

But it was, he felt, an implicit admission of failure. The case against each suspect on the list had huge, disqualifying holes. There was not one truly likely suspect that Burakov could cite. The first six places were occupied by Kalenik, Tyapkin, and their various friends from the *internat* for retarded youth. Then came Nikolai Byeskorsy, the drunken baggage handler at the Rostov airport who had had an assignation in the woods in Aviators' Park. Artur Korshenko, the drug user from Aksai who killed Tatyana Polyakova, was next; but he had type A blood, and Burakov was already satisfied that he was guilty only of the single murder to which he had confessed. The ninth suspect was Andrei Chikatilo, the man whom Aleksandr Zanasovsky had shadowed through the Rostov bus and train stations. But Chikatilo also had type A blood.

Sergei Kolchin, the *militsioner* from the shelter for the homeless in Shakhty, ranked fourteenth. But the investigation had established his connection to only one victim: Inessa Gulyaeva, who had last been seen at the shelter. There was a possible connection to Vera Shevkun, who had last been seen in a *priton* visited, according to one witness, by an unidentified *militsioner*. But the investigators had failed to link Kolchin to any of the other victims. He was still on the list because his blood type was AB.

Burakov supervised the completion of the booklet and its binding in red covers. His department mailed it to all the *militsia* departments in the country, and waited for a response.

The booklet project had one immediate side benefit. The flow of data into the *militsia* building on Engels Street had already become voluminous, as the investigators turned up hundreds, and eventually thousands, of potential suspects. The *militsia* had no computers, which was in keeping with the generally low level of computerization in Soviet society. The information being gathered in the field had begun to overwhelm the filing system, which consisted primarily of manila folders locked in safes. Faced with the task of collating all the data for the booklet, Burakov had requested help from Moscow. Several filing experts were dispatched to help organize the material.

They created an alphabetized card file, rather like a library's card catalog. Each person who became involved in the investigation got a card. Suspects with blood type AB had cards with a red stripe. Other suspects had cards with yellow stripes. People who discovered bodies or otherwise provided information had cards with blue stripes. Relatives and friends of the victims were denoted by a green stripe. Some cards had no stripe. If, for instance, the *syshchiki* got a tip that an unidentified man had been seen bothering children in a Shakhty park, they filled out a stripeless card on the incident.

The card on each suspect was supposed to have the individual's name, address, blood type, and date of birth. It was supposed to indicate whether he had a car and, if so, its license plate number. There was a line to indicate why the man had fallen under suspicion. And there were lines to indicate where he was on the dates when murders had occurred. Very quickly, the file grew to include several thousand cards.

In fact, that was one of the investigation's major problems. It was quite easy to convene a meeting and decide on plans: checking all drivers with AB blood or identifying all convicted sex criminals and former psychiatric patients. It was much harder to complete the tedious work of checking out each theory, each suspect. And the more successful they were at generating theories and suspects, the less successful they became at checking each of them out thoroughly.

In a way, their problems mirrored the general problems of the Soviet system. It was easy for the members of the Politburo, sitting in the Kremlin, to decree that the central economic plan for 1986 would be adjusted to provide a twenty-percent increase in shoe production. But that didn't assure that the shoemaker sitting in a cramped, dark little workshop in Rostov got the leather and thread he needed, or that he showed up for work sober, or that he completed each shoe properly. As any Soviet consumer could attest, the system all too often broke down somewhere between the Politburo meeting and the shoe store.

Similarly, Burakov knew, much of the work being done on the *lesopolosa* case was suspect. To begin with, many of the cards in the card file should not have been there. His own name turned up as that of a suspect when he renewed his internal passport and entered his blood type, which was, ironically, AB. Someone filled out a red-striped card with his name on it. Yet, if the investigation were to follow its own rules, some *syshchik* would have to waste dozens of hours verifying Burakov's whereabouts on the days of the murders.

More often than not, Burakov knew, *syshchiki* in the field did a superficial job of checking things out or didn't do it at all. They might, for instance, simply assume that because someone was employed at a given factory he was in the factory on the day of a murder, rather than going onto the factory floor, finding the foreman, and checking his records. Assignments tended to slide or be superseded by new assignments; there were, after all, more than four hundred murders a year in Rostov oblast. A year after the murder of Natalia Pokhlistova in Moscow, the investigators still did not have a complete list of business travelers from all three hundred forty-two Rostov enterprises that traded with Moscow enterprises. Nor had the investigators completed numerous other assignments.

This was no secret to Fetisov, Kostoyev, or anyone else who monitored the investigation. Virtually every internal document criticized the performance of the investigation. "There have been serious inadequacies and organization omissions in the work of different city and local *militsia* organs, and there have been instances of failure to perform work and failure to carry out orders," read a typical internal critique, written in September 1986.

The *militsia* authorities in Moscow remained unhappy. But at the time, Mikhail Gorbachev was struggling to get a handle on the growing national problems of crime and corruption, and he frequently fired his Ministers of the Interior. The turmoil at the top helped protect Fetisov and those below him on the ladder, including Burakov.

Kostoyev's superiors at the office of the Russian procurator in Moscow were also unhappy. In April 1987, I. S. Zemlyanushin, a deputy procurator of the Russian Republic, flew to Rostov with Kostoyev for one of the meetings of the in-

vestigative group. Moscow was concerned about the failure
to solve the case, Zemlyanushin said. The Central Committee of the Communist Party had decided to monitor the progress of the investigation. Zemlyanushin would, in turn, be
monitoring Kostoyev's work.

Kostoyev, by that time, had been on the case for eighteen
months, though he spent most of his time outside Rostov. He
took the floor and tried to shift the blame to his predecessors.
Stupid mistakes made in 1983, such as the fixation on Kalenik, Tyapkin, and their "gang" of mentally retarded youths
had delayed and complicated the search for the real killer, he
said.

They would, Kostoyev promised, catch their man by working through five hypotheses. He predicted that the killer
would turn out to be: someone with a previous conviction
for a sex crime; a homosexual; someone with a mental illness
characterized by a sexual perversion; a present or former law
enforcement officer; or a railroad worker.

At his orders, Kostoyev said, the investigation was focusing on the operation to identify drivers with type AB blood
and on people from Rostov who were in Moscow at the time
of the Pokhlistova murder. But, he complained, the *militsia*
were guilty of sometimes sending out unqualified people who
hindered his work. They had tramped all over the scene of
Irina Pogoryelova's murder, possibly obliterating the killer's
footprints. And, he complained, he was finding it hard to
supervise the work, since he had other assignments, which
took him away from Rostov.

The frustration, backbiting, and recriminations began to affect the emotional stability of both Mikhail Fetisov and Viktor Burakov. The split within the *militsia* over the case against
Yuri Kalenik had gradually healed as more victims turned up
and the theory of a retarded "gang" became more obviously
untenable. But in its place came a more general fear that the

case might never be solved, to the lasting discredit of those who had worked on it.

Other men had joined the investigative team, retired, been reassigned, or quit because the pressure of the case became more than they could bear. Fetisov's original deputy, Vladimir Kolyesnikov, had been transferred to the Ministry of the Interior's academy in Moscow for advanced training.

Fetisov was the only person who had been on the case since its beginning in 1982. But even he had other duties to occupy some of his time. Burakov had been assigned to the *lesopolosa* case virtually full time since the beginning of 1983. He had been given command of a special unit, his killer department, established specifically to handle the investigation. He bore the responsibility with no respite.

Fetisov found that he could not sleep well. He would awaken in the middle of the night and tiptoe compulsively to the bedroom of his eight-year-old son to check and make sure that the boy was still there. And when he could sleep, his dreams were filled with blood and bodies.

Occasionally, it would seem to him that he was living in a nightmare. The thought would occur to him that he himself got up in the middle of the night, went outside, committed the murder, and then returned home and fell asleep, remembering nothing in the morning.

Fetisov confided this only to Burakov.

"Listen, Viktor," he said quietly one day. "Does it ever seem to you that something—that we're committing these crimes? You and I?"

"I've thought of it," Burakov said.

Burakov could not, in fact, stop thinking about the case. At night, he would go home and try to relax. But he could not sleep. He would try to read, and toss the book away. He watched television until the last program signed off after midnight, trying to distract himself. Then he would slip into bed and stare at the ceiling, thinking about suspects that had not yet been checked out. Or, worse, he might think about the bodies.

Finally, at the end of 1986, he had what in the West would be called a nervous breakdown. He recognized only the physical symptoms—a debilitating lassitude that felt like a general weakness. He found that he could not climb the flight of stairs to his office on the second floor of the *militsia* headquarters without grabbing the banister and literally dragging himself up.

He checked himself into the hospital. The doctor told him that due to nervous stress and exhaustion, he had weakened his heart. For three days, he was kept in an intensive-care room, receiving injections. They did not tell him what the drug was, but eventually it caused him to sleep. For the better part of a week, he slept. When he awakened, he could tell that his body was returning to normal. But he was kept in the hospital for three more weeks, and then sent to a *militsia* rest home called Salyut, on the Black Sea near Sochi, for another month.

Svetlana Burakova asked her husband to let someone else take his place in the *lesopolosa* investigation. He refused. He had already invested four years of his life in the search for the *lesopolosa* killer. He could not leave the job undone. It would be like pounding the mat and submitting in a *Sambo* match just because something had snapped in his knee.

He had no new ideas for catching the man. In fact, he had a sense of powerlessness, a sense that the investigation had reached a dead end. But it had become a personal matter between him and X, the man Bukhanovsky said felt superior to the investigators.

He *would* catch the man.

9

The Killer Surfaces

In a way, Viktor Burakov wanted the killer to murder again. Thinking about the case as he lay in the hospital, then recuperating by the Black Sea in January 1987, he grew increasingly certain that none of the methods they were using was likely to work. They could identify all the drivers in the oblast with type AB blood, but they might be looking for a man who didn't drive or a man who had bought a false blood-type stamp for his passport. They could check out all the convicted rapists, all the homosexuals, and all the former psychiatric patients in the Soviet Union, but they might be dealing with a man who had kept himself off all those lists.

He felt like a fisherman who sees a big fish surface and casts repeatedly toward that spot without getting a bite, until he is convinced that the fish has gone elsewhere. He can only hope that his fish breaks the surface again.

In the same way, Burakov felt that he would catch his prey only if the man killed again. Surely, if he continued to kill, he would eventually slip up. He would leave a fingerprint, or he would be seen in the act by a witness, or he would pick a victim strong enough to fight back, escape, and tell the story to the *militsia*.

But during all of 1987, no corpses turned up in Rostov that unmistakably bore the *lesopolosa* killer's signature.

On April 6, 1988, railroad workers near the station at Krasny Sulin found the body of a young woman. It lay on a flat, weedy piece of ground near the tracks. There was no question of how she had died. The entire left side of her skull was bashed in. The *militsia* who first got to the scene speculated that the killer might have used one of the chunks of concrete that some construction workers had tossed away. They littered the ground not far from where the body lay. The woman was naked, and her hands had been bound behind her.

Burakov drove up to Krasny Sulin, a farming and logging town about fifteen miles northeast of Shakhty, and helped conduct the examination of the crime scene.

The first task was to identify the remains. Though the woman's wounds were massive, enough remained of her skull to permit a photograph. Her fingerprints were intact.

Burakov's crew prepared a circular with the woman's photograph, fingerprints, and body measurements, then mailed it to *militsia* departments throughout the Soviet Union. They compared her characteristics with all those on the missing-persons lists. Nothing matched, and no one sent word that they were looking for a woman of that description.

Burakov, by this time, could make an intelligent guess about the victim. She might be an orphan or she might be totally estranged from her parents. She might have lived in an *internat* until she was eighteen, and then been assigned to a menial job. She might have quit the job or been fired, and lived a few years in the ranks of homeless women who spent their time going nowhere on the *elektrichka*. When she was murdered, she had no one to miss her.

None of the Krasny Sulin station workers, the investigators soon found, remembered seeing the woman get off the train. None had heard a cry. None had seen a man walking away from the scene of the crime. Their search turned up only one bit of physical evidence: a muddy footprint, size twelve or thirteen, that could be a match for the footprint found near Dmitri Ptashnikov's body four years previously.

Burakov could not decide whether to place this victim on the *lesopolosa* list. Her wounds differed significantly from those of the other women in the series. She had been stabbed many times, and her nose had been cut off. But it was clear that it was the blow to the skull that had killed her. Her eyes and genitals were untouched, and there was no semen on the body. More significantly, Burakov thought, she had not been killed in the woods, as nearly all of the *lesopolosa* victims had been.

Before this question could be settled, the *lesopolosa* investigators heard on May 17, 1988, of a murder in Ukraine that did seem to bear the clear signature of the killer they were seeking. The victim was a nine-year-old boy named Aleksei Voronko, who lived in a town called Ilovaisk, some thirty miles west of the border between Ukraine and Rostov oblast. What attracted Burakov's attention was the fact that Ilovaisk was a regional rail hub. Trains to and from Rostov passed through it. Crews from Rostov handed off their trains to Ukrainian crews at the Ilovaisk station. And Aleksei Voronko's body had been found in the woods near the station.

Burakov mobilized his department. With a group of *sledovatyeli* from the procurator's office, he drove to Ilovaisk. The details of the killing, they quickly learned, coincided with those of the killings they had seen before. The boy had apparently been sodomized. His mouth and anus were stuffed with dirt. His penis had been cut off, and he had died of a multitude of knife thrusts and a blow to the head. The body was discovered two days after his parents reported him missing.

This time, though, the investigators turned up a witness.

A classmate of Voronko's had been playing near the tracks on the afternoon when Aleksei disappeared. This boy had encountered Aleksei walking toward the woods in the company of a man. The witness had spoken to Aleksei, and Aleksei had told him he would soon return. And when the boy pointed out the place where he had last seen Aleksei, it fit. It was on the way to the spot in the woods where the body had been found.

Carefully, mindful of what had happened in the Fischer

case when a boy of a similar age had made up a story about seeing the killer, they asked if the boy could describe the man.

He was a *dyadya*, the boy said, using the Russian word that literally means uncle but frequently is used in reference to any middle-aged man. He was perhaps thirty-five years old, well built, athletic-looking, with a wispy mustache and a mouthful of gold teeth. He had been carrying a sports bag over one shoulder.

Finally, Burakov thought, the killer might have tripped up. He had given them several solid leads to work on.

The first was the gold teeth. Russian dentists quite frequently dotted their patients' mouths with metal crowns. White smiles were a relative rarity among adults. But so were mouths completely full of gold crowns. Burakov directed the *syshchiki* in the killer department to assemble a list of all the dentists and dental labs in the region. If someone had all his teeth crowned, they should be able to find him.

Perhaps, Burakov speculated, the killer had been sent to Ilovaisk from a Rostov enterprise on a business trip. The investigators had tried to pursue a similar theory three years before, after the murder of Natalia Pokhlistova in Moscow. That effort had become a chronic embarrassment. Burakov and Fetisov had badgered the *syshchiki* in the field for more than a year to complete the survey of all Rostov enterprises for a list of all business travelers to Moscow at the end of July 1985, then check them out. The *syshchiki* had never completed the task. But this time, it might be easier. Only a few Rostov enterprises traded in Ilovaisk. Burakov ordered a new effort to come up with a business travelers' list.

Or it might be, Burakov reasoned, that the killer had moved from Rostov oblast to the Ilovaisk area. Or he might have been visiting relatives. Burakov and his team could think of only one way to find out. In coordination with the local *militsia*, they conducted a door-to-door inquiry. During the course of the next six months, they interviewed at least one person in every household in the town, which had a population of twenty-five thousand people.

But by the end of 1988, it had become clear that all the leads had combined to produce nothing. No one with gold teeth had turned out to be a viable suspect. Neither had any of the Rostov business travelers to Ilovaisk, or the people with relatives there, or the people who had moved there.

It seemed that they were back to where they started when Aleksei Voronko's body was found. But in fact, by the end of 1988, they were back further than that.

Dr. Svetlana Gurtovaya, the head of the biology lab of the bureau of forensic medicine of the Ministry of Health in Moscow, sent a disturbing letter to all Soviet law enforcement agencies at the end of 1988.

The letter said that investigators of sex crimes should no longer assume that blood types and secretion types were always identical. In very rare cases, she said, her laboratory had found that suspects could have blood of one type and semen of another. Therefore, she concluded, the only completely reliable way to determine if a suspect's semen type matched the semen type found at a crime scene was to get a semen sample from the suspect and test it.

Gurtovaya's assertion that blood and semen types could differ had no support in the world community of forensic scientists and physicians who specialize in the matter. Their opinion was that, given proper testing, only two results are possible. Either a person will have the same antigens in his or her blood and secretions—that is, a person with type A blood will have type A secretions. Or he or she will be a "non-secreter," with no antigens at all in the semen, saliva, and other bodily secretions.

In addition, studies were calling into question the competence of Soviet laboratories, suggesting a different explanation for the discrepancies Gurtovaya had found. Successful testing required not only skill and care on the part of the laboratory worker, who had to mix the semen sample with reagents and peer into the microscope to determine whether the cells were clustering or not. It also required proper procedures and a supply of accurately manufactured, consistent, and uncontaminated laboratory reagents. In the decaying Soviet Union of the late 1980s, none of that could be assumed.

A study published in 1989 by a scientist named T. V. Stegnova, in a Soviet journal called *Forensic Medicine Expertise*, reviewed nineteen Soviet sex crime cases and found that in eight of them, the laboratories had incorrectly analyzed semen types. In some cases, they had failed to use proper controls or to follow other vital test procedures. In some cases, Stegnova wrote, it appeared that the reagents used on semen falsely showed the presence of the B antigen. Criminals with type A blood and secretions had left semen that Soviet laboratories had typed AB.

As a practical matter, it made no difference to Burakov and his team whether Gurtovaya had discovered a new medical phenomenon or whether the laboratories that had been working on the case had simply botched their testing. In either case, the fundamental postulate of the investigative strategy could no longer be considered completely reliable.

For more than four years, since Dr. Gurtovaya's definitive statement that the semen found at the murder scenes was type AB, the investigators had grouped suspects by blood type. The operation to check drivers had screened one hundred sixty thousand men, selecting those with type AB blood for further checking. All the lists the investigators had compiled—business travelers, homosexuals, psychiatric patients, convicted rapists, cashiered *militsionery*—went through the same filter. Now, Dr. Gurtovaya was saying that there was a chance, albeit a small chance, that the killer's blood and semen types differed, and that he might have slipped through that filter.

Redoing all the work of the previous four years presented two difficulties that seemed overwhelming. The first was the sheer volume of suspects. The card file in Burakov's office by the end of 1988 had nearly fifteen thousand entries, and about half were men who had been eliminated from suspicion because they had A, B, or O blood. More important, there could be only one way to recheck, reliably, all the thousands of suspects: each would have to submit a semen sample.

The Soviet *militsia* followed a simple method for obtaining semen samples. They gave the suspect pornography and access to an empty room and tried to persuade him to masturbate. In routine criminal cases, this often worked. They could convince a suspect that they had enough evidence to convict him without the sample, and that therefore the sample could only help him. But the method relied on the suspect's cooperation and on the investigators' ability to show that they had other evidence against him.

Burakov could not imagine calling thousands of men into the *militsia* station and persuading them all to cooperate. Apart from the logistics of such an operation—Where would they get enough pornography and enough empty rooms?—there was the question of leverage. Soviet law did not give the investigators the right to demand a sample. In Stalin's time, it might have been possible to demand one anyway; a suspect would have known that the alternative to cooperation might be Siberia. In the era of perestroika and glasnost, the *militsia* could not make that threat. And suspects would soon hear, via rumor or the press, that it was in their best interests not to cooperate, and that there was nothing the *militsia* could do to force them. So, testing the semen of all the old suspects was not an option.

With increasing certainty, Burakov believed that they would have to catch the *lesopolosa* killer in an old-fashioned way. Either they would finally get a witness who could identify him or they would watch the railroads and bus stations so thoroughly that they would catch him in the act.

But the investigation was floundering in a miasma of frustration, confusion, and recrimination. Periodically, Isa Kostoyev, the procurator from Moscow, would arrive in Rostov and conduct a meeting. Burakov, Fetisov, and the local *sledovatyeli* would recite statistics about how many people they had checked out and how many more they planned to screen. Kostoyev would upbraid them for something like failing to coordinate their efforts. "Everything that's been said here, the enormous numbers cited, is all fine," he said at one meeting. "But I can't agree that this is a thorough investigation. Information comes in here and it doesn't go to the right investigator. It just sits in a pile."

Burakov, for his part, found it increasingly difficult to tolerate the sloppy work that was the standard for some of his colleagues. Several months after Aleksei Voronko's murder, he tried to have a *militsioner* fired. The man was a veteran of the Rostov city *militsia* who had been assigned to the *lesopolosa* team. Burakov had found that instead of doing the tedious work of checking out suspects, this officer was likely to absent himself from work. On one occasion, Burakov had heard that the man was drunk on duty. He complained to Fetisov that the officer's example was affecting the work of other investigators. If he could be sloppy, why couldn't they?

Fetisov did not fire the man. Firing someone in the USSR was a bit like firing a government worker protected by one of the more muscular Western labor unions. It required an enormous amount of red tape. Instead, Fetisov transferred him out of the *lesopolosa* group. That solved the particular problem of this officer's poor performance. But his work was only one egregious example of investigative assignments completed carelessly or not at all.

As the snows melted in the spring of 1989, Burakov and his team waited to see whether the killer would give them another chance to pick up his trail. They were not disappointed. On April 10, 1989, lumbermen in a forest near the Donleskhoz railroad station, midway between Shakhty and Krasny

Sulin, found the body of a missing boy named Yevgeny Muratov. His wounds left no doubt that he had become a victim of the *lesopolosa* killer. The corpse was badly decomposed, but the medical examiners were able to establish that someone had stabbed him dozens of times and cut off his penis and testicles.

Muratov was, at sixteen, the oldest of the male victims, though he had the body of a younger boy. He was slightly built, dark-haired, and dark-eyed, and only a couple of inches over five feet. In contrast to many of the earlier victims, he was an excellent student. He came from Zverovo, a small town a short distance up the line from Gukovo, where the *internat* for retarded children was located.

Muratov had disappeared in the summer of 1988 after going to Rostov to fill out the papers to enroll in a school that trained workers for the railroad. On the day after he registered, he and his family were scheduled to go off on vacation, but he never returned home. The *militsia* in both Rostov and Gukovo had mounted an intense search; they had broadcast his picture on the oblast television station, asking for information. They had found nothing. And that was not surprising. The Donleskhoz station was some seventy miles north of Rostov and thirty miles east of Zverovo, in a remote area frequented mostly by woodcutters and mushroom gatherers. It had one thing in common with the sites where many of the earlier victims had been killed. It was on the *elektrichka* route between Rostov and Gukovo.

Most likely, Burakov thought, the killer had met Yevgeny Muratov on the train. He had come up with a convincing pretext to persuade the boy to get off at Donleskhoz. They had walked into the woods together until they reached the secluded spot where he killed the boy.

But this hypothesis frustrated Burakov all the more. Since 1986, the *lesopolosa* investigative group had been ordering special patrols on that very *elektrichka* line. They could not cover all the cars on every train, but they were supposed to be riding frequently and observing. They had particular orders to look for adult males leaving the train with women or children. But none of the *militsionery* on duty the day Muratov disappeared had reported seeing him—alone, in the company of the *dyadya* with the gold teeth, or with anyone else. Somehow, Burakov thought, the killer had a way of protecting himself from their surveillance. He felt the same disquieting suspicion that had troubled him when they questioned Sergei Kolchin, the *militsioner* at the shelter for the homeless in Shakhty. What if the killer was one of his colleagues?

The investigators had two leads to go on. Yevgeny's parents had said the boy was wearing a wristwatch inscribed "To Zhenya on his birthday, from Uncle Tolya and Aunt Raya." They had not found the watch at the scene of the murder. Presumably, the killer had taken it with him, and perhaps he had tried to sell it. Burakov ordered a thorough check of all the watch repair and second-hand stores in the oblast. It turned up nothing.

The ticket clerk at the Donleskhoz station, a woman named Lyudmilla Yepisheva, offered a second lead. In the summer of 1988, she said, she had seen a suspicious-looking man hanging around the platform. He had, in fact, tried without success to persuade her son, Slava, to go off into the woods with him. The police soon found this man, living in a nearby village. But he denied any knowledge of the Muratov murder, and they could find no evidence to contradict him. In fact, he had been a patient in a prisonlike hospital for alcoholics from December 1982 until November 1984, the period when most of the *lesopolosa* killings had occurred. That effectively ruled him out.

Almost from force of habit, the investigators checked out an old suspect, Yuri Kalenik. Kalenik had, by then, been released from prison, and he was back in Gukovo, working as a boiler stoker at the *internat* for retarded children where he had spent his adolescence. He was, the *internat* director assured them, a good worker who caused no trouble. Only the fact that he lived not far from Muratov made him a possible suspect. But Kalenik denied any knowledge of the crime. This time, mercifully, the *syshchiki* believed him.

And there the trail they had hoped to find petered out. The Muratov murder, far from helping to narrow the list of possible suspects, in fact expanded it. Since 1986, the investigators had found two victims that they felt certain belonged to the *lesopolosa* series: Aleksei Voronko at Ilovaisk and Yevgeny Muratov near the Donleskhoz station. They were still not sure about the unidentified woman killed near Krasny Sulin in 1988. This buttressed, in the minds of some of the investigators, the old theory that there had been at least two killers in the *lesopolosa* series, one killing males and the other females, and probably working independently of each other. The killer of boys, they suggested, was the one still active. The killer of women might have gone inactive for any number of reasons: imprisonment on another charge, suicide, or fear of capture.

Isa Kostoyev, who arrived in Rostov to supervise after the discovery of Muratov's body, leaned toward this two-killer theory. "I'm not sure these murders were committed by one man," he said at an investigators' meeting on May 11, 1989. "From these corpses, it's impossible to conclude that."

Burakov still believed in the theory advanced by Dr. Aleksandr Bukhanovsky that a single, uniquely twisted individual was killing both males and females. But he did not argue with Kostoyev. Burakov had been working on the case, unsuccessfully, for more than six years. He was not in a strong position to dispute someone else's theory.

On the same day the investigators met, May 11, another young boy disappeared. Aleksandr Dyakonov had turned eight the day before. But his birthday had not been a happy occasion. Aleksandr lived in Rostov, where the schools were overcrowded and the pupils attended in two shifts; he went to the afternoon session. He was supposed to come home right after school, to the two-room apartment in a five-story building on Second Five-Year-Plan Street, not far from the helicopter factory where both his parents worked. But Aleksandr was not particularly obedient. As the days warmed up and lengthened, he liked to stay out with his friends, playing on the street or in a vacant lot. His father often beat him for doing this. He had beaten him on May 10, his birthday. On May 11, Aleksandr did not come home. Both his parents went out to look for him, but they found nothing.

The Dyakonovs called the *militsia* the next day, and a search was organized. There was no secrecy about this disappearance. The *militsia* printed a flyer with a picture of the little boy—smiling, wearing sandals and his blue school uniform, and carrying a book bag decorated with two Russian cartoon characters, a mouse and a cat. It was a picture bound to cause anyone who looked at it to wonder what kind of man could harm such an innocent-looking child. The *syshchiki* carried it door to door in the Dyakonovs' neighborhood. But they found neither the little boy nor his remains.

Much of the investigators' initial attention focused on the missing boy's father, Vladimir. Relatives were always among the first to be questioned when a child disappeared, and Vladimir Dyakonov aroused suspicion by his responses. He said nothing about beating his son; the *syshchiki* heard about it from the neighbors. Then he admitted beating the boy, but denied he had anything to do with his disappearance. The local *syshchiki* suspected otherwise. They called him down to the station for questioning nearly every day. After one session, Vladimir Dyakonov told his wife that they had promised him a light sentence if he admitted to killing his son and showed them where to find the body.

Two months later, on July 15, a Rostov taxi driver stopped to urinate in a bushy triangle of empty land formed by the fork of two roads, Nansen Street and Stayonnaya Street. Five feet from the edge of the road, he saw some bones and a book bag that bore the pictures of a mouse and a cat. The process of decomposition had gone so far that the Dyakonovs said they were not sure the corpse was that of their son. The *militsia*, comparing the skeleton's size with the size of the boy they were looking for, and considering the presence of the book bag, came to a conclusion less driven by parental hope. It was Aleksandr Dyakonov. The medical examiner soon told them what they needed to know to put him on the list of the *lesopolosa* victims. He had died from several dozen knife wounds, and his sexual organs had been cut off.

To Viktor Burakov, the discovery of Aleksandr Dyakonov's body suggested a change in the killer's behavior. In the Voronko and Muratov cases, he had stalked his victims on or near a train. The *militsia* had responded, in part, by increasing their presence on the trains and in the stations. Now it seemed that the killer had noticed. He had, to the best of the investigators' knowledge, found Aleksandr Dyakonov on a city street. He had killed the boy, under cover of darkness and in a thicket of bushes, within a couple of yards of cars whizzing past. Once again, he had shown an almost preternatural ability to avoid being seen. But he also seemed, to Burakov, to be showing the behavior of a man growing increasingly desperate, compulsive, and careless.

But the next victim, who disappeared on August 19, 1989, showed that the killer shared none of the investigators' desire to impose a current pattern on his actions, either in the sex of his victims or the place where he killed them. She was Yelena Varga, nineteen years old, and she strongly resembled the string of young women who fell victim to the *lesopolosa* killer in his early years, from 1982 to 1986. They found her body in a woodland near the village of Rodionovo-Nyesvetaiskaya, thirty miles north of Rostov and far from any railroad. As far as the *syshchiki* could determine, she used buses when she traveled. But there was no doubt that she belonged in the series. Her killer had slit open her abdomen and removed her uterus. He had sliced off her nose and her breasts.

Nine days later, attention shifted to a ten-year-old boy,

Aleksei Khobotov, who lived in Shakhty. He disappeared much as Aleksandr Dyakonov had, from Karl Marx Street in the center of the city. The investigators in Shakhty grilled Khobotov's father so intensely that at one session he fainted. But they could not find the boy.

The killer's rage subsided for a little more than four months. On January 14, 1990, an eleven-year-old boy named Andrei Kravchenko disappeared from the streets near his home in the center of Shakhty. His body, with the sexual organs cut off, was found several days later in one of the wooded strips not far from where he disappeared.

On March 7, 1990, a ten-year-old boy, Yaroslav Makarov, disappeared from a park near the Rostov railroad station. His body was found a few days later, the tongue and sexual organs missing.

Two months later, woodmen found a female's corpse, which could not be identified, near the Donleskhoz railroad station, not far from the spot where Yevgeny Muratov had been found a year earlier. The woman's uterus and breasts had been removed.

On July 30, 1990, in some woods on the left bank of the Don, near the city beaches that were filled with bathers in midsummer, workmen found the body of a thirteen-year-old boy, Viktor Petrov. He had disappeared on July 28 from the Rostov railroad station. He was a big boy, standing about five feet, six inches. But his body was mutilated just as those of the previous victims had been.

At that point, Burakov's list of probable *lesopolosa* victims numbered thirty-two. The number was still an official secret, as were the details of the wounds the victims suffered. But the existence in Rostov of a serial killer, or killers, was not. By 1989, thanks to Mikhail Gorbachev's glasnost policy, newspapers and the oblast television station were no longer the docile instruments of state control they had been when the *lesopolosa* killings began. Censorship still existed, and editors still responded to suggestions from the local Communist Party hierarchy, but they no longer feared to publish anything not specifically authorized by the Party. They carried reports and pictures on each victim, generally urging witnesses to come forward and help the *militsia*.

The panic that had set in during the killer's most feverish period in the summer of 1984 had subsided during the years from 1985 to 1988, when he had taken only a couple of victims in Rostov oblast. But by summer of 1990, after the discovery of the mutilated bodies of Yevgeny Muratov, Aleksandr Dyakonov, Yelena Varga, Andrei Kravchenko, Yaroslav Makarov, and Viktor Petrov, the cities were full of fearful rumors. The most persistent, reflecting the political tension among ethnic groups in the rapidly decaying Soviet Union, had it that a gang of cutthroats from one of the Transcaucasian republics was bent on killing and mutilating as many young Russian boys as possible.

Mikhail Fetisov felt intense pressure to solve the crimes. The turmoil of the perestroika era had been a blessing to Fetisov. The leadership of the Ministry of the Interior in Moscow changed hands half a dozen times in the late 1980s. No single minister was in office long enough to set a deadline for solving the case and enforce it. The turnover was high in Rostov oblast as well, opening up chances for advancement. General A. N. Konovalov retired. Deputy Chief Pavel Chernyshev was transferred to a new post in Moscow. In the spring of 1990, the oblast Party designated Fetisov as its choice for commander of the entire oblast *militsia* and promotion to major general.

But the Party could no longer place its choices automatically in plum jobs. The oblast had a new Supreme Soviet, or council, chosen for the first time in competitive elections. Just as the Supreme Soviet in Moscow was demanding, and receiving, the right to vote on Mikhail Gorbachev's choices for the Council of Ministers, the Rostov oblast legislators demanded and got the right to approve the Party's choices for the top administrative positions in the region. Fetisov, for the first time in his life, had to face the elected representatives of the people.

He prepared a careful and constructive speech, outlining a program that he thought would allay the growing concern over street crime. He recommended purchasing a computer network for the department; by that time it had a handful of personal computers, but they were not connected in a network and played a very limited role. In Burakov's office, clerks had just begun the task of copying the information in his card file into a program that could sort and group suspects by criteria such as address, previous convictions, and, still, blood type. Fetisov recommended the construction of new apartments for the *militsionery* to help in the effort to recruit better-educated men and women. He recommended new radio equipment for the fleet of *militsia* cars to help them respond more quickly to calls for help. It was, he thought, just the right speech at a time when Russia was looking for new leaders with pragmatic and popular programs.

But that was not on the minds of the legislative committee members who questioned him.

"When are you going to catch the *lesopolosa* killer?" one of them asked.

And the best Fetisov could do was to answer them as he answered Isa Kostoyev when he arrived from Moscow to check on the investigation. He recited the statistics: the number of investigators working on the case, the number of people already checked out, the number of people convicted of crimes that came to light because of the investigation. And he assured them that the case would be broken soon. They endorsed his candidacy, and he took over the big office on the second floor of the building on Engels Street and had a single golden star sewn onto each of his epaulets.

But privately, Fetisov was seething. The investigation seemed to be falling into the same slough of incompetence and irresponsibility that afflicted the entire Soviet system. At a meeting of the investigation leaders on March 11, 1990, he thumped his heavy fist on the table and shouted, "Do I have to give one hundred and one orders before people start looking for Khobotov, and then Kravchenko? You people aren't carrying out orders! You're not supervising the work your subordinates are doing! Some of you are taking missing-persons reports on children lightly. When Makarov was reported missing, the *militsionery* didn't even find out what clothes he was wearing when last seen!"

Then he threatened all of them, including Viktor Burakov. If the investigators' performance didn't improve, he warned, "people are going to be fired."

But nothing the investigators tried worked against a killer who seemed to have the ability to select, mutilate, and kill his victims invisibly.

On the warm, lingering evening of August 17, 1990, Burakov received word that another victim had been found, this time at the municipal beach in Novocherkassk, thirty miles north of Rostov. Recreational facilities were never high on the priority list of any of the towns in Rostov oblast, and the Novocherkassk municipal beach reflected it. To get there, Burakov's car had to slalom over one of the worst roads in the Soviet Union, a collection of razory ridges and cavernous potholes interspersed with crumbling bits of pavement. The beach itself was a spit of sand at a bend in the sluggish, turbid tributary of the Don called the Aksai River. A couple of rough, concrete booths served as changing rooms, and a pair of faded metal umbrellas provided some shade. Green reeds grew six or seven feet high along the bank on the beach side; the railroad tracks occupied the opposite bank. When he saw the setting, Burakov wondered immediately where the closest *elektrichka* stop might be; it turned out to be about a mile away.

The victim was an eleven-year-old boy named Ivan Fomin, stabbed forty-two times and castrated, then left in the reeds about fifteen yards from the beach. He had last been seen on the street outside his grandmother's cottage on a bluff over-looking the river and the railroad tracks. It had been a hot day, and his grandmother, who was looking after him, allowed him to go down to the beach alone to swim. The little spit of sand was crowded that day with the usual crowd of Soviet bathers— small children and their mothers and grandmothers, splashing and wading, taking the sun in their underwear if they could not find a bathing suit big enough to fit them.

But only the *militsionery* and the *sledovatyeli* were there by the time Burakov arrived to examine the corpse and the scene. The reeds were thick by the river. As Burakov pushed his way through, they closed behind him; a few feet into them and he could turn around and not see the beach or the river. He knew, from experience with similar beaches, that bathers would use the reeds as a quick alternative to waiting in line for the changing booth or the toilet. The reeds afforded a certain privacy. But it was still hard to imagine a man so reckless as to kill in these reeds on a summer day, a stone's throw from dozens of potential witnesses. How could he be sure no one would hear his victim's cries? The image that flashed into his mind was that of a wolf—brutal, quick, and cunning.

The body lay in a small hollow in the reeds. As Burakov knelt down to examine the wounds, he thought of his own son, Maksim, who was about the same age and size as this boy. He bit his lip until he tasted his own blood. Frustration and anger reverberated inside his chest until his heart started to ache sharply, and he thought that this time he might be having a true heart attack, more serious than the coronary weakening that went along with his breakdown in 1986. He put his hands on the wet ground to steady himself. Sweating, he shook his head, then got slowly to his feet. Gradually, the pain passed. The anger and frustration remained.

10

The Snare

The *elektrichka* dominated Burakov's thoughts. So many of the killings had occurred near railroad tracks and railroad stations. So many of the victims had been riding the trains. Ivan Fomin was not one of them; he had, as best the investigators could reconstruct his movements, walked to the site of his murder. But the killer might well have used the *elektrichka* to get to the little beach. And the rumble of a passing train, fifty yards away, might well have drowned out the boy's last screams. The investigators had to find a way to make the *elektrichka* work for them rather than for the killer.

Burakov ordered the usual steps after Fomin's death. *Syshchiki* questioned everyone who lived in the area. They released the news of the murder to the newspapers and the oblast television, asking for anyone at the beach that day, anyone who saw anything, to come forward. They found no witnesses.

They checked out all the former mental patients, all the convicted rapists and perverts, all the known gay men in Novocherkassk. Nothing came of it.

After seven years of fruitlessly checking such leads, Burakov was not surprised. And after the pain of his team's failure to prevent yet another murder had subsided somewhat, he was even slightly encouraged. The killer had murdered five times already in 1990, more than in any eight-month period since the summer of 1984. Whatever it was that triggered his rages—hormones, as the experts in Moscow had suggested, or weather patterns, as Bukhanovsky had postulated—was obviously peaking again. The risky circumstances of Fomin's murder suggested that the killer was approaching a point of desperation and might soon make a major mistake.

They might, Burakov thought, be able to arrange things on the *elektrichka* and at its stations in such a way as to induce the killer to make that mistake where they could see him. That was the essence of the plan that he and Fetisov put into operation as the summer of 1990 ended.

Since 1984, they had been keeping watch at railroad stations and bus terminals, because that was where the killer most often selected his victims. Since 1986, they had assigned special units, both uniformed and in plain clothes, to ride the *elektrichka*, though these units had not covered every train every day. And though not all of Burakov's men knew it, some investigators had, since the discovery of Yevgeny Muratov's body in 1989, been secretly filming and photographing passengers on the trains, with the help of the KGB. Some *elektrichka* cars had dummy compartments packed with cameras. The investigators' luck had not been good; not once had they been able to go back to their film or to the reports of the operatives on the trains and find a picture or report of a victim or the man riding with him or her.

Part of the problem, Burakov thought, was the sheer number of people who used the trains and stations, particularly around cities as large as Rostov and Shakhty. It was impossible for the operatives there, whether in uniform or plain clothes, to notice everyone. The discovery of two corpses—those of Yevgeny Muratov and the unidentified woman found in May 1990—near the Donleskhoz station suggested a way to improve the odds.

Donleskhoz was one of three *elektrichka* stations in the middle of a forestry sovkhoz—the Soviet equivalent of a national forest. The station consisted of a ticket booth and two low concrete platforms, with weeds sprouting through the cracks. Except on weekends in late summer, when Russians descended on the forest to pick mushrooms, very few people used it. Express trains on the Rostov-Moscow line passed it by; only the slow *elektrichka* stopped there.

They could, Burakov thought, prod the killer into using that station again. They could blanket all the larger stations on the line with an obvious uniformed presence that the killer could not fail to notice. At Donleskhoz and the other two forest stations, Kundryucha and Lesostep, they would have only plainclothes operatives. If the killer selected a victim on the *elektrichka*, Burakov reasoned, he would want to lure the victim off the train at a station where the *militsia* were not in evidence. Only the three forest stations would seem safe to him. But the plainclothesmen there would have instructions to take the name of every person who left or got on the trains at those stations, particularly if they saw a single man with a woman, girl, or young boy. Other plainclothesmen would be stationed in the forest itself, disguised as sovkhoz workers.

Fetisov approved the plan. It would be a major undertaking, requiring three hundred sixty men, both in uniform and plain clothes, to cover all the stations during the hours when the trains ran. He ordered the men deployed. By this time, the *lesopolosa* working group had grown from its original complement of ten men to include twenty-seven *syshchiki* working out of the Rostov headquarters under Burakov's supervision and twenty-eight *sledovatyeli* working from the Rostov procurator's office. Local *militsia* stations in Shakhty, Novoshakhtinsk, Gukovo, and Krasny Sulin had assigned seventy-two additional men to work full time on the case. Normal patrols were left unmanned and other work was left undone to provide the manpower for the operation, even though the overall crime rate in Rostov was rising. If the plan failed, Fetisov knew, he would have a very difficult time explaining his orders to his new masters in the oblast soviet.

It was a very Russian plan. Marshal Kutuzov, who led the

Russian army that defeated Napoleon in 1812, or Marshal Zhukov, who led the armies that rolled back the Nazi Wehrmacht in 1943, would have understood and appreciated it. They had both given ground to the enemy, sustained horrible casualties, and triumphed in the end primarily by throwing overwhelming numbers of men into the battle. They relied on numbers and persistence rather than brilliant tactics.

The operation plotted by Burakov and Fetisov was imbued with a similar spirit. It recognized, tacitly, that the killer had thwarted all their efforts to identify him through the shrewdness of their deductions or through the work of their forensic laboratories. It accepted, tacitly, the fact that if the killer did show up at one of the three forest train stations, it might very well be in the act of luring another victim into the woods. The forest was vast, with many secluded groves. The plainclothesmen there might not stop the killer before another victim died. That was a risk the investigators felt they had no choice but to take.

Just to make certain that there would be no mistakes, Fetisov called a special meeting of the officers supervising various aspects of the plan on October 27. He warned them that anyone who fouled up would be fired.

By then, though Fetisov did not know it, the killer had already struck again, near Donleskhoz, one of the three stations targeted by the plan. On October 30, workers in the forest near the station found boy's clothing as they worked in a grove of pines. They alerted the *militsia*, and a search began in a cold, heavy rain. The next day, the searchers found the short, slightly built body of a boy. He had been dead, it appeared, about two weeks. The wounds on the corpse left little doubt about the killer. The boy had been choked, then killed with twenty-seven thrusts from a knife. His left eye had been stabbed and his testicles removed. The tip of his tongue was also missing.

A check of the missing-persons reports quickly established the corpse's identity. The boy's name was Vadim Gromov, aged sixteen. He suffered from mental retardation and he had, until April, been a student at an *internat* in Shakhty. Then he dropped out and lived, officially, at least, with his mother. She saw him only sporadically. He spent most of his time riding the *elektrichka*. On October 17, he had taken seven rubles from his mother and said he intended to ride the train to Rostov or Taganrog, where word had it that some of the stores still had candy; the stores in Shakhty were out. His mother had not seen him again.

The discovery of Gromov's body embarrassed and enraged Mikhail Fetisov and Viktor Burakov. The killer had gone to one of the three stations they wanted him to go to, killed, left a body, and gotten away. He did it ten days before the inception of their snare plan, but there were still standing orders to keep close track of stations up and down the *elektrichka* line. The surveillance records held no reports of anyone unusual at the Donleskhoz station on October 17, particularly not of anyone exiting the train with a sixteen-year-old and returning alone.

Kostoyev, Fetisov, and Fetisov's newly appointed deputy chief, Vladimir Kolyesnikov, all left Rostov for Shakhty, where they set up field headquarters. Burakov remained in Rostov, monitoring and analyzing the information that began to come in from the dozens of *syshchiki* who questioned everyone living on the sovkhoz and from the watchers at the various stations.

But that same day, the investigators got more bad news, this time from the local *militsia* in Shakhty. On October 30, a boy named Viktor Tishchenko, also sixteen years old, had gone to the Shakhty railroad station to pick up some tickets for a family trip to Novorossisk, a city almost three hundred miles to the south, where his aunt lived. He did not return. The next day, his distraught parents reported him missing.

Alarmed, Fetisov ordered a thorough search of the woods near the railroad station. Three days later, they found the body, in some thick woods about two miles south of Shakhty

station, closer to the next station on the line, called Kirpichnaya. The body was not far from the place where Tatyana
and Svetlana Petrosyan, the mother and daughter victims,
had been found six years previously.

Tishchenko was bigger than any of the previous male victims—almost a man. He stood five six, and weighed about
one hundred thirty pounds. The woods near the corpse
showed the evidence of a long struggle: branches were broken and leaves churned up. But his struggle had failed. He
had forty knife wounds, including a long slash that ripped
open his abdomen. His testicles, like Vadim Gromov's, were
gone. His eyes, however, had not been touched.

The *militsia* surveillance had failed. Four *militsionery* had
been on duty at the Shakhty station that day. None could
remember seeing Tishchenko. Burakov and Fetisov could
understand why. Thousands of passengers went through the
Shakhty station every day. Some bought tickets and got on
trains, some got off. Some simply hopped quickly off trains
that stopped en route to Moscow or Leningrad and bought
some mineral water or apples from the peasant hawkers on
the platform. Then they got on the train again and left. It
would be hard to pick out or spot anyone in this swirl of
faces. Moreover, the men on duty in Shakhty had been told
to be especially watchful for a middle-aged man with a girl,
a woman, or a young boy. Tishchenko, nearly full grown, fit
none of those descriptions.

But the failure to catch the killer at Shakhty intensified
Kostoyev's anger and the *militsia*'s own discomfiture. Burakov and Fetisov did not have to be told that they had better
not fail again. Pressure was piling on the investigators like
snow from an avalanche.

Burakov's office churned out lists of potential suspects to
check out. There was a boxing instructor from Novoshakhtinsk with homosexual tendencies. He was checked out.
There were some recently released convicts with type AB
blood. They were checked out.

Once more, the *syshchiki* questioned every potential witness they could find. The ticket seller at the Shakhty station said she thought she remembered Tishchenko, and she thought she remembered seeing a middle-aged man with glasses standing behind him. But her description was vague. The woman's daughter, interviewed separately by a *sledovatyel*, said that she, too, had seen a bespectacled, middle-aged man in suspicious circumstances a week or so earlier. He was riding an *elektrichka* train, conversing animatedly with a young boy who suddenly jumped up and bolted from the train at Shakhty. Her description was also vague, but it could have fit the man seen walking, in 1984, in front of Dmitri Ptashnikov before he died. But who was the man?

In desperation, without consulting Fetisov or Burakov, the Shakhty *militsia* turned to a psychic, whom they identified in their written report only as "K." They escorted the psychic into the morgue where Tishchenko's body was being kept and allowed him to commune with the spirit of the dead boy. Thereupon K. gave them a remarkably detailed portrait of the killer. He was a man in his early thirties, married, with a son between the ages of four and six. He was an athlete, perhaps a former physical education teacher. He had a scar on his upper left lip and a birthmark on his right cheek. He had had surgery on his right knee. He drove a Moskvich automobile and he lived in Shakhty, probably on either Shkolnaya or Koshevo streets. And he would be attending Tishchenko's funeral. The Shakhty *syshchiki* looked carefully for a man fitting this description at Tishchenko's funeral. They found no one.

The rest of the USSR, meanwhile, slowed down in preparation for the long holiday in observance of the seventy-third anniversary of the Bolshevik Revolution of 1917. Wednesday, November 7, was the actual holiday, and the following day, November 8, was traditionally also a day off. In every city and town in the nation, factories and offices worked an extra day in the first week in November in order to add Friday, November 9, to the vacation; Saturday and Sunday followed. In effect, the nation took a week off.

Once, the November 7 parade in Moscow had been the high point of the Party's annual calendar. Tanks and missiles rolled through Red Square under the stern eyes of the Politburo members and military leaders standing atop Lenin's mausoleum. Carefully selected marchers carried thousands of portraits of the general secretary and his colleagues in the leadership. Crack troop units goose-stepped crisply across the cobblestones. Diplomats and foreign journalists carefully studied the slogans in the parade and the arrangement of faces atop the mausoleum for clues to policy or personnel changes in the Kremlin.

In 1990, this stern glory was fading quickly. Mikhail Gorbachev had done away with the portraits in 1988 and then with the military hardware in 1989. The parade of November 7, 1990, made clear that he had not won the gratitude of his countrymen for doing so. In fact, it showed that the Party had lost control of the streets. Unofficial marchers got into Red Square and walked through with placards denouncing both Gorbachev and the Party. Gorbachev retreated from the platform atop the mausoleum well before the parade ended.

In provinces like Rostov, there were no such provocative protests. The population reacted to the political situation by taking its holiday vodka rations, holing up in cottages or apartments, and relishing the chance to spend five days in potted oblivion.

After the holiday ended on November 11, the workers on the forestry sovkhoz where the snare had been set went back out into the woods to cut lumber. On November 13, they found that the *lesopolosa* killer had not been idle. There was yet another body in the woods near the Donleskhoz station— the thirty-sixth victim on the *lesopolosa* list.

Mikhail Fetisov, as it happened, was only a few miles away from Donleskhoz when he heard about the latest corpse. The chief of the *militsia* in Gukovo, a man named Alik Khadak-hyan, had dropped dead of a heart attack on November 12. Fetisov decided to attend the funeral. He was en route, near Shakhty, when he got the news via radiotelephone from Ros-tov. He sped to the scene. It was a typically cold, drizzly November day in southern Russia, and the mud stuck to his shoes as he slogged toward the glade where the body lay.

When Fetisov arrived, the corpse was lying just as it had been found. He could see that the victim was a young woman with dirty-blond hair, cropped short and ragged. She lay on her back, naked, her hands at her sides. Her face was swollen and blackened by bruises, one eye open and one eye shut. Her mouth was agape, as if she had died with a scream on her lips. Her lips were caked with blood; medical examiners would later determine that the killer had sliced off her tongue. He had also sliced open her abdomen, leaving a deep, ver-tical gash from her breastbone to her genitals. The body looked, to his eyes, as if it had been lying there about a week.

There had been, Fetisov knew, no reports of any man exiting a train with a young woman at Donleskhoz during the previous week. The snare had failed again. Fetisov's body shook with rage. He ordered his driver to take him to the Krasny Sulin *militsia* department, the local station with the responsibility for organizing the surveillance of Donleskhoz.

He summoned Vasily Panfilov, the officer directly in charge of the Donleskhoz operation, and demanded to know how the killer had slipped through the surveillance. Were there plainclothesmen on duty all the time?

Well, Panfilov replied, nearly all the time.

"Nearly all the time?" Fetisov demanded.

"Except for their mealtimes," Panfilov said. "They have to eat."

There were no restaurants, of course, in the middle of the woods. Sometimes, a plainclothesman left his post and went back to Krasny Sulin to eat. But there was always supposed to be at least one left on the platform, Panfilov assured him.

Fetisov, furious, began shouting that Panfilov would be fired.

Why had no reports been filed by the men on the platforms, regardless of when they ate, he yelled.

Blushing, Panfilov handed him a pile of papers. There had been reports, he explained. But during the holidays, no one had bothered to send them to Burakov's office in Rostov.

Angrily, Fetisov began to read the names of the mushroom pickers and forest workers who had been stopped and asked to identify themselves. Ivanov, Petrov, Sidorov . . .

One name seemed familiar to him: Andrei Romanovich Chikatilo, stopped and identified on the Donleskhoz platform on November 6.

Fetisov telephoned Burakov. He told him about the unfiled reports. Then he told him the name that had caught his eye.

''Do you have anything on a guy named Chikatilo?''

As soon as he heard the name, Viktor Burakov felt an enormous sense of relief. The long hunt, he began to hope, was over.

Fetisov had been on vacation in September 1984 when Chikatilo had been arrested, interrogated, and cleared because he had type A blood. The name was only vaguely familiar to him.

But Burakov had searched the man's apartment. He had placed him ninth on the 1987 suspect list. This was the first time a reliable witness had placed one of the chief suspects at the scene of a murder.

Chikatilo must be, Burakov felt, the *lesopolosa* killer. The snare had worked—barely.

As Burakov later discovered, the investigators had almost missed Chikatilo on the afternoon of November 6. Two plainclothesmen were assigned to the Donleskhoz station at that hour. But only one, a *militsioner* named Igor Rybakov, assigned from Donetsk, was at his post. The other had gone to eat. And Rybakov had not been wearing civilian clothes.

The day was cold and drizzly, and his uniform overcoat was the warmest and driest garment he had. So he wore it.

Late that afternoon, Rybakov noticed a tall, bespectacled man carrying a briefcase walk up one of the paths out of the woods to the platform. Just before he reached it, he stopped at a well, pumped some water up, and washed his hands. The man walked up onto the platform, where a few late-season mushroom hunters were gathered, waiting for the next *elektrichka*. Rybakov had already checked their documents.

The tall man started to chat with the mushroom hunters. How many had they gotten? Where were the best ones?

Rybakov walked up and, in the manner of Soviet *militsionery*, gave him a half-salute, flashed his badge, and said, "Documents."

Wordlessly, the man handed over his passport.

Rybakov wrote the name down: Andrei Chikatilo. He looked the man over. He saw a pale red smear on the man's cheek. It seemed to him that Chikatilo had perhaps washed some blood off his face.

But Rybakov had no grounds to arrest him. He jotted a few words about the smear in his notebook.

The train clattered in. Chikatilo and the mushroom hunters boarded and rode away.

It had been a near thing, Fetisov and Burakov realized as they reviewed the report a week later. If Chikatilo was in fact the killer, they were very lucky that Rybakov's gray *militsia* overcoat, which might have been recognizable from the edge of the forest, had not frightened Chikatilo back into the woods.

Isa Kostoyev had by then arrived in Krasny Sulin. Fetisov showed him the report on Chikatilo. They agreed that he should be placed under immediate, twenty-four-hour surveillance. And they ordered a thorough investigation of his record.

To the embarrassment of the *militsia*, the *syshchiki* sent out to tail Chikatilo could not find him immediately. The card file in Burakov's office had data from 1984. It said the suspect lived at 5 Fiftieth Anniversary of the Communist Youth League Street in Shakhty and that he worked at Spetzenergoavtomatika in Rostov. But it turned out that he had not lived in Shakhty nor worked at Spetzenergoavtomatika for four years. The *syshchiki* had to be circumspect about looking for him; they did not want friends or relatives tipping him off that the *militsia* had asked about him. It took three days to track down his whereabouts. He lived in Novocherkassk, in Apartment 68 in a large, prewar building at 36 Gvardeiskaya Street. He worked in Rostov, at a locomotive repair works called Elektrovozoremontny Zavod.

Now that they could focus on one man, the investigators quickly gathered information on Chikatilo. What they found persuaded them that they had the right man. Chikatilo had worked for several years as a teacher at Vocational School No. 32 in Novoshakhtinsk. According to the official records, he had voluntarily resigned. But an interview with the director established that he had, in fact, been asked to leave quietly after the director received complaints that Chikatilo had molested several of his female students. He had drifted into work as a *snabzhenyets*, a supply specialist, at several Rostov enterprises. But he had been fired from one job after another, in part because he would frequently go off on business trips and return without the supplies he was supposed to be getting. His arrest in September 1984 and the three months he subsequently spent in jail coincided neatly with one of the killer's periods of inactivity.

Most significantly, the *syshchiki* found travel records at a locomotive factory called NEVZ in Novocherkassk, where Chikatilo had worked from January 1985 to January 1990. At the end of July 1985, during the period when Natalia Pokhlistova was killed, the factory had indeed sent him on business to Moscow. But he had apparently gone by train, which explained why the check of the Aeroflot tickets had not turned up his name. There was no good explanation for the investigators' failure to find the travel records at NEVZ in 1985. They had simply not completed their assignment. It was not, in the context of the general collapse of discipline and efficiency in the Soviet Union, an altogether unusual failure.

Other NEVZ travel records placed Chikatilo at the scene of other murders. He had, for instance, been traveling back to Rostov from Ukraine when Aleksei Voronko was murdered in Ilovaisk in 1988. As Burakov relayed the new data to him, Fetisov shook his head. Everywhere the man had been, it seemed, he had left bodies behind.

Once the investigators had located Chikatilo, they watched him for four days, hoping that he would do something to strengthen their case. Ideally, they wanted to see him select a victim as the *lesopolosa* killer had done, then follow secretly as he lured his prey into the woods. They wanted to arrest him just as he was on the verge of killing.

Otherwise, they knew, their case was weak. They had no witnesses who could say they actually saw Chikatilo kill someone. They could place him at or near the scenes of many murders, but that was circumstantial evidence. And the only physical evidence they had, the semen samples typed AB, might work against them. Suppose Chikatilo gave them a semen sample and it was, like his blood, type A? Then everything would depend on extracting a confession from the man. And he had not confessed in 1984. It would be best to catch him in the act.

But Chikatilo did not kill anyone or do anything else illegal during the days he spent under constant surveillance. He went to work at the locomotive repair works. He went home. He put out the garbage. He went to the stores on Gvardeiskaya Street. He walked in the park that lay between his apartment and the huge NEVZ factory that dominated that side of Novocherkassk. Three times, the watchers reported, he approached a boy or a girl and struck up a conversation. But each time, either he or the child broke off the contact and Chikatilo walked away alone. When the *syshchiki* questioned the children later, they all reported much the same thing. The man had asked them how things were going, where they went to school, what sports they played—nothing overtly malign.

By November 20, Burakov and Fetisov felt the time had come to bring him in. The evidence gathered about Chikatilo's business trips, though circumstantial, would be a powerful lever in an interrogation, as would his presence on the Donleskhoz platform at around the time of the murder of the still-unidentified woman found November 13. Moreover, Fetisov was afraid of another mistake. Chikatilo might notice the tail. He might slip out of his home under cover of darkness and flee. He might commit suicide. Kostoyev agreed and signed the arrest order.

Fetisov asked Kostoyev for one favor. Once the man was brought in, the *militsia*'s primary job—to find the suspect and arrest him—would be done. The next step, the interrogation, would be primarily Kostoyev's responsibility. But before turning him over, Fetisov wanted a chance to see the man for himself. He asked that the preliminary interrogation and examination of the suspect be conducted in his office, on the second floor of the *militsia* building. There was no precedent for doing so, but Kostoyev agreed.

Fetisov ordered his deputy, Vladimir Kolyesnikov, who had been reassigned to Rostov after completing his courses at the academy in Moscow, to organize the arrest. Fetisov told Kolyesnikov to stay on Chikatilo's tail during the daytime, giving him one more chance to be caught in the act. But before nightfall, Fetisov wanted Chikatilo under arrest. He wanted the arrest, if possible, on film, as part of a videotape archive they would build for the case. Kolyesnikov consulted with Burakov, and they picked two experienced undercover surveillance men, Vladimir Pershikov and Anatoly Yevseev, for the assignment. They also detailed a young *militsioner* named Slava Vinokurov, who operated their newly acquired video camera; they wanted to get as much of this arrest as possible on film. Then Burakov and Fetisov settled in to await the arrival of the suspect.

Half an hour later, Kolyesnikov and his crew arrived in Novocherkassk in an unmarked, light blue sedan and checked in with the local surveillance detail. Chikatilo, they were told, had emerged from his apartment half an hour before they arrived and taken a walk in the park adjacent to his home. He had strolled half a mile through a grove of linden and acacia trees to a small metal beer kiosk. There, he had pulled a large jar from the bag he carried over his shoulder and had it filled. He had begun to walk back toward his apartment.

Kolyesnikov deployed his men on Chikatilo's homeward route, standing outside a small café called Snezhinka, or Snow Fairy. It catered to the children in the park, serving them ice cream and cookies. Behind the café was the park's playground, with dozens of children shouting and clambering over the teeter-totters and swings. Kolyesnikov's crew had not yet seen Chikatilo, but they had a description, augmented by two details radioed in by the men on his tail. He was carrying the jar of beer, and he had a bandage on one hand. They lit cigarettes and assumed the guise of four men killing time in the park.

They spotted him ambling slowly through the alley of black, bare trees. He did not look like a man capable of killing thirty-six people. He was thin, bespectacled, and stoop-shouldered, about six feet tall. He wore a dark brown coat and a cap; the hair beneath the cap was graying and a little scraggly. Carrying a small leather satchel, he looked like just another Soviet bureaucrat, walking home from work, thinking, perhaps, about the time he had left until retirement.

As he reached their position, Chikatilo turned and entered the children's café, walking over a faded little red-and-yellow footbridge that spanned an empty fountain. Kolyesnikov let him go in. They would give him a last chance to be caught in the act. Through the large glass windows in the front of the café, they watched him approach a boy and begin to talk. The conversation lasted for only a couple of minutes. Chikatilo ambled out of the café and turned toward his apartment. Kolyesnikov gave the signal. The three *militsionery* surrounded him, and he stopped. Vinokurov stepped out from behind some trees and began to film.

"What's your name?" Kolyesnikov demanded, quietly.

"Chikatilo, Andrei Romanovich," the man answered.

"You're under arrest," Kolyesnikov said.

Silently, the man offered his hands to be cuffed.

Chikatilo's reaction pleased Kolyesnikov. Innocent people, he believed, responded to the same approach in a different way. They might demand to know who he was, and why he wanted to know their name. But Chikatilo, he felt, acted like a man who had been waiting a long time for the moment of his arrest. He was calm and subdued, almost exhausted, it seemed. Pershikov handcuffed him, and Yevseev took the leather bag and the jar of beer. They bundled him into the car and headed back to Rostov.

Squeezed into the back seat between two *militsionery*, Chikatilo waited until they were on the Rostov highway before saying anything.

"Why am I being arrested?" he asked.

The *militsionery* did not reply. That was not their job.

Darkness had fallen by the time they returned to Rostov. The scene in Fetisov's office bordered on chaos. Kostoyev, Burakov, and a dozen others clustered around the suspect as they booked him.

With his coat and hat off, Chikatilo looked even more like an intellectual and less like a brutal killer. His graying hair was thin on top, but he wore it brushed straight back, revealing a broad forehead; the skin of his scalp shone through under the lights that Slava Vinokurov had set up. He had on blue trousers, a violet shirt, and a thin brown tie that seemed calculated to give his clothing a touch of dignity. His neck was long and thin, his nose beaky. He still seemed subdued, almost depressed.

He answered questions for the standard arrest form in a low monotone. He was born in Yablochnoye, Ukraine, in 1936. His education included a degree from the liberal arts school of Rostov State University, as well as a technical education in communications and electronics. He spoke German. He had a wife and two children. His wife was fifty-two. He recited the list of places where he had worked, and he began to sweat.

A physician took over the questioning. Did he have any diseases?

No, the suspect replied.

The doctor ordered him stripped to his white undershorts. Chikatilo suffered this in silence. He had a bony body with a middle-aged man's pot belly. Carefully, the doctor removed the bandage from the middle finger of Chikatilo's right hand, revealing an ugly cut, stained by green disinfectant. The middle joint was broken.

"How did you get this?"

It was an accident at work, Chikatilo replied. A box fell on his finger.

The doctor ordered him to strip completely. Humiliation etched on his face, Chikatilo complied. Carefully, the doctor examined his penis, focusing on a patch of irritated skin.

"What's this? How did it get there and when?" the doctor demanded.

Chikatilo mumbled that he did not know.

"When did you last have sex with your wife?" Kolyesnikov broke in.

"I don't remember," Chikatilo replied.

The doctor ordered Chikatilo to bend over so that his anus could be examined. Then he let him put on a pair of gray prison pants with an elastic waistband but no belt. A nurse took a blood sample.

Kolyesnikov stepped in front of the camera to display what he had found in Chikatilo's satchel—a folding knife.

Viktor Burakov watched the scene for a while, then walked back down the hall to his own office. He had occasionally daydreamed about the moment the *lesopolosa* killer was arrested, and he was fairly confident that this was that moment. But he had never imagined that he would feel nothing as he watched it. But nothing was in fact what he felt, or what he would allow himself to feel. There was no anger, no elation. The man, he found, barely interested him. Closing the case interested him. And that would depend on the success of the interrogation, which would begin the next day. If they failed to extract a confession, their case against Chikatilo would rest only on a flimsy chain of circumstantial evidence. Without a confession, even a Soviet court might acquit the man.

11

Confession

As soon as everyone in Fetisov's office had had his chance to look the suspect in the eye, Isa Kostoyev decreed that he would handle the interrogation alone. No one else—not the *militsia*, not the other procurators, not any of the psychiatric experts—would participate until Kostoyev had cracked the suspect. Under the Russian legal system, as procurator he had the power to determine who questioned the suspect. Kostoyev was not a man unmindful of his own talents. Nor was he unaware of the spotlight that would inevitably fall on the *lesopolosa* case. He was determined that Andrei Chikatilo's confession would be his show.

They put Chikatilo in a cell in the KGB building, adjacent to the *militsia* headquarters on Engels Street. He had a cell mate—a *stukach*, or informer, named Vladimir Titorenko. Titorenko was, in Viktor Burakov's judgment, the most capable of the convicted con artists then in the Rostov prison system. His job was to engage Chikatilo in conversation as much as possible and elicit whatever information he could. In return, Burakov promised Titorenko he would receive whatever help the *militsia* could legally provide him, such as support for parole after serving the minimum time.

The next day, Kostoyev called the office of the local version of the bar association, the Rostov College of Lawyers, and asked it to send a defense attorney to witness the interrogation and represent the suspect. Under reforms enacted late in the Gorbachev era, criminal suspects had the right to counsel as soon as their interrogation began. If they could not pay, the local college of lawyers paid from a fund amassed by taking a percentage of the fees collected from solvent clients. This was a significant reform; in the old Soviet system, a suspect got a lawyer only after the procurator had compiled the evidence against him. Defense attorneys had generally confined themselves to arguing that, while the state's case was irrefutable, their clients regretted their mistakes and deserved mercy.

But the perestroika of criminal law had not gone so far as to produce an adversarial system. All the defense lawyers had been trained to believe that they served the state, not their clients. Even the most conscientious of them felt that their job was first to help the court get at the truth, then to help their clients. Their training told them it would be unethical to advise a guilty client to refuse to talk to investigators.

The Rostov bar association appointed a thirty-two-year-old criminal lawyer named Viktor Lyulichev to represent Chikatilo. Lyulichev already had some knowledge of the *lesopolosa* case. After completing the law school at Rostov State University, he had spent several years as a *sledovatyel* in the local procurator's office. He had worked on both the Lyudmilla Alekseyeva and Aleksandr Chepel investigations before resigning and going to work in a lawyers' *kollektiv* in the town of Aksai.

Lyulichev drove to Rostov and presented his identification to the guard at the entrance to the KGB building. Admitted, he made his way to the interrogation room, a harshly lit office, furnished with a desk and a table and a couple of wooden chairs. Kostoyev was already there.

They had, Kostoyev informed him, a suspect in the *lesopolosa* case. The first day's interrogation would be brief and general. Chikatilo came into the room, escorted by a guard, wearing the jailhouse clothing and the same subdued, humiliated expression caught by the video camera the night before. He looked, Lyulichev thought, about as he had expected the *lesopolosa* killer to look—ordinary and harmless. No one who looked more conventionally malevolent, he was certain, could have escaped detection for so long.

Kostoyev began his interrogation with rudimentary questions, reestablishing Chikatilo's name, address, and place of work.

Would he like to make a statement about the case?

Yes, he would, Chikatilo replied. The suspicion against him was a mistake. He had committed no crimes. Six years ago he had been detained and questioned about the same murders. That was an illegal detention and so was this. He suspected that the authorities were after him because of a dispute he was in over a construction project in Shakhty, at the apartment his son lived in. Someone had started to construct a garage in the courtyard, cutting off light to his son's apartment. He had been writing letters to bureaucrats from Shakhty to Moscow, protesting. He had accused some of them of taking bribes. That must be why they were after him.

How did he hurt his finger?

It was at work, Chikatilo replied. He'd been out on the loading dock, helping to pass along boxes. One of them had fallen on his finger.

And had he cut his face in the last fifteen days?

No, Chikatilo replied.

And where was he on November 6?

He had been, he insisted, at work nearly all day. Then he went home to his wife.

Why, then, had a *militsioner* at the Donleskhoz station reported seeing him on November 6, with what looked like an injury on his cheek?

Chikatilo said he didn't know.

That was enough, Kostoyev decided, for the first day. He handed Lyulichev and Chikatilo the written notes he had made of the questions and answers. These notes, called protocols, would be the basic record of the interrogation. Chikatilo and Lyulichev both signed, indicating that the record was accurate.

Lyulichev had said nothing during the interrogation. Now Kostoyev left the room and gave him a chance to talk to Chikatilo alone. Lyulichev introduced himself and told Chikatilo he had been assigned to his defense.

Did Chikatilo have any objections?

Chikatilo shook his head. He either had no objections or he didn't care enough to voice them.

They had a one-sided, ten-minute conference. Lyulichev told Chikatilo that he had to devise a defense strategy. It might, he suggested, be in his best interests to remain silent. But Lyulichev stopped short of advising him to stonewall, to refuse completely to cooperate with the interrogation. That would have been unethical.

Chikatilo did not reply.

After the conference, Lyulichev sought out Kostoyev.

Would the charges against Chikatilo involve the Alekseyeva or Chepel cases?

They well might, Kostoyev replied.

In that case, Lyulichev said, he would have to recuse himself from the case. He had a conflict of interest.

Kostoyev agreed. He said he would seek another attorney from the College of Lawyers. But the next day, Chikatilo signed a waiver of his right to counsel, prepared by Kostoyev. He would have no more legal advice for the next seven months.

The next afternoon, Chikatilo said he wanted to make a written statement. He was clearly a man burdened by something; it might have been guilt. Kostoyev decided to give him writing materials and see what he produced. Some two hours later, Chikatilo turned over a three-page essay, written in a cramped, nearly illegible hand. For the work of an educated man, the paper was a grammatical disaster, replete with incomplete sentences and missing punctuation. It betrayed the stress he was under.

TO: THE PROCURATOR OF THE RSFSR
FROM: CHIKATILO, ANDREI
DECLARATION

On 20 November I was arrested, and since that time I've been under guard. I want truthfully to tell about my feelings. I am in a difficult, depressed situation. I am conscious that I have committed, that I have unsettled sexual feelings. I earlier went to psychiatrists for my headaches, loss of memory, insomnia, sexual distress. But the treatment did no good.

I have a wife and two children, sexual weakness and helplessness. Because of my psyche, everyone laughs at me, that I don't remember anything, that I touch my sexual organs I didn't notice until they told me. I felt humiliated and I was subjected to laughter by my peers at work and in other companies. From childhood I have been subject to humiliation and always suffered. In my school years, with my belly swollen from hunger, dressed in rags, they laughed at me. I studied till I dropped and finished the university. I wanted to get work in production and I gave everything to work. I was appreciated but the administration suddenly because of my weak character demanded that I leave without a reason. And this frequently was repeated. I complained to higher organs. They chased me out shamefully. This, too, happened often. Now, with age, the sexual function isn't necessary, but the psychological distress manifests itself. Again I nervously write complaints to Moscow to vulgar boors, who decided to put garages and toilets in my son's courtyard. And as much as I can bear.

In perverted sexual manifestations, I feel a certain rage, out of control, and I can't control my actions.

Because since childhood I could not show myself as a man and a complete person, this (i.e., perverted sexual activity) gave me not sexual but psychic and spiritual calmness for an extended period. Particularly after looking at video films of any sexual—this shows where they show any perverted sexual activities and any violence or horror.

A. Chikatilo

The essay was tantalizing. Chikatilo admitted to a set of psychological symptoms remarkably consonant with those predicted years before in the psychiatric portrait drawn by Dr. Aleksandr Bukhanovsky. He all but admitted that he was the murderer they were looking for. What else could he have meant when he wrote of his rage, of being out of control? Some of what he had written seemed to be self-serving. His suggestion that pornographic videos triggered his rages, for instance, was not in accord with the fact that nearly all the *lesopolosa* murders occurred when pornography was still banned and very scarce in the USSR. Pornographic videos had become widespread only in 1989 and 1990. But almost every criminal in the Soviet Union sought to shift the responsibility for what he did; it was expected. The real problem with Chikatilo's statement was that he had danced around specific admissions of murder.

After he read the statement, Kostoyev set out to get those admissions.

Do you want to talk about your first murder, he asked.

Chikatilo said he did not feel too well, and would prefer to wait until the next day. Kostoyev agreed.

But the next day, Chikatilo was once again in the mood to write. The essay he produced was again disjointed and confusing, but it revealed a few more of the convolutions in his mind.

In my difficult, depressed condition, I remember my life with all its suffering and humiliations. As it happened, my work was connected with movement and business trips to various cities around the Soviet Union. I had to be often in stations, trains, *elektrichki*, and buses. I saw the situation in the stations, on the trains. There are a lot of homeless, young and old. They demand and beg and take things. They're drunk by mid-morning, and they drink in kiosks, at the stations, beer and vodka, until late at night. We workers can't get this, or afford it, because we work.

These bums attract minors into their dark net. They head from the stations in different directions on the trains. I had to watch scenes from the sex life of these bums in the stations and on the trains. And I remembered my humiliation that I couldn't ever prove myself a complete man.

And a question arose. Do these rotten elements have a right to exist, in full view of the whole population? People are embarrassed by them. And I thought to myself, where were these bums earlier? They worked somewhere and lived somewhere. Why aren't they identified so they can live by themselves and work for themselves? Many of them are not mentally right, they're handicapped. But there are also probably normal people. The question arises, why do they get to freeload? And more than that, they are quickly multiplying, having lots of children. They use their children to give themselves a luxurious life by begging. And their children then fall into the same criminal world. Getting acquainted with these people is not hard. They themselves aren't shy, they ask for money or food, vodka, beer and offer themselves for sex. I saw how they walked away with partners into nooks and corners and groves of trees. I heard about people and in the press a lot of stories that corpses were found around cities and along highways and railroads. All these circumstances—humiliation, being laughed at all my life at work, working under various boors, I always had an internal battle because of my humiliation and this injustice. I felt that I was a professional, normal worker, but they humiliated me because of my weak memory. Therefore, I always walked around with a pen and pad and everyone laughed because I wrote everything down. In the most recent time, I had to deal with social injustice. I was depressed because my son's apartment was old, dark, and wet. The director decided to put toilets and garages right next to it.

I wrote complaints and sought justice—to the city Party committee, to the oblast executive committee, and to President Gorbachev. In the end, they threatened me with legal action. This complaint was made in Shakhty against the procurator and the procurator of the Rostov oblast. All my failures, and, in health, a heart attack, I bore. My legs are arthritic. My sexual impotence, although in my old age that's not necessary, often brought me to think of suicide and attempt it. On Monday [this was only Thursday, but Chikatilo may have thought it was Friday] in the presence of my lawyer, I will give evidence about everything I've done.

A. Chikatilo

This essay, like the first one, lacked coherence. But it established a rationalizing motive for the murders. He was laying out why, in his own mind, he had killed, and how he justified those crimes to himself. He was only, he seemed to think, preventing the reproduction of the dregs of society.

But again, Chikatilo had danced away from a direct admission of guilt. And the next day—Friday, November 23—he renewed his written request that the critical interrogation be postponed until November 26. At that time, he promised, he would give a detailed and truthful account of both his own crimes and the crimes of others, which he did not specify.

Kostoyev's records indicate that he believed the suspect. He recorded no interrogations on November 24 or November 25.

On November 26, the protocols indicate Chikatilo forgot

his interest in having a lawyer. Kostoyev did not remind him of his right to counsel, and Chikatilo's initial waiver remained in effect. Kostoyev asked Chikatilo if he was ready to make a detailed statement about his crimes. But Chikatilo abruptly confounded his interrogator.

He had committed no crimes, Chikatilo replied. Yes, he had ridden on the *elektrichka* a lot, but he had committed no murders. Yes, he had written on November 23 that he would testify about his crimes, and no one had forced him to write that. But today, he was declaring that he had committed no crimes.

Kostoyev changed tacks and began asking Chikatilo questions about specific dates and places.

Had he been at the Kirpichnaya station on the night of October 30—31? (This was the approximate time and place of the murder of Viktor Tishchenko.)

No, he hadn't, Chikatilo said.

How often had he visited the city beach in Novocherkassk (site of the murder of Ivan Fomin)?

Never, Chikatilo replied.

Where had he been between March 6 and March 8 of 1990 (when Yaroslav Makarov was killed)?

He had been home with his wife in Novocherkassk, Chikatilo replied. There had been a long weekend because of International Women's Day, a holiday the Soviet Union observed on March 8.

Where had he gotten the folding knife confiscated after his arrest?

Sometime in 1987, Chikatilo replied. He had gone to Sverdlovsk on a business trip and bought it there. He carried it for everyday needs, like cutting sausage.

Had he been in Moscow around the time of the World Youth Festival in 1985 (when Natalia Pokhlistova was killed)?

Chikatilo, probably aware that there were records to show that he had made this trip, confirmed that he had indeed been in the capital on business at that time. He had traveled back and forth by train.

Had he ever had occasion to go to Domodedovo Airport?

Chikatilo said he didn't remember, and Kostoyev concluded the session.

He had not wasted his time. Even if a suspect lied in response to such questions, the lies could be useful tools. If the *syshchiki* could subsequently find witnesses to put Chikatilo in places he had denied visiting, Kostoyev could confront Chikatilo with the refutation of his lies and, perhaps, persuade him that it was futile to lie about the larger question of the murders.

But the next day, Chikatilo modified his posture of denial.

He had thought the situation over, he said, and he wanted to talk about his criminal activity.

Fine, Kostoyev replied. Talk about the murder on November 6, the last in the *lesopolosa* series, committed near the Donleskhoz station. The *syshchiki* had, by then, established the victim's identity. She was Svetlana Korostik, a twenty-four-year-old veteran of shelters for *bomzhe* and nights on the *elektrichka*.

But Chikatilo did not have Svetlana Korostik on his mind. He did not know her and he did not kill her, he said. What he wanted to talk about was something that happened, as he recalled it, in 1977.

He had been working then as an instructor of Russian language and literature at an *internat* in Novoshakhtinsk, which taught students mining trades. One of his students, a girl named Gultseva, had aroused him. One day he gave her a make-up assignment and told her to do it after regular classes. When she was alone in the classroom with him, he had grabbed her and fondled her breasts and buttocks. When she screamed, he locked her in the classroom and left, but the frightened girl had jumped out a window (the classroom was on the first floor) and escaped. The school's director had found out and asked Chikatilo to resign.

But that was not the only crime he had committed during those days, Chikatilo went on. He remembered another, earlier occasion, when he took a group of students swimming in a lake. He had grabbed and fondled another young girl, whose name was Lyubov Kostina. She also cried out.

He had, he told Kostoyev, difficulty controlling his passions when he was around children.

Did he have any other sex-related concerns, Kostoyev prompted.

No, Chikatilo replied. Those were the only instances he could remember in which he had lost control.

The next day, November 28, Chikatilo asked to write again.

He had, he wrote, lived through years of insomnia and nightmares. He had tried to get help, but without success. He had even watched some of the charlatan healers who had made their way onto post-glasnost Soviet television and purported to cure ailments by sending out psychic energy through the airwaves. That hadn't helped him.

"Everything irritates me, even conversations about the weather," he wrote. "I'd like to be treated if I'm abnormal."

He wrote that, back in his cell, cut off from his work and family life, the rage would sometimes suddenly revisit him and he would tremble with it.

"I've felt this during many crimes," he wrote. "I truly haven't wanted to hinder the investigation, but I couldn't tell everything I've done. It would throw me into trembling."

And that was as far as he would go, no matter what approach Kostoyev tried.

Nine days had passed since the arrest. Chikatilo had revealed a great deal about himself that suggested he was, in fact, the murderer. But, paradoxically, he had confessed only to two child molestations that had happened long ago. Clearly, he was a man racked by guilt and anxious, in some respects, to unburden himself. But Isa Kostoyev had yet to find a way to use that guilt and anxiety to get the confession he needed.

Viktor Burakov monitored the progress of the interrogation with growing concern. Officially, his role was confined to assisting while the investigation tried to uncover as many details as possible about the suspect. The day after the arrest, he led a team of *syshchiki* to Novocherkassk to search the one-bedroom apartment where Chikatilo lived with his wife. The investigators had confiscated everything that had the slightest potential to be useful in building their case: twenty-two knives from the kitchen, all the clothing from his closet, lengths of cord and strips of cloth, an attaché case, some bus tickets. But the most remarkable thing they found they could not remove. Chikatilo's apartment, like most Russian apartments, had small, separate rooms, the size of stalls, for the toilet and the bathtub. Chikatilo had recently moved the bathtub from its stall into the kitchen, where it stood awkwardly, taking up space in an already cluttered room.

Burakov, from the repair work he had done on his own apartment, knew how much time and effort would be required to find and buy the pipes and plaster Chikatilo had needed to relocate the bathtub and create, in effect, a small private room for himself where the bathtub had been. The little room had been empty and bare; it was a work in progress. But the man who was building it, Burakov thought, must have been obsessed by the desire to create a little sanctuary from which he could wall off his family and the rest of the world.

The removal of the bathtub, like the papers Chikatilo was writing for Kostoyev, hinted at a mind that might belong to a serial killer. But what did this prove? Chikatilo could claim that he moved the bathtub to give him privacy to write or study.

Similarly, the interrogation of Chikatilo's neighbors and family tantalized the investigators and proved nothing.

Chikatilo seemed orderly but not very sociable, said a woman who lived upstairs, Irina Zakharenko. If she saw him on the staircase, he would smile and say hello, but nothing more.

There was one thing, she added. She recalled that he seemed to spend a lot of time in the building's courtyard, watching the children play.

Burakov did not handle the interrogation of Chikatilo's family; it was left to Kostoyev's deputies in the procurator's office. But the reports said that Chikatilo's wife, Feodosia, and his grown children, Yuri and Lyudmilla, denied knowing anything at all about any murders. They were insisting that Chikatilo was an upstanding family man.

The investigators could not, Burakov knew, rely too much on the handful of witnesses they had found before arresting Chikatilo. The witnesses in Novoshakhtinsk who had reported seeing a man of Chikatilo's size walking in front of Dmitri Ptashnikov back in 1984 had conflicting recollections of what the man had been wearing. Their memories were not likely to have grown sharper after six years. And the boy in Ilovaisk had insisted that the man with Aleksei Voronko in 1988 had a mouth full of gold teeth. Chikatilo had normal teeth.

The physical evidence would be helpful, Burakov thought. Dr. Gurtovaya had flown to Rostov the day after Chikatilo's arrest. She reported a few days later that tests of Chikatilo's saliva and semen had found a weak B antigen. He was, she declared, an example of her newly discovered phenomenon, which she called "paradoxical secretion." His blood type was A, and his secretions were type AB. Burakov had no particular confidence in the laboratory's work, but he knew that Dr. Gurtovaya's testimony would probably be the only forensic expertise presented at the eventual trial. While the analysis of his semen samples would not prove Chikatilo guilty, it would at least not exclude the possibility.

Still, they needed a confession badly, and from what Burakov was hearing, they might not get one. Kostoyev did not share the reports on the interrogation with Burakov. But the *stukach* in Chikatilo's cell gave Burakov daily reports of what Chikatilo said when he returned from his interrogations.

According to the *stukach*, Kostoyev was badgering Chikatilo in ways that did not appear in the official protocols of the interrogation. He asked repeatedly about the grisliest aspects of the murders. He demanded to know why, for instance, Chikatilo had cut out the uteri of his female victims. This questioning, the *stukach* said, had made Chikatilo deeply ashamed and defensive. He might not open up to Kostoyev for a long time, if ever.

And Burakov did not want to take a long time. Under Soviet law, the *militsia* and procurators could arrest and question a suspect for only ten days before they had to accuse him of a specific crime and inform him of the charges. The standard for evidence for making an accusation was not as strict as the standard for proving guilt in the eventual trial. It was roughly analogous to the "probable cause" standard that grand juries in Western legal systems use in deciding whether to indict a suspect. But if the procurator could not make an accusation after ten days, he was supposed to let the suspect go.

Soviet investigators, of course, had ways of getting around this ten-day deadline when they wanted to. They could, as they had done numerous times during the *lesopolosa* investigation, find some petty accusation that served as a basis for keeping the suspect in jail and under interrogation.

Alternatively, in Burakov's opinion, they could charge Chikatilo with the last murder in the series, that of Svetlana Korostik near the Donleskhoz station on November 6. It was the one case where they had an irrefutable witness to place Chikatilo at the scene of the crime. They could add the other murders to the accusation later, as they developed evidence.

But all the investigators wanted badly to have a more solid basis for an accusation. They knew that everything they did with Chikatilo would be reviewed very carefully in Moscow. They did not want to provide anyone with yet another basis to criticize their performance.

What they needed, Burakov thought, was a different interlocutor, someone who knew how to turn Chikatilo's obvious feelings of guilt and shame into a confession. He had a candidate in mind: Dr. Aleksandr Bukhanovsky.

He first broached the idea to Kostoyev on November 27. The procurator's initial reaction was negative. But Burakov kept pressing him on it. On November 29, with the ten-day deadline period on the eve of expiration, Kostoyev agreed. That morning, he sent a car to the Institute of Medicine to fetch Bukhanovsky to the interrogation room in the KGB building.

Chikatilo's arrest had been kept secret from the media and the public; none of the investigators wanted to risk more embarrassment by announcing a premature end to the case. Bukhanovsky, until Kostoyev told him, had not heard about the arrest. The entire investigative staff, Kostoyev said, was certain that they had the right man. But the suspect, Kostoyev went on, had proved difficult to interrogate. He rambled on incoherently in response to some questions. He refused to answer others. The investigators still needed answers to a long list of critical questions. Had he committed the murders? How had he selected his victims? How had he lured them into the woods? What had he done with their missing clothes and their excised organs?

Could Bukhanovsky help?

He could and would, Bukhanovsky said, under one condition. He would talk to the suspect as a psychiatrist, not as an investigator. He would try to get the man to open up. But he would compile no protocol that could be used as evidence against Chikatilo in court.

Kostoyev agreed. He put his copy of Bukhanovsky's 1987 profile on the table, then left the room. In a few minutes, a guard ushered Chikatilo into the room and then left Bukhanovsky and Chikatilo alone.

Confronting the man he had so often theorized about, Bukhanovsky felt vindicated. Chikatilo's appearance and background were close enough to the parameters Bukhanovsky had sketched to make the psychiatrist feel that his profile would stand up to professional scrutiny not only in Russia, but anywhere in the world. He felt, as well, a surge of excitement at the opportunity to study such a uniquely aberrant mind.

Bukhanovsky gave Chikatilo his visiting card and told him that he was a psychiatrist. He had, he said, been thinking about Chikatilo for a long time. And he opened the copy of the profile and began to show the suspect how thoroughly he already knew him.

It took Bukhanovsky about two hours to establish rapport with Chikatilo and begin to elicit the confessions of murder that the investigators needed. In subsequent interviews, the psychiatrist refused to discuss the precise questions he had asked. It was a matter, he said, of understanding what Chikatilo wanted to talk about—the feelings of shame, humiliation, and rage that filled his essays. Once Bukhanovsky had established himself as a sympathetic man who understood those feelings, the confessions followed. They talked, according to Bukhanovsky's recollection, well into the evening. Then Chikatilo went back to his cell. Bukhanovsky reported to Kostoyev that Chikatilo was ready to confess.

That night, armed with the handwritten notes that Bukhanovsky had made, Kostoyev prepared a formal accusation of murder, dated November 29, just before the expiration of the ten-day period since Chikatilo's arrest. In it, Chikatilo was accused of killing thirty-six people, beginning with Lyubov Biryuk and ending with Svetlana Korostik. These were all the murders the investigators knew of that bore the basic *lesopolosa* signature: dismembered victims left in wooded areas, with type AB semen, if any, found on the remains.

Kostoyev also noted Bukhanovsky's success in his interrogation protocols.

"In your declaration of November 28, you stated that psychological barriers prevent you from giving testimony," he quoted himself as saying to Chikatilo. He then noted that he offered Chikatilo a chance to talk alone with Bukhanovsky.

"I don't know him, but I would like to be able to tell him about some psychological manifestations I've suffered. I indeed feel I can't explain some things I've done," he quoted Chikatilo in reply.

"This request was granted," Kostoyev's protocol went on. "He talked alone with Bukhanovsky. After that, he said he would testify about the circumstances of crimes he had committed."

In Room 24 of the *militsia* building, Viktor Burakov felt an enormous sense of relief when he heard what Bukhanovsky had accomplished. For the first time, he had a sense that the job was done. For the first time since Chikatilo's arrest on November 20, he felt safe to celebrate. He pulled out a bottle of vodka he had been saving for the occasion and poured a shot for each of the half dozen *syshchiki* still at work. Quietly, they toasted their success.

But they were, in fact, only beginning to learn the extent of Andrei Chikatilo's activities.

The next morning, Kostoyev resumed the interrogation. The protocol of the session depicts an abjectly contrite Andrei Chikatilo.

"I have read and become familiar with the declaration of charges lodged against me on November 29," he said. "I fully acknowledge my guilt in the commission of the crimes listed. Now, deeply regretting what I have done, I want to truthfully tell about myself, and my life, and the circumstances leading me to these serious crimes."

He talked for a while about his early life. He mentioned the molestations of the two girls while he was a teacher at the *internat* in the 1970s. Then he revealed something that shocked and embarrassed the Rostov oblast procurators and *militsia*. His first murder victim was not Lyubov Biryuk, he said. It was a little girl named Yelena Zakotnova in 1978.

If the admission was true, it was cause for a scandal. The authorities in Shakhty had convicted and executed another man, Aleksandr Kravchenko, for Zakotnova's murder.

According to Chikatilo's account, he had moved to Shakhty that year and begun teaching at Technical School No. 33, which trained workers for the mining industry. The school had given him an apartment on the first floor of a dormitory on a street named for the Fiftieth Anniversary of the Communist Youth League. His family temporarily remained behind in Novoshakhtinsk, so for a few months he was free to spend his spare time as he pleased, virtually unobserved.

"In that period, I was just overwhelmingly drawn to children, by the desire to see their naked bodies," he told Kostoyev. "I used to hang around the women's toilets downtown, and when no one was watching, look at the girls in there. I used to buy chewing gum for them in order to meet them."

At about that time, Chikatilo bought a hut on one of the meanest streets in Shakhty, Mezhovoy Street, at the other end of the city from the school. The street, unpaved, dirty, and dark, was like a slice of a Third World slum transplanted to southern Russia. The huts along it generally had one room and no plumbing. A creek called Grushevka ran along a little ravine below the street. The poorest of Russians lived there. Chikatilo bought the hut at No. 26, ostensibly to fix up as a place to live for his aging father. (Soviet citizens were permitted to buy small dwellings in certain areas, but not the land they sat on.) In fact, Chikatilo used it not for his father's retirement, but for the secret life he was developing.

"At the end of December 1978, in the evening—I don't remember the exact date—I took a streetcar from the center of town to the Grushevsky Bridge station and headed down Mezhovoy Street toward my hut," he said. "Completely un-

expectedly, I saw that I was walking next to a girl about ten
or twelve years old. [Yelena Zakotnova was in fact nine years
old.] She was carrying a school bag. We walked together for
a while, and I started to talk to her. I remember she said she
was going either to a girlfriend's house or from it. When we
got close to the creek and a bit farther away from the houses,
I was seized by an irresistible urge to have sex with this girl.
I don't know what happened to me, but I literally started to
shake. I stopped the girl and shoved her into some high grass.
She tried to get away, but I was literally like an animal.

"I pulled down her panties and put my hands on her sex
organs. Right after that, wishing to keep her quiet, I evidently squeezed her throat. I tore at her sex organs with my
hands. Lying on top of her, I ejaculated. There was no sex
as such. The sperm came out on her abdomen. Then I realized that the girl was dead. I dressed her again and threw her
body into the river."

Kostoyev ordered up the files on the Zakotnova killing and
read them. In many respects, they corroborated Chikatilo's
account. The body had indeed been found in the river. But
the girl had died of knife wounds, not strangulation. How
could that be, he asked Chikatilo.

"I said that I hit her a few times. I meant with a knife.
But in my opinion, she was already dead when I stabbed her.
I thought she died from the strangling," he said.

Kostoyev pressed on. The body had been found blind-
folded. Did he have an explanation?

"After I attacked her and pushed her to the ground and
strangled her, I covered her eyes with her scarf. I did this
because I had heard that the image of the murderer remains
in the eyes of his victim. For that reason, I tried to wound
my other victims in the eyes with my knife. In later years I
became convinced that this was just an old wives' tale, and
I stopped wounding eyes," Chikatilo said.

It was an explanation of the clue that first suggested the

presence of a serial killer in Rostov back in 1982, the striations in the eye sockets of the victims.

But there were still other discrepancies between Chikatilo's account of the Zakotnova killing and the 1978 case files. Kostoyev continued to press him.

There were, Chikatilo finally admitted, a few details he had tried to hide. He had killed the girl inside the hut, not out on the creek bank. He lied about it in the initial interrogation, he said, because he feared that an investigation among the neighbors on Mezhovoy Street would reveal his identity to the people of Shakhty; he wanted, he said, to protect family members who still lived in Shakhty. That explanation made little sense; his admission was going to reopen the Zakotnova case regardless of where, specifically, he said he killed the girl.

More likely, he had tried to hide the role of the hut in the killing because the hut was connected, in his mind, with his true intent when he first approached the little girl. He had wanted to rape her. But admitting this entailed an admission evidently more shameful to him than murder. He had not been able to achieve an erection, and his knife had become a substitute.

Eventually Kostoyev extracted an amended account.

"It was about five or six o'clock, dark and cold," Chikatilo said. "I saw her alone on a dark street and I asked her why she was out so late. She was either coming or going from a girlfriend's, and she said she wanted to fix her hair. I said, 'Come to my place.'

"As soon as I turned on the lights and closed the door, I fell on her. The girl was frightened and cried out. I shut her mouth with my hands. I couldn't get an erection and I couldn't get my penis into her vagina. The desire to have an orgasm overwhelmed all else and I wanted to do it by any means. Her cries excited me further. Lying on her and moving in imitation of the sex act, I pulled out my knife and started to stab her. I climaxed, as if it had happened during a natural sex act. I started to put the sperm into her vagina by hand."

But the little girl, remarkably, was still alive.

"She said something very hoarsely, and I strangled her," he said.

He also changed his story about the blindfold.

"During this act, I covered her eyes with her scarf because it was terrible to see her gaze."

The amended confession corresponded remarkably well with the analysis of the *lesopolosa* killer's perversions and rituals that Bukhanovsky had written in 1987. It convinced Kostoyev that Chikatilo had indeed killed Yelena Zakotnova and that a terrible miscarriage of justice had occurred in Shakhty in 1979. He put Zakotnova's name on the list of victims and asked how Chikatilo had avoided suspicion during the earlier investigation by the authorities in Shakhty.

"After a few days, they called me into the police station and interrogated me. They asked me where I spent the night of the killing. I said I spent it at home, and my wife confirmed it," Chikatilo recalled.

In fact, the case was more complicated than that. A witness had given the *militsia* a description of a man she saw walking with Yelena Zakotnova. A drawing was made, and it resembled Chikatilo enough that the director of Technical School No. 33 responded, "It's Andrei Chikatilo" when a *syshchik* showed it to him.

What saved Chikatilo, apparently, was the presence in the neighborhood around Mezhovoy Street of a suspect the investigators viewed as a more plausible killer. Aleksandr Kravchenko was a convicted murderer, out of prison on parole. He was the sort of person who would immediately fall onto a suspect list.

The case file, not unexpectedly, did not specify the means used to interrogate Kravchenko. But he had confessed, he had been convicted, and he had been executed. His was another name to add, retroactively, to the list of collateral victims in the *lesopolosa* case.

After Yelena Zakotnova's death, Chikatilo related, images of her agony filled his mind. He could not stop thinking of the sight of his hands on her. When he was alone, the urge to relive the experience all but overwhelmed him. He had, he told Kostoyev, struggled against it. Sometimes he would cut short a business trip and return home rather than face the temptation to find a victim and kill again.

But in the fall of 1981, he said, he had succumbed. "At a bus station in Novoshakhtinsk, I saw a girl alone, looking like a vagrant, going up to one car after another and asking the driver to give her a ride. I followed her for a while and watched her. Then she came up to me and asked for money for beer or wine. She said I could have sex with her in exchange. I said that I'd give her the money.

"We left the station and crossed the road into a grove of trees. We walked for a mile or so and sat down. She took off all her clothes and invited me to have sex with her. I loosened my pants and pulled out my sexual organ and tried to get it into her. But nothing happened. I couldn't get excited. And she kept saying I should hurry up and get it over with and give her her money. I got enraged. I remembered a video with sadistic moments and I pulled my knife out and started to stab her in different parts of her body, completely at random. At the moment of cutting her and seeing the body cut open, I involuntarily ejaculated."

This woman, he said, became the first victim from whom he excised sexual organs. "I can't explain why I had this desire; at the moment of committing the crime, I wanted to tear everything. I did cut open the abdomens of my victims and cut out the uterus or other sexual organs. As I left the scenes of the killings, I would throw them and the victims' clothing away. I was in an animal fever and I remember some of my actions only vaguely.

"How long I was with the victims is hard to say. It seems to me that everything happened quickly, although leaving the scene, I felt a terrible physical fatigue. I became apathetic. There were times when I would come out of the woods and onto a road and almost get run over because I was too tired to react to the horns of the cars and the buses."

He had never, he said, learned the last names of any of his victims. "It's possible that someone told me his or her last name, but I don't remember them. The last names didn't interest me."

This admission did not fit the facts of any outstanding Rostov murder cases. Burakov set his staff to work trying to determine who this second victim was.

Speaking in a low mumble, looking most often at the table or the floor, Chikatilo began, over the ensuing days, to tell the story of the thirty-six murders on the initial list of *lesopolosa* murders. He had, as it turned out, a remarkable memory.

"There were instances," he said, "when I learned about the way people were planning to go, watched them, and killed them along the way. This is what happened with [Lyubov] Biryuk, the first name on the list of charges. This was the beginning of the summer, 1982."

He recalled the day of the week when she died, a Saturday. He had the day off, and he decided to take a bus from Shakhty to an area on the opposite bank of the Don called the Bagayevsky Raion. It was, he said, locally famous for the quality of its cucumbers and other vegetables. He wanted to buy some.

He remembered that he had to change buses in Donskoi, and discovered that the bus had broken down. He decided to set off on foot.

"When I had gone a little way down the left side of the street, I noticed that a girl of twelve or thirteen was coming along behind me, carrying some kind of bag in her hand. I slowed down and let her catch up to me. We walked together beside the woods. I started talking to her, about whatever I thought might interest her. I remember she said she was going home from the store. When we had gone about a quarter of a mile, I pushed her off the road and grabbed her by the waist and dragged her into the woods. I pushed her onto the ground and tore her clothing off and lay on her. At the same time, I was stabbing her, imitating sex. From that, I ejaculated. When I had done that, I threw leaves and branches on the girl's body and left. I threw her clothes and bag away somewhere, but I don't remember where.

"After the killing, I had blood all over my hands. I cleaned them off sometimes on grass, sometimes on the victims' clothing. Sometimes I found a lake or a pond or something."

The account fit the known facts in the Biryuk killing. It was remarkable that Chikatilo had managed to murder the girl without attracting attention, a few yards away from a public road, on a sunny Saturday afternoon. But apparently, he had an instinctive ability to assess the surroundings and avoid witnesses.

Like the Stavropol serial killer, Anatoly Slivko, Chikatilo said he had learned to cope with the problem of shedding his victims' blood without getting it all over his own clothes, so that he could leave a murder scene without attracting attention. He squatted beside his victims until they died and their hearts stopped beating. After that, the blood did not flow much from their wounds. If he arrived home disheveled or even scratched and bloody, he would claim that he had gotten that way unloading a shipment at work.

Steadily, Chikatilo worked his way down the list of victims, connecting names and dates with events.

"After a while, this was at the Shakhty train station, I saw a girl maybe eighteen or twenty, and it was obvious she was a tramp. I see from the charges that her name was Karabelnikova. [Irina Karabelnikova was one of the unidentified victims found in the autumn of 1982. Her corpse was identified in 1985.] I saw how she walked around the station with various guys who had bottles. When the men around her had gone off, Karabelnikova came up to me, and we agreed to get together in the woods—to have sex for money. We went together across the tracks, and when we had gone a few meters into the woods, Karabelnikova squatted down to relieve herself. At that moment, my instinct took over and I pulled out my knife and started beating her.''

That account of the Karabelnikova murder was not entirely correct, Chikatilo admitted in a later interrogation. He still found it easier to admit to murder than to impotence.

In fact, he acknowledged, ''I lay with her but nothing happened. She started to yell at me, to insult me, to push me off with her legs. I got angry and I got my knife out. We fought. In the midst of the struggle, I ejaculated. I started to stab her harder in the abdomen, then got up. I cut her in the eye sockets, in the breasts, in her sex organs.''

The moment of shameful, rage-triggering impotence figured in many of Chikatilo's confessions, particularly when the victims were mature women. ''As a rule,'' he said, ''I couldn't complete the sex act with a woman in the normal way. I was brought to a rage by the fact that my victims—I mean, the tramps—would demand that we get started as soon as we got together. Because of my condition [his impotence], I couldn't do it immediately. Gradually, I understood that for sexual excitement for myself, I had to see blood and wound the victims.''

He seemed compelled, however, to seek out the humiliation he would find when he failed to get an erection with one of the women he lured from a station into the woods. He repeated the pattern again and again. One evening in the summer of 1983, he said, he hung around the bus station in Novoshakhtinsk, watching a young woman about twenty years old trying to find a man who owned a car. Maybe she thought a man with a car could also provide her with shelter for the night. Maybe she just didn't want to sell her body in an alley or a grove of trees.

"She was trying to connect with men who had their own cars, but she couldn't attract anyone," Chikatilo recounted. "Then I suggested that we go off into the woods together.

" 'Do you have a car?' she asked.

" 'No,' I said.

" 'Without a car, I won't do it,' she said.

"But she couldn't get a man with a car, so she came back to me and said we could go into the woods. We walked into a grove and lay down, but I couldn't get started."

At this point, the young woman made a joke. In Russian, the word for "car" is *mashina*. The diminutive form, *mashinka*, means "little machine."

"You don't have a *mashina*, and your *mashinka* doesn't work either," the woman taunted.

Whereupon, Chikatilo said, he pulled out his knife and killed her, taking care to inflict a lot of shallow cuts in her neck and breasts before she died. The body was found, but never identified.

With the boys he killed, the ritual was somewhat different. Chikatilo did not, he stated, think of himself as a homosexual, and there was no evidence that he had ever engaged in homosexual relations with an adult. But a male victim offered the same potential for an arousing bloodletting as a female victim did. When he lured a boy into the woods, he often fantasized that he was a Soviet partisan during the Second World War. The victim, in this fantasy, played the role of a captured Nazi.

This was a common fantasy among people of Chikatilo's generation. Too young to have participated in the war as soldiers, they grew up listening to and watching tales of heroism by partisan guerrillas during the years from 1941 to 1943, when German soldiers occupied the western quarter of the Soviet Union. Quite often, the tales involved torturing the

Nazi to force him to reveal some secret about troop movements or ammunition caches. Evidently, these tales had made an enormous impression on young Andrei Chikatilo, because he relived them with his male victims.

He spotted Dmitri Ptashnikov, he related, as the boy looked at stamps in a kiosk in Novoshakhtinsk. Chikatilo struck up a conversation, pretending to be a stamp collector. He invited the youngster to come home with him to see his collection. The boy agreed.

Once in the woods, Chikatilo said, "I started to shake and get dry in the mouth. I stopped trying to control myself and attacked him. I tied his hands. This was a mania with me. It seemed to me that I was a partisan and was taking my victims to prison camp. I would yell at them, 'Hands up!' The victim would say he couldn't because his hands were tied. Then I'd start cutting them. I stripped Ptashnikov and tried to sodomize him. I stabbed him a lot and I cut off his penis. I don't remember why, but I cut off his tongue as well. He wasn't the only one I tied up. I cut out their tongues and cut off their sex organs. I can't say why I did it all. But the whole thing— the cries, the blood, and the agony—gave me relaxation and a certain pleasure."

He had, he said, often tasted the blood of his victims. "At the sight of blood, I felt chills. I shook all over. Sometimes, I would tear at my victims' lips or tongues with my teeth. With women, I bit off their nipples and swallowed them. I'd cut out the uterus with my knife; with boys, I would slit open the scrotum and take the testicles. I gnawed at them, then threw them away. It gave me some animal pleasure and satisfaction," he said.

Through the first week of December 1990, Chikatilo confessed in detail to all the murders on the list of thirty-six. His recollections, in each instance, fit the known facts of the case. He knew that Aleksandr Dyakonov had been killed near a busy street in Rostov. He remembered, in fact, that the noise of the passing cars drowned out the little boy's cries. He remembered that Ivan Fomin died in the reeds near the beach in Novocherkassk; he recalled being surprised that none of the bathers heard him. In most cases, when asked, he could draw a rough sketch of the crime scene that accurately placed roads, bridges, and the place where the investigators later found the body.

Then he began to add more victims to the list.

At the end of August 1989, he said, he met a boy about ten years old in the center of Shakhty. Chikatilo was hanging around a salon that showed videos when he spotted the boy. He struck up a conversation. The boy complained that he had seen all the videos in town. Chikatilo said that he had some videos at home, and the boy agreed to follow him there. Chikatilo led him into Shakhty's central cemetery, and there he killed him. But in this case, he said, he altered his usual ritual. Normally, he covered male victims with pieces of their own clothing, and he covered female victims with leaves and branches. But this time, he spotted a shovel nearby, probably left by someone who had been tending a relative's grave. He dug a shallow grave and buried the victim.

Kostoyev relayed the information to Burakov, who quickly responded that the date, place, and the victim's description in Chikatilo's account matched the missing-persons report filed for Aleksei Khobotov. He had disappeared at the end of August 1989 and never been found.

Kostoyev decided to call a temporary halt to the questioning and see whether Chikatilo could verify his story and help the investigators recover the boy's body.

On December 7, a group of investigators, including Kostoyev and Burakov, took Chikatilo outside the KGB building for the first time since his incarceration. They manacled his hands and flanked him with two burly men. Slava Vinokurov, the *militsia* photographer, videotaped the process. The suspect, wearing the clothes he had been arrested in, looked gaunt and troubled. His head hung low, and he responded to questions without raising his eyes to meet his interrogator's. He seemed ashamed.

They took Chikatilo to the cemetery in Shakhty, and he led them to a thicket, a few yards away from the nearest tombstones. At his direction, they began to dig in a slight depression in the muddy earth. Within a few minutes, they uncovered a boy's sneaker.

It was getting dark, too dark to film, and Kostoyev ordered the operation halted for the night. The next morning, under a cold gray drizzle, it began again. Slowly, the investigators finished the excavation, uncovering the yellowing skeleton of a boy, lying face down in the mud. It was, medical records later confirmed, the body of Aleksei Khobotov.

On December 11, Chikatilo agreed to write down the particulars of all the murders he had committed that were not on the initial list of thirty-six.

"There was a woman in Krasny Sulin in about 1987 in a field of high grass," he wrote. He gave them directions toward the remains. "From the Krasny Sulin station, go right and up the road. Second, a boy from Zaporozhe [Ukraine]. About 1986, in the woods near the railroad. Third, a boy from an *internat* in the city of Shakhty, around 1985 in the woods near the Shakhty station. Fourth, a woman in Shakhty, in 1989, near the Shakhty station. She was from Kamensk. A boy in Leningrad, who studied at a vocational school, around 1986. Sixth, a boy in Sverdlovsk oblast, in Revda, in the woods near the Revda station, about 1986. Seventh, a boy in the town of Kolchugino, Vladimir oblast, whom I took from the beach into the forest in 1987. Eighth, a boy in Krasnodar in 1986, approximately, in the forest outside of town. Ninth, a girl from Krasnodar, in an orchard near the airport. Tenth, a woman in Tashkent, in 1984, on the bank of a river. Eleventh, a girl in Tashkent, in some farmland outside the city; she was from Alma-Ata."

Other admissions came almost haphazardly. It occurred to Kostoyev that Chikatilo might be responsible for the killing of a woman found in the beach area on the left bank of the Don in 1988, a murder whose signature did not fit the *lesopolosa* pattern and which therefore had not been on the list of thirty-six murders.

No, said Chikatilo, but he did seem to recall killing in that area a different woman, who also had not been on the victims' list; it was, he thought, in 1987 or 1988. Chikatilo was taken over the bridge to the general area and asked to point out the site. He led the investigators to the spot where, in 1981, the *militsia* had found the body of a woman named Larisa Tkachenko, stabbed to death. On second thought, Chikatilo said, he probably had committed that murder in 1981 or 1982.

The Tkachenko case had never been added to the *lesopolosa* list because the medical examiners in 1981 had concluded that the killer probably had type B blood. Now, with all the laboratory analyses called into question and Chikatilo's confession at hand, the Tkachenko case was added to the accusation.

Other cases Chikatilo mentioned had not made the original accusation because the killer's method had been at variance with the usual *lesopolosa* signature or because they occurred far from Rostov.

The young woman from Kamensk that Chikatilo mentioned turned out to be a sixteen-year-old student named Tatyana Ryzhova. He described meeting her in the Shakhty station at the end of February 1989. He had taken her to an apartment that his daughter, Lyudmilla, had vacated a few months previously, when she married a man from Kharkov, Ukraine. The Chikatilos, like nearly all Soviet families, knew better than to give up an apartment they controlled, and they kept paying rent in the expectation that their son, Yuri, would move into it when he got out of the Soviet army.

Inside the apartment, a familiar scene unfolded. The woman had a drink and agreed to have sex. She undressed. "I tried to get an erection and to put my penis into her with my hands," Chikatilo recounted. He failed. "Evidently, this hurt her, because she started to get angry and demand five hundred rubles, or else her gang would come and destroy the apartment. I tried to calm her down, but saw that I couldn't. So I hit her and she lost consciousness." Soon, he recounted, he realized that he could not simply leave the body there, as he had done in the woods. So he dismembered the corpse.

Chikatilo went outside and walked around until he saw a sled sitting behind an open gate. He stole it. He remembered that a dog had barked, and he had a fear that someone could catch him in the act of theft. No one did. He took the sled back to the apartment and found some old cloths in a garbage pile. Furtively, in the dark, he laid the body parts on the sled and covered them with the cloths. Then he set out into the night to try to find a place to dispose of the body. He headed toward the Shakhty station, thinking he would take the corpse into the same woods where he had left other victims. At one point, he recounted, the sled got stuck and a stranger helped him pull it across the street, never suspecting what lay under the pile of cloths. Before Chikatilo got to the forest, he saw an open sewer main. Quickly, he pushed the body parts inside. He left the sled in a gutter a few hundred yards away.

Ryzhova's body, found ten days later, was never associated with the *lesopolosa* killings until Chikatilo's confession, because it had been dismembered, rather than disemboweled, then left in a sewer pipe, not in the woods.

Chikatilo's disclosures about the murders of Aleksei Khobotov, Larisa Tkachenko, and Tatyana Ryzhova solidified Burakov's conviction that they had indeed found the *lesopolosa* killer. After untangling no fewer than five false confessions between 1983 and 1986, Burakov did not want to have to rely on confessions obtained for crimes the investigators already knew about. He had seen how easy it was to coerce an admission of guilt, and there was always the possibility that Chikatilo, reacting to the list of accusations, had fabricated a story about each of them, or been prompted.

No investigator, however, had known with certainty that Aleksei Khobotov was dead, much less where the body was buried. Only the killer could have shown them to the site.

As the weeks passed and more information came in, other parts of Chikatilo's confession checked out. Small details corroborated some confessions. He knew, for instance, that Marta Ryabenko, the drunken woman slain in February 1984, was the granddaughter of a famous Soviet general. The general's name had not been Ryabenko, and it was presumably a detail Chikatilo had learned in conversation with the victim. Chikatilo recalled that one of the victims, Anna Lemesheva, had threatened as she struggled with him that a man named Bars would get Chikatilo for what he was doing. Lemesheva, it turned out, had a boyfriend with the nickname "Bars" tattooed on his fist.

In Leningrad, Tashkent, Sverdlovsk, Krasnodar, and other Soviet cities where Chikatilo said he had murdered, the *militsia* dredged up records of unidentified remains or missing persons that fit Chikatilo's descriptions. For some of the cases, Chikatilo traveled, under guard, to the sites of those murders and correctly pointed out where the remains had been found years before.

Chikatilo had, it became clear, been affected by his 1984 arrest. From 1985 to 1989, he did nearly all his killing while traveling on business outside Rostov oblast. Gradually, though, his obsession had overpowered his caution, and he had resumed killing close to home.

Chikatilo also eventually confessed to three killings that Burakov and his crew could not verify. Chikatilo said these murders were committed in the Shakhty area between 1980 and 1982, and he showed the investigators the sites where he remembered leaving the bodies. The *militsia* spent three months combing the areas Chikatilo designated. In one instance, they drained part of a swamp. But they found no human remains, and the times and places Chikatilo remembered did not correspond to any missing-persons reports.

By the end of the interrogation, Chikatilo had confessed to fifty-six murders. The investigators found sufficient corroborating evidence to charge him with fifty-three, thirty-one females and twenty-two males. Burakov, however, believed that the true total might never be known. There were, he suspected, victims Chikatilo had not remembered or had chosen, for some reason, not to reveal. Though he had no proof, Burakov thought that the true total of victims might be much higher.

12

Portrait of a Killer

Andrei Chikatilo himself wondered what had made him the man he was. "The more I've thought about it," he told Kostoyev during an interrogation in early December, "the more I've come to the conclusion that I suffer from some kind of sickness. It was as if something directed me, something outside me, something supernatural. I was absolutely not in control of myself when I committed these murders, when I stabbed people, when I was cruel. Therefore, I have a request for the investigators. I want you to show me to specialists in psychology and sexual pathology. I am ready to discuss my condition in detail with these specialists and I'm ready to answer all their questions. I want the specialists to know the truth."

Chikatilo's eagerness to undergo a psychiatric evaluation suggested that he could recognize his own best interests. Given the confession that he had made, the psychiatrists were the only ones likely to be able to save his life. Only if they found him criminally insane was he likely to escape the death penalty.

The investigators, on the other hand, had no choice but to comply with Chikatilo's request. At his trial, the question of his sanity was certain to come up. They would need a psychiatric evaluation to rebut the insanity defense. In August 1991, after completing the interrogation and all the attendant crime scene trips, the investigators transferred Chikatilo, under guard, to the Serbsky Institute in Moscow for a sixty-day evaluation.

The Serbsky is located at 23 Kropotkinsky Pereulok, in one of the capital's oldest neighborhoods. Some of the neighboring buildings are graceful prerevolutionary merchants' mansions, with pastel walls, arches, Palladian doorways, and white Doric columns, now used by foreign embassies. But the Serbsky is a product of the Soviet era, and it has neither warmth nor polish. High granite walls, topped with barbed wire, surround its buildings. Inside, the walls are sheer and intimidating, with tiny barred apertures for windows. Guards and doctors carry rings with heavy iron keys to unlock the whitewashed doors leading to the Serbsky departments.

In the Brezhnev years, the Serbsky Institute had a reputation for malevolence. It was known for inventing diagnoses of schizophrenia that the KGB could use to lock up dissidents who had violated no criminal laws. By the time Chikatilo arrived, perestroika had changed the Serbsky's orientation. It was still the government's leading institution for diagnosing aberrant criminals, but it no longer provided a legal pretext for confining dissidents.

Chikatilo was sent to the Third Department at Serbsky, the one that deals with what Russian psychiatry defines as *psychogenia*—personality disorders that seem to arise in reaction to environmental factors. Other sections deal with schizophrenia and with organic brain disorders like epilepsy. In the Third Department, Chikatilo lived in a cell with high, dingy green walls, a bunk with a mattress that was leaking stuffing, and a single window, mounted high on the wall and painted over so that only a little light shone through.

There, he fell under the authority of Andrei Tkachenko, a thin young psychiatrist with freckles, blue eyes, and an unruly shock of strawlike blond hair. Dr. Tkachenko had come from medical school to Serbsky in 1985, the first year of Mikhail Gorbachev's tenure in office. He helped to organize an informal group of psychiatrists from Serbsky and other institutes who work on sexual disorders like pedophilia and exhibitionism, about which he published a book. If Dr. Aleksandr Bukhanovsky in Rostov was a maverick who practiced modern psychiatry in spite of the Soviet system, Andrei Tkachenko represented a younger generation of psychiatrists, who began to practice as the system changed and became more receptive to Western ideas and methods.

Tkachenko made certain that Chikatilo received a battery of tests that are familiar to Western practitioners. The prisoner took the Minnesota Multi-phasic Personality Inventory. He looked at the ink blots in Rorschach tests. He had an electroencephalograph and other physical examinations. The psychiatrists also had access to the protocols of Kostoyev's interrogation and to the reports of the other investigators' interviews with Chikatilo's relatives. Finally, they interviewed him every day and felt that he willingly answered their questions.

From the work done by Tkachenko and other specialists, from the protocols of the confessions, and from interviews conducted for this book with many of Chikatilo's associates and relatives, it is possible to piece together a portrait of the accused killer.

"I was born in Yablochnoye, in Sumskaya oblast," Chikatilo said in one of his first post-arrest interrogations. "There were two children, myself and my sister, Tatyana, who was born in 1943. Until the end of secondary school, I lived in that village with my parents. My father was at the front [in World War II] and was captured. After the war, as a prisoner who returned, he was condemned and sent for a time to Chuvashkaya [a region on the lower Volga in Russia, the site of many prison camps]. My mother, a kolkhoz worker, raised me and my sister. Despite hunger and poverty, I was a good student."

Behind that sparse and factual account of his early life, however, lay an enormous burden of suffering.

Sumskaya oblast is not in Russia but in Ukraine, midway between the cities of Kiev and Kharkov. Ukraine, when Andrei Chikatilo was born in 1936, was the scene of one of this century's worst crimes against humanity, Joseph Stalin's genocidal collectivization of agriculture. Beginning in 1930, Stalin decided to crush private agriculture in the Soviet Union. Communist zealots went out into the countryside and, backed with bayonets, forced the small farmers to give up their land and their animals to collective farms. Simultaneously, the state began draconian requisitions of grain, intended to provide food for the new proletariat that was filling the cities in response to the First Five-Year Plan's manic quest for steel mills and smokestacks. Sometimes, the requisitions seized even the peasants' seed grain, and terrible famines resulted.

In Ukraine, Stalin seemed bent as well on making the people, who represented the largest ethnic minority in the Soviet Union, so fearful of Communist power that an independence movement would be unthinkable. Half a million of the most capable Ukrainian peasants were sent to the Gulag in Siberia, where most of them perished. An estimated six million Ukrainians died in the ensuing famine. Then, in 1941, Ukraine was invaded and occupied by Nazi troops. The Soviet army drove them out during 1943.

The precise impact of these events on Roman and Anna Chikatilo can only be guessed. Their daughter, Tatyana, said in a 1992 interview that she and her brother heard in their childhood that there had been another child, an older brother named Stepan, born several years before Andrei. He died during Stalin's famine. Their parents told them, Tatyana said, that Stepan's body was eaten by starving neighbors. There is no way of knowing if the story is true. But there were hundreds of documented cases of cannibalism in Ukraine at the time. It quite likely happened.

Andrei Chikatilo, the doctors at Serbsky discovered, was born abnormal. "His electroencephalograph [a reading of electrical activity in the brain] showed certain disturbances

associated with the early period of brain development,"
Tkachenko said. "It was probably the result of something
that happened in the uterus, during his mother's pregnancy.
We found other symptoms characteristic of this. He had a
slightly hydrocephalic skull. The pupils of his eyes were of
different sizes. When he stuck his tongue out, it didn't come
out straight, but to the right."

For Chikatilo, unfortunately, this brain abnormality man-
ifested itself in his genitalia. Until he was twelve years old,
Tkachenko learned, he was unable to control his bladder.
Later, the abnormality would manifest itself as a tendency
toward extremely premature ejaculation, often before Chikatilo achieved an erection.

But in his early childhood, his bladder problem was
paramount. The circumstances of the Chikatilo family magnified its importance. The family was, as he said in his confession, very poor. They lived in a one-room hut. There was
only one place to sleep—a wooden platform they called the
divan; their bodies, in the winter, were often the only source
of heat. When Andrei Chikatilo wet the bed, everyone in the
family knew it and suffered.

And his mother, Anna, was not the sort to suffer in silence. Perhaps because of the traumas she had suffered herself, she was a woman with a cruel, nasty temper. Twenty
years after Anna Chikatilo died, her daughter, Tatyana, could
not find a good word to say about her when an interviewer
broached the subject.

"We were very poor and we were hungry. My parents
worked day and night and got nothing for it," she recalled.
"My father was kind despite it all. But my mother was very
harsh and rude. I suppose it was because of the difficulties
of her life. But she only yelled at us and bawled us out,
bawled us out. She never had a kind word. When girlfriends
came to visit me, she'd bawl them out and ask them why they
didn't have anything to do at home. I left home when I was
fourteen."

Andrei Chikatilo slept with his mother from infancy and, presumably, repeatedly wet her bedclothes. Roughly from the time he was five or six, when his father went off to war, until he was seven, when his sister was born, he slept with her alone, and there was no one to protect him from her rage. His father did not return permanently to the family until after the war and his stint in a postwar camp had ended, when Andrei was about ten years old.

Tkachenko could only imagine how this period might have affected Andrei Chikatilo. He could imagine Chikatilo wetting his mother's bed at night and the consequences—the words and blows occasioned by his undiagnosed physical weakness and his mother's foul temper. But he could not get Chikatilo to talk about it. During his time at Serbsky, Chikatilo talked of many things, including murder. But his memories of that childhood period were locked so tightly away that the doctors could not get to them.

"He wouldn't talk about how his mother reacted, although we asked about it," Tkachenko recalled. "He didn't refuse to answer. He would say he didn't remember or he would talk about something else. And maybe he really didn't remember. Maybe he repressed it."

Chikatilo did recall for his doctors two childhood memories that apparently had imprinted themselves quite deeply in his mind.

"His sister [Tatyana], when she was a newborn, had a falling out of the colon," Tkachenko recalled. This is a relatively common event in infancy, when a section of the large intestine protrudes from an infant's anus. In the West, a doctor can usually reinsert it without surgery. In Ukraine, in 1943, Anna Chikatilo did it herself as her seven-year-old son watched. "He saw that and had feelings of fear and hot flashes of blood," Tkachenko recalled. "He spoke of it very clearly, as an event he clearly remembered."

Chikatilo also told the psychiatrists of traumatic wartime memories. He said that he recalled the aftermath of a German bombing raid, a vision of dismembered corpses and pools of blood. "It was one of the strongest experiences of his childhood," Tkachenko said. "When he saw them, he felt a mixture of fear and excitement, an excitement that in this type of person is almost sexual."

Tkachenko had heard a similar memory from Anatoly Slivko, the serial murderer from Stavropol whom Burakov, Fetisov, and Kostoyev interviewed before his execution in 1986. "Slivko also lived under the [German] occupation, and he remembered seeing a German kill a dog, and he had the same emotional reaction. He didn't feel sexual excitement as such, but a beginning kind of excitement."

Nothing went well for Andrei Chikatilo in childhood. He did not make friends easily. In fact, his boyhood peers ridiculed him and bullied him. Tatyana, seven years younger, has vague recollections of her brother during this time that indicate how unhappy he must have been. "I only remember that they picked on him and chased him," she said. "I would sometimes see him hiding in the vegetable garden next to the hut, afraid to go out."

"He has never been able to have a good relationship with his peers," Tkachenko said in more clinical terms. "His personal qualities hindered him. He feels inadequate, and he is extremely sensitive. He didn't have the qualities boys respect, like aggressiveness or physical strength."

Tkachenko found the roots of sadism in this period of Chikatilo's life. Not only were the boy's relationships with his mother and his peers suffused with humiliation and repressed anger, he had also seen the fearful bloodshed of war and found it exciting. After the war, pervasive propaganda reinforced the message of redeeming cruelty and violence.

"Chikatilo loved the novel *The Young Guard*, about underground partisans during the war who beat up Germans and threw them in mine shafts. One of his repeated fantasies was that he was a partisan and he was torturing a German prisoner for information, then killing him. This kind of fantasy is quite common among sadists of that generation. The common root is that the fantasizer sees himself in the role of a person with power over another person,'' Tkachenko recalled.

Chikatilo himself, as he sorted through his boyhood memories, focused most of all on his nearsightedness, which he recalled as a humiliating weakness. ''Until I was thirty years old, I felt inadequate because of my nearsightedness,'' he wrote in one of his essays for the procurator. ''I couldn't wear glasses because I was ashamed to. But without them I often fell into awkward situations.'' When he was thirty, Chikatilo went on, he bought a motorcycle. He could get a driver's license only by correcting his vision. For the first time in his life, he bought and wore eyeglasses.

He had other compensating mechanisms in childhood. He sat close to the blackboard in school and he studied very hard. ''Schooling did not come easy to me, because of my bad vision and the fact that I had trouble remembering a lot of the material the instructors taught me,'' Chikatilo wrote. ''But by virtue of perseverance, I finished ten classes [the Soviet equivalent of high school] successfully. Not many people in my village did so.''

Chikatilo was, in some respects, a model student as he struggled to find some niche for himself. He got good grades. He was chairman of one of the approved student activities, a committee that helped the elderly. He drew placards glorifying Stalin for the rallies organized by the Komsomol, or Communist Youth League. He worked on Komsomol wall newspapers for his fellow students.

But in one important respect, Chikatilo could not keep up with his peers. His brain abnormality, Tkachenko found, delayed his sexual maturation. Chikatilo gave slightly varying accounts of his early sexual experience to different examiners. But the accounts had enough common elements to enable the examiners to establish a history. Chikatilo's sexual development started quite late. He did not masturbate until he was seventeen. And, apparently, his sexual development frightened him. He told the psychiatrists at the Center for the Study of Sexual Pathology in Moscow that he had vowed, when he was fourteen or fifteen, not to touch a woman until he was married. It was not, of course, a vow he could keep.

His few experiences with girls were nearly all traumatic. When he was about sixteen years old, a friend of his sister's came to the Chikatilo hut. No one else was at home. Chikatilo had been watching, enviously, as his peers in the village were initiated into sex. This visitor was much younger than Andrei Chikatilo—about ten or eleven years old. Apparently, he felt a sudden and overpowering urge to rape her. He grabbed the girl, pushed her to the floor, and, as she struggled, had his first ejaculation. Then he let the girl up. This event, according to Dr. Vyacheslav Maslov of the Center, cemented in Chikatilo's mind the connection between sexual satisfaction and overpowering a victim.

At the end of his adolescence, a critical academic failure intensified his feelings of inadequacy. Chikatilo had set his sights on following the same path out of rural poverty that Mikhail Gorbachev had taken five years previously. Gorbachev, from Stavropol Krai in southern Russia, had made it off the kolkhoz by winning admission to the Law Faculty at Moscow State University, the most prestigious school in the Soviet Union. Chikatilo, though he, of course, had never heard of Gorbachev, applied to the same faculty at the same school. Admission (except for those whose parents had sufficient influence within the Party) was by a highly competitive examination. The exam, Chikatilo pointed out, was in Russian, which gave him a further disadvantage. In his part of Ukraine, the people generally spoke a mixed dialect of Ukrainian and Russian, which differ from each other about as much as Spanish and Portuguese. Chikatilo traveled to Moscow and took the examination. He passed, he would recall, with good-to-excellent grades. But they were not high enough to make the cut for Moscow State.

Chikatilo recalled his rejection as yet another humiliation. He told the doctors at the Serbsky Institute that the director of his high school had advised him that he would never get into Moscow State because of his father's tainted war record. This may have been true, although by this time Stalin had died and an ideological thaw was beginning under the leadership of Nikita Khrushchev. Whatever the reason, Chikatilo's failure was hardly the disgrace he deemed it. It was as if a bright farm boy from Nebraska had been turned down at Harvard. That boy might enroll at the University of Nebraska instead. Chikatilo, similarly, could have applied to a less prestigious university. He could have studied on his own for a year and taken the exams in Moscow again. But he chose not to.

Andrei Chikatilo was not prepared to risk further humiliation. "I decided to find work somewhere," he told Kostoyev. "I took the train to Kursk, and I worked there for three months as a laborer." Then he enrolled in a vocational school, where he was trained to become a communications technician. The boy who had aspired to a career as a lawyer in Moscow had settled for becoming, in effect, a telephone repairman.

Once he had completed this school, the army drafted him. He was assigned to a special KGB communications unit, where he served for three years in the enlisted ranks. After the army, he bounced around for a couple of years in technicians' jobs in Rostov oblast. His chief distinction was membership in the Communist Party, which he joined in 1960.

He remained painfully inadequate with women. Occasionally he would meet a woman, work up the nerve to ask her out, and try to demonstrate his manhood. In some cases the women were willing. "We checked and corroborated one account he gave us," Tkachenko recalled. "He tried to have sex with a woman in 1960, just after he got out of the army. She said that when he tried to have sex with her, he couldn't manage it. And there were a few other attempts he made earlier than that that were unsuccessful. Either he didn't have an erection or he very quickly ejaculated.''

Tkachenko described two distinct problems in Chikatilo's sexual makeup. ''The inability to get an erection was the result of his personality problems. He didn't believe in himself; he felt inadequate, and so on. But the premature ejaculation was the result of a physical condition. Because of the peculiarities of the organic functioning of his brain, he had what sexual pathologists call a lowered threshold of excitement. He could become excited without sexual stimuli or with asexual stimulation. He could ejaculate without an erection.''

Afflicted with these related, but distinct, sexual disabilities, Chikatilo grew more withdrawn and introverted. ''I was shy and silent,'' he told Kostoyev. ''I never had sexual relations with a woman and I had no concept of a sex life. I always preferred to listen to the radio, watch television, or read the newspapers.''

In 1961, when she was eighteen, Chikatilo's sister, Tatyana, finished her schooling. Rather than see her return to Yablochnoye, to their impoverished hut and to the mercies of their mother, Andrei invited his sister to live with him. They shared his one-room apartment for six months, and Tatyana felt grateful to her brother. ''He cared for me,'' she said. She noticed nothing abnormal about his behavior, except that he had no girlfriends.

Very soon, Tatyana married a laborer named Vasily and moved out. But she was intent on trying to help her older brother find a wife and have a family. Andrei Chikatilo had some attractive attributes. He was a serious young man who continued taking correspondence courses after finishing his schooling. He belonged to the Party. Most important, he drank very little. In the Soviet Union, male drunkenness was by far the leading cause of divorce. Many women dreamed of nothing more than a sober, reliable working man for a husband.

In 1963, Tatyana and her husband's family found such a woman for Andrei Chikatilo. She was Feodosia Odnacheva, the daughter of a coal miner from Novoshakhtinsk. Feodosia was a stocky young woman, not particularly attractive, with a secondary school education. At twenty-four, she was a bit past the age when most Soviet girls married.

It was, Andrei Chikatilo recalled, basically an arranged marriage. "The decisive role was played by my sister, Tatyana," he told Kostoyev. "She and her relatives on her husband's side set me up with my wife. They agreed on everything among themselves. After two weeks, we were married."

Chikatilo could not, at first, get an erection and consummate his marriage. But, eventually, he had his first sexual intercourse with his wife. Sex was, for him, infrequent and difficult, Tkachenko learned. But it occurred often enough for Feodosia to become pregnant. Their first child, a girl named Lyudmilla, was born in 1965. Their second, a boy named Yuri, was born in 1969.

Both families were quite pleased with the match. "I had a very good impression of Feodosia," Tatyana recalled. Feodosia's family looked at their new in-law as an intellectual. "We saw him every Easter, when they would visit to help us tend our parents' graves [a Russian custom]," recalled Ivan Odnachev. "He would have a drink or two, eat, then go off and read a newspaper. I thought very highly of him. He read a lot. He was a member of the Party."

Chikatilo maintained the facade of a normal family man until his arrest in 1990. In 1985, his daughter married Pyotr Moryakov, a young man studying to be a ship's engineer. Moryakov and Lyudmilla Chikatilo lived with his parents, but they saw her parents often. Moryakov had more personal experience with Andrei Chikatilo than perhaps anyone outside the immediate family.

He found his father-in-law to be a quiet man who was submissive to his domineering wife. The marriage between Andrei Chikatilo and Feodosia did not seem to their new son-in-law to be a particularly warm one. He could not remember ever seeing them kiss. Feodosia, Moryakov thought, was the dominant partner. "The women played the bigger role in that family," he recalled. "Feodosia decided what to do and told him to do it."

Moryakov's recollections about Andrei Chikatilo's wife, in fact, resembled Tatyana Chikatilo's recollections of their cruel mother. "Feodosia liked to yell and to bawl him out," Moryakov recalled. "It was nothing that seemed really serious. She'd complain that the water was not running or the gas was off and tell him to do something about it. And he would not say anything at all, usually, and would just go and do what she said."

Moryakov suspected nothing of his father-in-law's secret life, and he saw no evidence that anyone else did. Everything seemed to be quite normal. He and Chikatilo played chess together. The older man, Moryakov recalled, usually won. They talked about Russian literature and of Chikatilo's regret that he did not have a good library. When he was not off on a business trip, Chikatilo seemed often to be working on a home improvement project in the family's apartment, and gave his son-in-law occasional lessons in carpentry and plastering.

Lyudmilla, he recalled, respected her father enormously. "She held him up to me as a model. I paint as a hobby, and she suggested that I paint her father's portrait. I didn't, because I like to paint only women. But she thought he was a very cultured individual."

In 1986, Pyotr and Lyudmilla had their first child, a son. Andrei Chikatilo reacted like a normal grandparent, his son-in-law recalled. He was proud of the newborn boy's size and good health. As the baby got older, his grandfather would take him to the park and treat him to rides on the carousel.

* * *

Moryakov was not aware of it, but a few people in fact did know a little about what lay beneath Andrei Chikatilo's facade of normalcy. They had, however, long ago decided tacitly to ignore it.

In 1964, the year after his marriage, Chikatilo made another effort to get a higher education. He was accepted in the liberal arts school of Rostov State University as a correspondence student. This meant that he attended classes two months a year and did the rest of his course work on his own, through the mail. It took much longer to complete a degree this way, but Chikatilo persisted. In 1970, he was awarded his degree, with a specialty in Russian literature. He had made it from the kolkhoz of his birth into the ranks of the Soviet intelligentsia.

Immediately, he looked for work befitting his new status. He had reasonably good contacts within the Party; he had been to the Party school in Rostov for course work in 1968 and 1969. He called on an acquaintance from that school, Pavel Voznikov, who was directing an evening school in Novoshakhtinsk. Voznikov called a friend of his named Aleksandr Sorochkin, the director of Vocational School No. 32 in Novoshakhtinsk. Sorochkin agreed to take Chikatilo on as a deputy director and a teacher of Russian language and literature.

But Chikatilo failed as an administrator and failed as a teacher. "I was too shy to be a deputy director," he recounted. The job involved supervising other teachers. Sorochkin soon asked Chikatilo to give it up and simply be a teacher. Chikatilo agreed.

But he could not handle that, either. "I couldn't maintain discipline in my classes," he recalled. "Some of the students took advantage of my weak character and acted rudely. They laughed at me and called me 'Antenna.' Sometimes they even smoked cigarettes in class. The director heard about it, and I was warned several times to maintain discipline in class. I tried, but I couldn't do it.''

Vocational School No. 32 had an *internat* section for boarding students, and part of Chikatilo's work involved supervising their dormitories. What he saw there inflamed him. ''I noticed that a few of the stronger boys were committing acts of sodomy with the weaker ones. Despite the measures we took, girls started to have sex at an early age. There were cases where we caught boys and girls together in bed. This disturbed me. I could see children doing what I had not done even when I was thirty years old.''

Teaching was obviously a terrible career choice for Chikatilo. It subjected him daily to humiliation and ridicule. The sexuality of his adolescent charges seemed to taunt him. Sorochkin suggested that he might do better going back to technical work. Chikatilo resisted. He had his university degree, and he thought it would be shameful to go back to working with his hands.

In the spring of 1973, Chikatilo's mother died. In his interviews with the psychiatrists, he did not ascribe any particular importance to it. But it was only a month later, in May 1973, that his perversion first slipped the chains of legality and began claiming victims.

He was then thirty-seven years old. In the United States, serial killers generally begin to act out their internal rage at a much younger age—from late adolescence to their midtwenties. Chikatilo's later start is probably attributable, in part, to the constraints of the marriage his sister helped arrange, and to the generally repressive and limiting aspects of Soviet society. He could not, for instance, have been constantly exposed to the sexual stimuli in the media that assail American serial killers.

Dr. Andrei Tkachenko saw in Chikatilo's history a steady but gradual descent into perversion. ''His libido became distorted,'' Tkachenko said. ''His sexual inclination gradually turned from normal, heterosexual activity, which no longer brought him satisfaction, because it didn't respond to his true desires. To get satisfaction and relieve the tension within him, he needed aggressive, violent, and destructive acts with his object."

But Chikatilo did not begin by killing. From 1973 to 1978, he confined himself to acts of molestation. Dr. Tkachenko saw in these acts an intermediate stage in the development of Chikatilo's sadism. "They were sadistic in the sense that there was a moment of power that he could experience when he forced someone to undress or submit. He said he wanted to touch them or pinch them. That is sadistic."

In his confessions, Chikatilo outlined the growing power of his perversion. It began with hanging around near the public toilets, hoping to catch glimpses of young girls with their clothes in disarray. In May 1973 (although in his initial confession, he remembered it as 1977 or 1978), he took some pupils swimming at a pond in the woods around Novoshakhtinsk. In the pond, he swam up behind a fifteen-year-old student, Lyubov Kostina, and grabbed her breasts and genital area. She yelled and struggled and Chikatilo had an immediate ejaculation.

Later in the same month came the incident with Tonya Gultseva that he first recounted to Kostoyev. He forced the girl to stay after school to do some remedial work. "I noticed that her skirt had ridden up," he recalled, "and I could see her panties and bare legs. This excited me. I got a passionate desire to touch her breasts, her sex organs. She resisted, pushed me away, and cried out."

Chikatilo left the room, locking the girl inside. But she escaped by climbing out a window. She told her parents about the incident. Her parents complained to the school's director.

This was the first time that Chikatilo's perversion came to the attention of the Soviet authorities, and it was the first chance they had to do something about it. But the school's director, Aleksandr Sorochkin, chose to cover up the scandal rather than confront it. He asked Chikatilo to resign quietly.

In return, Sorochkin said nothing to the *militsia* and did nothing to prevent Chikatilo from getting a job at another school, Vocational School No. 39 in Novoshakhtinsk. In 1978, he lost that job when the staff was reduced. But he quickly arranged yet another teaching position, this time at Technical School No. 33 in Shakhty, a training institution with a dormitory.

There he lost control of himself again. In 1978, he entered the dormitory room of a boy named V. I. Shcherbakov while the boy was sleeping, and fellated him. According to Chikatilo's confessions, the boy woke up and Chikatilo fled in shame. The incident, he recalled, became a topic of gossip among the boys in the school, and he became an object of constant derision.

Two years later, three girls, ranging in age from six to thirteen, came to the Chikatilo apartment in Shakhty to collect old newspapers for a communal bonfire. Andrei Chikatilo was the only one home. He grabbed them, pulled their panties down, and groped at their genitals. The children ran away.

These children told their parents, but the reaction of the adults in the neighborhood spoke volumes about why Andrei Chikatilo was allowed to develop from a molester into a murderer. The idea that one of the men in the neighborhood could molest children was not something that the other men could cope with. Their instinct was to deny that such a thing could happen.

Viktor Smirnov, a shop master at Technical School No. 33, lived in the same building with the Chikatilos. He considered Chikatilo a decent individual—not a fishing buddy, but someone whom he occasionally sat next to at teachers' meetings in the school. "He didn't have a vulgar streak. He wasn't a drinker," Smirnov recalled. Chikatilo had an unflattering nickname—"Goose." But that was a reference to his long neck and squinty eyes.

There were rumors, Smirnov recalled in a 1992 interview,

that Chikatilo had molested children. "The women talked about it, but I didn't believe it," he recalled. "I got angry at my [late] wife when she mentioned it. 'How could a man do that?' I said. I thought the children must have made the story up as a prank."

A few members of Chikatilo's own family also had reason, in these years, to know of the aberrant tendencies beneath the facade. But they also kept silent.

One of them was his niece, Marina Odnacheva, the daughter of Feodosia's brother Ivan Odnachev and his wife, Tayisia. In 1973, when Marina Odnacheva was six, her Uncle Andrei stuck his hands down her pants and groped at her genitals. He warned her to say nothing, and she didn't.

Five years later, Marina was again visiting her cousins. In the middle of the night, she awoke to find her Uncle Andrei standing over her, his penis in his hand. He rubbed his sexual organ over the girl's skin and ejaculated. Again, he warned her not to tell anyone. She kept the secret for twelve years, until she heard that her uncle had been arrested. Only then did she tell her parents what he had done.

It was not entirely a surprise to her mother, Tayisia Odnacheva. Tayisia believed her daughter because she herself had a painful memory of Andrei Chikatilo. "At about the same time, in 1978, he tried to force himself on me," she recalled in a 1992 interview. She resisted, and Chikatilo stopped short of raping her. Tayisia went to her mother-in-law, Matrena Odnacheva, who was also Feodosia Chikatilo's mother and the matriarch of the family. She told the old woman what had happened. But Matrena Odnacheva, to the best of Tayisia's knowledge, said and did nothing about it.

Couldn't she have told her husband?

Tayisia snorted. "What good would it have done? Men only think of themselves." Her voice quavered. "No one defends us women!" she wailed, and began to weep.

If any of the molestation incidents that occurred between 1973 and 1978 had resulted in a criminal prosecution, Andrei

Chikatilo probably would not have been able to commit the more than fifty murders he had confessed to. He would have been jailed, or at least confined in a mental institution. Thereafter, his name would have been on the list of sex offenders that the *militsia* always compiled when they investigated individual *lesopolosa* murders. Most likely, after one or two murders, he would have been caught. But his name never made it into the sex crime files, until his arrest in 1990.

Soviet society, Dr. Tkachenko observed, was caught up in a syndrome of denial that inadvertently protected molesters and created favorable conditions for them to continue committing crimes.

"You have a situation where mothers and others hide the perverse behavior of their husbands toward their children, even though they know it's child abuse. People don't trust authority and don't come forward. The knowledge of these things is restricted to gossip and rumor," he said.

The failure of society to punish him severely for his early molestations, Tkachenko thought, emboldened Chikatilo.

"He might have feared something would happen, but it didn't. He was fired from one job, and he got another one right away. He was never prosecuted. The point is, he got away with it."

By 1978, occasional molestation was no longer satisfying him, and Andrei Chikatilo embarked in earnest on his secret life. His first step was the purchase of the hut on Mezhovoy Street in Shakhty, several miles from his family's apartment. Though state-owned high-rises were the preferred form of housing in the Soviet Union, there have always been privately owned houses. Often they are old peasant huts, some of which now stand in growing urban areas. Because of the shortage of building materials, these houses are hard to improve with conveniences like indoor plumbing, so they tend to be slum housing. The hut at 26 Mezhovoy Street certainly was. It was a miserable, one-room dwelling, with a sagging roof and a precarious set of steep, muddy steps hewn into the embankment that separated it from the unpaved street. It is in a neighborhood where, in 1992, Gypsies had begun to move in, signifying its status at the bottom of the Russian housing ladder.

Chikatilo told the neighbors that he bought the house, which probably cost a few hundred rubles, with the idea of fixing it up as a retirement home for his father. Later, he told them that his father had decided not to occupy it because of the steep steps.

Whatever Chikatilo's real intentions were when he bought the house, it soon became a hideaway where he could indulge in the kind of sex that appealed to him.

"Two girls showed up one day in 1978 and said they were 'renting' the place from him," recalled a neighbor named Mariya Khorkina, a hefty old woman with rheumy eyes. "They were young, and dirty. Probably station tramps who didn't have anyplace else to go. After a while, they left, but others appeared. Girls. Boys. I'd hear things occasionally in the evening. It sounded like debauchery."

She never called the *militsia*, in part because people in her neighborhood tried to have as little as possible to do with the *militsia*, and in part because Chikatilo had made a good first impression on her. "You'd have never suspected what he was. He was always clean, with pressed clothes. If I'd been younger, I might have gone over there myself if he'd asked. And he'd have killed me and sent me straight to hell!"

Actually, in these years, Chikatilo was most often attempting to have some kind of sex with the people he lured into the hut. Generally, because of his inability to get an erection, he would offer to perform oral sex on a woman, Tkachenko said. In the course of this, he would ejaculate without penetrating her.

Sometimes, the partner might be a boy. But Tkachenko did not conclude that Chikatilo had a homosexual tendency. He was, in effect, indifferent to the sex of his partner, as long as he could manipulate and dominate the partner in the way he desired. This manipulation and domination grew more and more violently sadistic over the years. But there was no indication that Chikatilo was ever attracted to an adult male. "He was not a homosexual, but a sadist," Tkachenko concluded.

Two of his partners during this time might have given Burakov and the *syshchiki* clues to the *lesopolosa* killer's identity, had they only known about them. One of them was Tatyana Petrosyan, the woman who was killed along with her daughter in the summer of 1984. She and Chikatilo had occasional contacts much earlier, although they were apparently confined to oral sex. Chikatilo had even visited the apartment where Tatyana lived with her mother. But he had identified himself as a teacher, though he was no longer teaching by the time Tatyana Petrosyan was killed. And, Tatyana had a lot of male visitors.

Another of his partners during this period was an older sister of Irina Dunenkova, the girl with Down's syndrome who became a victim in the summer of 1983; Chikatilo had gotten to know Irina slightly during the time he had a sexual liaison with the older sister. Irina Dunenkova and Tatyana Petrosyan were the only victims whom Chikatilo knew before he killed them. But in neither instance were the investigators able to establish the connection.

According to Pyotr Moryakov, Chikatilo's son-in-law, no one in the family knew what went on at 26 Mezhovoy Street. But there were indirect signs. According to Tkachenko, the frequency of Chikatilo's sexual relations with his wife dwindled to once every few months, beginning at around the time he bought the hut.

Chikatilo's sexual relationship with his wife ended completely in 1984, according to Tkachenko. Chikatilo told the psychiatrist that in that year, his wife unexpectedly got pregnant. He wanted her to have the baby, but she insisted on an abortion. Whether this was true or not—Feodosia Chikatilo was forty-five that year—it does seem likely that he found his sexual satisfaction solely through his secret life after that year.

As time passed, the facade of normalcy became increasingly difficult for Andrei Chikatilo to maintain. In March 1981, he decided to abandon his disastrous career as an educator. He found work as a *snabzhenyets* at an enterprise called Rostov-nerud.

Snabzhenyets means, literally, "provider," and it is a uniquely Soviet job category, reflecting the backwardness of the Soviet economy. Whereas the primary task of an enter-prise in a market economy is to sell its output, the primary task for a Soviet enterprise often boiled down to buying its inputs. Rostovnerud, for instance, produced construction materials. To do that, it required raw materials ranging from sand to nails. Given the inefficiencies of the Soviet economy, suppliers often failed to fulfill their contracts, and a Rostov-nerud production line for, say, concrete building slabs might shut down for lack of aggregate mix, or steel rods, or almost anything else. The job of the *snabzhenyets* was to minimize these problems by assuring the enterprise of a steady supply of raw materials. Informally, the *snabzhenyets* was also called a *tolkach*, or "pusher."

It was difficult work, for several reasons. First, a *snab-zhenyets* had to be on the road very often, visiting the fac-tories that supplied his factory and pushing them to make deliveries. Life on the road in Russia is a hard one. The hotels and restaurants are miserable, the trains are slow, and the airplanes sometimes fail to fly at all. Pushing a factory to make deliveries often entailed bribing its directors, either with gifts like vodka and caviar or with cash. And whatever a *snabzhenyets* did, he was likely to fail often, resulting in reprimands from his superiors. As a result, virtually any large enterprise had trouble finding and keeping good *snabzhen-yetsy*. Virtually anyone who wanted the job could have it.

It was, however, not a bad job for someone who wanted

to ride on lots of trains and buses, someone who didn't want to account for every hour of his working day.

"Andrei Chikatilo came here looking for work in 1981," said Nina Nasacheva, the chief clerk in the personnel department at Rostovnerud. "I don't remember what he said the reason was." He was hired, she remembered, because he had a technical education and wanted the job. No one checked his past employers. He got a desk in the office next door to hers.

Chikatilo did not fit in well among the fifty people who worked in Rostovnerud's administration office in the center of Shakhty. "He never looked people in the eye. He'd sit at his desk, lost in thought, and he'd constantly tap his pen on some paper or doodle and pretend to work. If someone asked him a question, he might take a long time to answer. Or he might not answer at all. He had no close friends here. He was peculiar," Nasacheva recalled.

He was sometimes the butt of practical jokes. Another personnel office worker, Rita Golovanova, remembered that co-workers began to notice that Chikatilo never went anywhere, even to the water fountain, without carrying his briefcase. ("And now I know why," she added in 1992.) One of his co-workers one day wrapped a brick in a newspaper and opened the briefcase while Chikatilo was distracted, during a staff meeting. Then he closed it, apparently seeing nothing unusual in it. Chikatilo left that afternoon on an errand in Rostov. He carried the briefcase and the surreptitiously placed brick with him. The next day, the jokers in the office expected that he would at least say something about finding a brick in his briefcase. But he returned to the office and said nothing. If he realized that his colleagues were mocking him, he suffered his humiliation in silence.

Chikatilo's work performance, however, won him two promotions in his first couple of years on the job. He became a minor supervisor, with five underlings in the supply department. But in 1983 and 1984, years in which his killings became more frequent, his work performance deteriorated. "He'd take money to purchase things and come back without them," Nina Nasacheva recalled. "It got to where, at the Monday meetings, the director was constantly bawling him out. He'd just say nothing and hang his head and doodle."

In the spring of 1984, Chikatilo finally gave his director, Pyotr Palagyn, an excuse to fire him. Chikatilo went to Moscow, charged with getting sixteen car batteries for the enterprise's car pool. (It was a measure of the inefficiency of the Soviet economy that he could not simply pick up the phone and order them from a distributor in Rostov oblast.) He came back and said he could get only fifteen batteries. But it was quickly determined that he had taken one battery for the car he owned jointly with one of Feodosia's brothers.

Across the Soviet Union, millions of workers behaved exactly as Chikatilo had, supplying their private needs by chiseling from a state enterprise. Normally, enterprise directors looked the other way. But Palagyn seized on the incident. After investigating, he added a charge that Chikatilo had also stolen a bit of linoleum flooring for his apartment. The Party committee at Rostovnerud began proceedings to expel Chikatilo.

But Chikatilo fought back. He wrote letters of complaint to Party officials in Shakhty and Rostov, saying that Palagyn was unfairly singling him out. According to Soviet practice, Palagyn had to answer to charges against him lodged with the Party. The director did not want the headache. He and Chikatilo reached a compromise not unlike the one Chikatilo had reached with Aleksandr Sorochkin at Vocational School No. 32 ten years earlier. He would resign quietly and find another job. The Party would expel him, but Palagyn would not press charges on the battery and linoleum thefts.

At about this time, Nina Nasacheva needed Chikatilo's work history booklet, a document maintained by all Soviet workers, to record that he was resigning. Since he was not at work, she stopped by the Chikatilo apartment to get it and for the first time met Feodosia Chikatilo. Andrei was not home, Feodosia said. Wasn't he at work, she asked.

Chikatilo, it turned out, had told her nothing of his problems at the office. That, presumably, would have skirted too close to his secret life.

The theft charges were revived by the *lesopolosa* investigators when they decided to hold Chikatilo a little longer after his arrest in September 1984. He spent three months in jail, and he lost his new job, at a factory called Spetzenergoavtomatika. Ironically, the charges also permitted Andrei Chikatilo to keep his family in the dark about his real activities. According to his brother-in-law Ivan Odnachev, he told them that the case had been trumped up against him by a vengeful boss with whom he had a personality conflict. That was an easy story to believe. Why else would a man be charged with something so petty? The family never learned about the nocturnal activities in the bus and train stations that had in fact led to his arrest.

Neither his conviction nor his expulsion from the Party prevented Chikatilo from getting still another job as a *snabzhenyets* when he was released from prison in January 1985. He found a place as a metals supplier at an enormous state enterprise, the Novocherkassk Electric Locomotive Construction Factory, known (because of its initials in Russian) as NEVZ. It employs eleven thousand workers, who turn out, if they are meeting their quotas, more than two hundred locomotives a year.

"He was a bad worker," recalled his boss there, a heavyset man named Aleksei Rezhko. "I don't know why he was hired, but he was here when I got here."

Chikatilo, Rezhko said, had trouble connecting with people. As his fellow teachers had done, his co-workers in the office called him "Goose" behind his back. Like the people at Rostovnerud, the people at NEVZ remembered him as a man who never looked them in the eye.

"Whenever people got together, like for a drink on

someone's birthday, he sat off to one side by himself. If you tried to talk to him, he'd smile a little and say something else. Like, if you talked about the prices in the stores, he'd say something about an illness. If you talked about cars, he'd say something about fishing. Some people felt sorry for him, but others didn't like him. He was an unattractive man,'' Rezhko said.

They also learned, obliquely, that he was a man keeping secrets. One day, Feodosia Chikatilo called the office to ask when her husband would return from his business trip. He was, at the time, on vacation. The secretary who answered the phone did not tell her.

Rezhko quickly grew dissatisfied with Chikatilo's work. Often, he would have to send another man out to a supplier's office to procure something Chikatilo was supposed to have gotten. "He was ill suited to the work," Rezhko said. "I tried to explain things to him, and I docked his bonuses, but it didn't help. Eventually, I started to gather material for a dossier of complaints to use in firing him. He was the first man to be fired from that job in at least thirty years.''

Again, the dismissal was disguised. The trade union at the factory interceded for him, and he was allowed to resign voluntarily. He got another job, again as a *snabzhenyets*, at a Rostov plant that repaired locomotives, and he was employed there when he was arrested.

Once, during the years he was killing people, Chikatilo sought help. In the summer of 1984, when his compulsion to kill was so intense that he was murdering at the rate of about once every two weeks, he went to the clinic in Shakhty, where he lived. According to Dr. Tkachenko, he wanted to consult a psychiatrist who worked there. But a *militsioner* happened to see him in the waiting room and recognized him.

"Why are you here?" the man asked. "Alcohol?" It was

the most common reason for a man of Chikatilo's age to go to the clinic.

The sight of a *militsioner* apparently unnerved Chikatilo. He left before ever speaking to the doctor.

His family life, meanwhile, was slowly deteriorating. In 1988, Pyotr Moryakov, his son-in-law, was hospitalized for a mental illness. Moryakov and Lyudmilla Chikatilo soon divorced. In 1985, Chikatilo's teenaged son, Yuri, developed a habit of taking the car owned jointly by his father and uncle without their permission. He drank, drove around, and had a couple of accidents. Chikatilo was forced to sell the car. Eventually, he began working on the strange little room in the middle of his apartment, the place where he would be able to retreat, undisturbed, with his fantasies.

Toward the end, he appeared to lose touch with reality. In 1989, Chikatilo began to be greatly agitated by the construction of the garage and the toilet in the courtyard by the apartment he was maintaining in Shakhty. It had been vacated by Lyudmilla when she remarried and moved to Kharkov, Ukraine. Feodosia wanted to keep it until Yuri got out of the army. Chikatilo wrote letters of protest to officials from Mikhail Gorbachev on down, complaining that the "Assyrian Mafia" (some Georgians believe they are descended from the biblical Assyrians) had bribed and corrupted the local government in an effort to despoil his living conditions. He traveled to Moscow and joined a protestors' encampment near Red Square. They were there to demand that the government do something to house Russian refugees from the growing ethnic conflicts in the Transcaucasus. That had nothing to do with Andrei Chikatilo's problems. Apparently, by that stage in his unfortunate life, Andrei Chikatilo just wanted to cry out.

At home, he would later tell Dr. Tkachenko, he read the newspaper accounts that began to appear about the *lesopolosa* killings. "He was prepared for arrest for a long time," Tkachenko said. "He perfectly understood that sooner or later it would end.'' Tkachenko had the impression that Chikatilo was anxious to unburden himself—that when the three *militsionery* finally surrounded him outside the children's café in Novocherkassk, Andrei Chikatilo felt something like relief.

13

The Trial

The most prominent feature in the courtroom where Andrei Chikatilo was tried was his cage.

The Rostov oblast courthouse is an ocher, Neoclassical building, set on a muddy lot a block from the city's central avenue, the name of which had been changed from Engels Street to Great Garden Street by the time the trial began on April 14, 1992. The courtroom, like nearly everything else in Russia, is a little threadbare. The stuffing is leaking out of the black leather padding on the door between the well of the court and the clerk's office. The clock in the back of the hall is stuck at 10:25. The seating for spectators and lawyers is a mishmash of old wooden chairs and metal benches that look like they might have been bought as surplus equipment from a Depression-era school. The presiding judge sits on a dais in a high-backed, carved wooden chair that still bears the hammer-and-sickle seal of the Soviet Union. Flanking him, in slightly smaller chairs, are the two citizens chosen as jurors for the trial. Though each has a vote under Russian law, the judge's opinion almost always determines the verdict.

All eyes were on the cage on the morning of April 14. The news of Chikatilo's arrest and a summary of his crimes had been released to the press by Kostoyev and Fetisov in December 1991. The newly liberated newspapers, both in Rostov and Moscow, sensed a story that would build circulation. They had published frequent articles about the upcoming trial. All two hundred of the courtroom seats were filled with people waiting to get a glimpse of the man the newspapers were calling "the Maniac."

A few minutes before ten o'clock, an escort of four uniformed soldiers from the Ministry of the Interior troops led Chikatilo up a stone staircase from a holding cell in the basement. The stairs led directly to the door of the cage, which is used for trials involving violent murders. The guards pushed Chikatilo into it, and he sat down on a bench. The cage door closed behind him.

Eighteen months in captivity had changed Chikatilo. He was gaunt, and he no longer had the little necktie and the eyeglasses that used to distinguish him as an intellectual. Instead, he had been issued a baggy gray suit and a slightly ridiculous red-white-and-blue sport shirt, in a checkerboard pattern that commemorated the 1980 Moscow Olympics. He would wear these clothes every day of the trial. Also gone was the thinning brown hair he had when arrested. His hair had gone gray since his arrest, and what was left of it had been shaved away by a prison barber. His bare, pale skull gleamed under the lights, giving him a diabolical look.

At the sight of him, an old woman in the spectators' section jumped up and screamed "Sadist! Murderer! What have you done?" She lunged dramatically toward the cage. A pair of *militsionery* gently restrained her, and she began pounding the chairs. Other spectators, many of them also relatives of the victims, joined in the wailing and screaming: "Murderer! Sadist!"

Chikatilo stared vacantly around the room for a moment, wide-eyed and open-mouthed, looking drugged. His head lolled on his neck. Then he turned and looked silently at the woman for a moment, almost smiling. He pulled a copy of a Russian tabloid called *Sobyesednik* from a sheaf of papers he was carrying and opened it to a full-page pinup picture of a seminude woman. He held the picture up in front of him like a shield as the old woman lunged against the grip of the *militsionery.* Then he yawned, theatrically, as if to say that this woman's anger and grief meant nothing to him.

Chikatilo's lawyer, Marat Khabibulin, had a table and chair in front of the cage. Khabibulin, who was thirty-seven as the trial opened, was a round-faced, amiable man. He had practiced law for fourteen years, and he had lost track of the number of accused murderers he had defended. He could, however, remember the number of his murder clients who had been found not guilty: two. He had, on the other hand, succeeded at getting judges to consider mitigating circumstances in his clients' cases and find them guilty of the Russian equivalent of second-degree murder. None of his clients had received the death sentence. They had gotten away with fifteen years in jail.

Realistically, that was about the best Khabibulin could hope to do for Andrei Chikatilo. He knew that, barring some kind of miraculous development, Chikatilo would be judged guilty. Khabibulin hoped, however, to save his client from the death penalty by persuading the court that Chikatilo was insane.

But Khabibulin faced handicaps that a Western defense lawyer would no doubt have considered intolerable. He had no right to call his own psychiatric experts, unless the court granted him special permission. He would have to content himself with cross-examining the state's psychiatric experts, led by Dr. Andrei Tkachenko. Nor could Khabibulin demand the right to call independent forensic science witnesses to challenge the state's explanation for the discrepancies between Chikatilo's blood type and the semen samples that had been typed AB. Unless the judge chose otherwise, the only evidence about the blood and semen analyses would come from Dr. Svetlana Gurtovaya.

Most important, he would have to confront the evidence amassed in two thick volumes—the protocols of Andrei Chikatilo's confessions. The Rostov bar association had appointed Khabibulin to defend Chikatilo in July 1991, shortly after the procurator, Isa Kostoyev, had concluded the interrogation and the visits to the various murder scenes. Prior to that, the only legal representation Chikatilo had was his hasty conference with Viktor Lyulichev, the attorney who then recused himself because he had worked in the procurator's office during the *lesopolosa* investigation. During the rest of the interrogation, Chikatilo signed various protocols, indicating that he had waived his right to counsel.

Not that Khabibulin's advice during the interrogation would necessarily have prevented Chikatilo from incriminating himself. In an interview during a trial recess one day, Khabibulin said that he considered it unethical to advise a client not to answer the procurator's questions. That was the way Khabibulin had been trained. Now that the Soviet Union has disintegrated, Russia may develop a more adversarial legal system. But such a system did not exist when Chikatilo's trial began. His confessions were considered legal, and Khabibulin had no hope of preventing their being introduced in evidence.

He also had little control over his client. The arrangement of the table and the cage prevented Khabibulin from seeing Chikatilo unless he turned around backward. It prevented any whispered conferences about responses to questions or restraining hands on the defendant's shoulder. To a much greater degree than a defendant in an American courtroom, Chikatilo was on his own.

That seemed to matter little to Chikatilo, Khabibulin said in an interview outside the courtroom.

"We first met in the cell at the KGB building. I introduced myself. He was polite, but I didn't sense that he was particularly interested in mounting a defense," Khabibulin recalled. "Sometimes a client will be overjoyed finally to have a chance to talk to a defense lawyer. He'll have a lot of questions. But Chikatilo seemed indifferent. I asked him, of course, why he had given such a detailed confession. He didn't really explain. He just said, 'Well, uh . . .' He basically avoided concrete answers. I had the impression that he felt that the fewer people he had around him, the better.''

The cacophonous wailing and screaming that greeted Chikatilo's first appearance lasted about five minutes, until Judge Leonid Akubzhanov entered the courtroom. The clerk and the *militsia* restored some order as Akubzhanov and the two jurors strode to their places.

Akubzhanov is a short, wiry, and intense man who often came to court with his necktie loosened and his shirtsleeves rolled up, revealing a tattoo on his left bicep. His manner was imperious and peremptory. If someone he didn't recognize showed up in the courtroom and began to take notes, he would stop the proceedings, summon the unknown individual to the bench, and check the person's credentials.

In addition to presiding, he often took on himself the function of prosecutor. He read long excerpts from the indictment and confessions into the record. If the questions posed to witnesses by the prosecuting attorneys did not strike him as tough enough, he asked his own. Western trials tend to become contests between opposing lawyers. Akubzhanov clearly saw this trial as a contest between himself and the Maniac.

The judge began by asking Chikatilo to stand and identify himself. Chikatilo complied. But that would be one of the last civil exchanges between them.

Over the next few weeks, Akubzhanov frequently hectored Chikatilo, who did not, of course, have the right to refuse to answer questions that might incriminate him. Akubzhanov's interrogations seemed to assume Chikatilo's guilt. They implied that the court's chief task was to understand how the crimes had occurred.

Why, he demanded to know one day, had Chikatilo cut the sex organs from so many victims?

Chikatilo stood mute for a moment. "I acknowledge what I signed [the confession protocols]," he finally mumbled.

How did you manage to lead away children from good families who should have known better than to go with you, the judge demanded on another occasion.

Chikatilo did not answer.

In May, Khabibulin had seen enough. He rose and made a formal complaint, charging that Akubzhanov was biased and asking that he be replaced by another judge. Akubzhanov turned to the prosecuting attorney, Nikolai Gerasimenko, and asked if he agreed. To Akubzhanov's evident surprise, Gerasimenko backed Khabibulin.

Akubzhanov rejected Khabibulin's complaint, and a few days later, he found a way to remove Gerasimenko. A relative of one of the victims stood up in court and protested that Gerasimenko was not being tough enough in prosecuting the case. Akubzhanov frequently tolerated this kind of spectator heckling during the trial. This time, he decided to take the remark seriously. He withdrew for a few moments, returned, and summarily dismissed Gerasimenko.

During the interval before Gerasimenko was replaced by a new prosecutor, named Anatoly Zadorozhny, Akubzhanov handled the prosecutor's role himself.

By June, the third month of the trial, the number of daily spectators had dwindled to a handful. The daily procedure involved reading into the record hundreds of pages of evidence, and after a few weeks, the entertainment value had diminished for the merely curious.

No one from Chikatilo's family ever showed up at the courthouse. After his name was published in the Russian press, Feodosia Chikatilo feared harassment from the families of the victims. She and her children changed their names and moved to an undisclosed city.

The confrontation between Chikatilo and Akubzhanov had by then degenerated into a shouting match in which Chikatilo seemed to be losing touch with reality.

On June 19, the defendant suggested that the judge might

want to engage with him in homosexual sex. When Akubzhanov told him to be quiet, Chikatilo refused.

"I'm the boss here," Chikatilo declared in a voice that was curiously both loud and indistinct. He spoke in a kind of deranged monotone that ran sentences together and lurched from one idea to another, with no apparent logical train of thought. "This is my funeral. Don't laugh at me. People have laughed at me all my life." He rambled on without pausing for breath, first talking about the death of his brother during the Ukrainian famine of the 1930s and then abruptly accusing Akubzhanov of being a member of the Assyrian Mafia that sided with the Communist Party's coup attempt of August 1991.

Akubzhanov, enraged, shouted for Chikatilo to sit down and be quiet. Chikatilo did not.

He had committed his murders in another life, on another planet, Chikatilo went on, shouting back. "This isn't a court. It's a farce!"

Akubzhanov then ordered the guards to remove Chikatilo from the courtroom and continued the trial without his presence. But the next morning, the guards trundled the defendant up the stairs and into his cage, and the confrontation resumed.

On June 24, Chikatilo stood up in his cage and began to unbutton his shirt. "It's time for me to give birth," he announced. Abruptly, he switched to another subject. Since he was Ukrainian by birth, he said he wanted a Ukrainian lawyer.

The next day, he stood up, his shirt again unbuttoned, and again demanded a Ukrainian lawyer. Then he opened his trousers and let them fall to the ground, exposing his flaccid penis. All the while, he yelled at Akubzhanov in his loud monotone. "You're laughing at me for engaging in onanism for forty years," he said. He broke into Ukrainian and said he was not a *khokhlushka*, a slang term for a girl. He might, it seemed, have been reliving some tormenting memory from his youth. Then the guards opened the cage door, jerked his pants back up, and hustled him down the stairs.

Opinions varied about the causes of Chikatilo's courtroom behavior. Marat Khabibulin said he warned Chikatilo several times, during conversations outside the courtroom, that his confrontation with the judge was not helping his case. Chikatilo responded by saying that he understood that, but was incapable of controlling his actions. The soldiers in Chikatilo's guard detachment said that the prisoner behaved calmly in his cell; they believed his outbursts were an effort to persuade Akubzhanov that he was insane and could not be held responsible for his crimes. Dr. Aleksandr Bukhanovsky, who observed many of the trial sessions, thought that Chikatilo's behavior was a response to the rough questioning by Akubzhanov. He believed Chikatilo had several distinct personalities. They included the submissive, incompetent husband and the enraged but calculating killer. Under the pressure of Akubzhanov's interrogation, he thought he had seen yet another emerge: the man of the incoherent monologues who exposed his penis to the court.

Bukhanovsky was prepared to testify that Chikatilo was in fact legally insane and could not be held responsible for his crimes. But Akubzhanov refused to allow Bukhanovsky to testify about Chikatilo's psychiatric condition. Nor did he grant Khabibulin's request that Chikatilo be examined by an independent panel of psychiatrists. In Bukhanovsky's opinion, Akubzhanov missed a chance to conduct a trial that would have illuminated the causes of Chikatilo's murderous behavior and perhaps would have educated the Russian people about some of the psychopathologies in their midst.

Instead, Akubzhanov relied entirely on the opinion of the official specialists at the Serbsky Institute and the Center for the Study of Sexual Pathology. Under Russian law, a criminal is legally responsible for his actions if the court reaches two conclusions: that the criminal understood what he was doing; and that he was capable of controlling his actions. Chikatilo, according to Dr. Tkachenko's testimony, met both conditions. He was legally sane and responsible for what he had done. Tkachenko made a special trip from Moscow to Rostov after the courtroom outbursts in June and examined Chikatilo again, for two hours. The doctor then repeated his judgment that Chikatilo was legally sane.

Tkachenko and the other psychiatrists based this judgment not so much on their examination of Chikatilo but on the way he committed his murders. Chikatilo was damned by the same cunning that had made him so hard to catch. He had shown that he was able select his victims carefully. He had shown that he could stop killing for nearly a year after his 1984 arrest. He had shown that he could refrain from killing anyone in Rostov for a year after that. "He always displayed well thought-out, controlled behavior that he could change in response to circumstances," Tkachenko said in an interview after his testimony. "I think Chikatilo could have refrained from killing if he had forced himself to. Or if the danger was real and strong that he would be caught. That's why he was able to stop for a while after his 1984 arrest."

Tkachenko readily acknowledged that the horrible nature of Chikatilo's crimes changed the standard for judging whether he was sane. "The more social significance the crime has, the more pathological the personality must be in order not to be able to abstain from that action," he explained. "A personality that is judged incapable of refraining from murder must be profoundly destroyed."

In other words, he was saying, if Chikatilo's crimes had been less horrible, if, for instance, his personality disorders had driven him merely to expose himself, he might have been found legally insane. But to be deemed incapable of refraining from murder, Chikatilo would have had to be all but foaming at the mouth. He would certainly have had to be incapable of the kind of care and planning required to commit fifty-three murders over a period of twelve years. It was a catch-22 of sorts for serial killers. To be capable of avoiding detection long enough to commit a series of murders, a person would have to be sane, at least by the definition imposed by Dr. Tkachenko and Judge Akubzhanov.

This standard of sanity would have been exposed to a stiff challenge in an American courtroom. Since the FBI, under the direction of ex–special agent Robert Ressler, began compiling and analyzing data about serial killers, many American criminologists have come to recognize two broad categories. Some serial killers are disorganized; they tend to be sloppy in the commission of their crimes and careless about the details of the murder scene and ritual. Others are highly organized, with precise rituals that are repeated time and again. Chikatilo, for the most part, fit the "organized" category. But that would not have meant, in an American courtroom, that he was sane. To take one example, Jeffrey Dahmer, the Milwaukee serial killer, also had an organized murder pattern. But he was judged insane.

Dr. Aleksandr Bukhanovsky had spent somewhat less time with Chikatilo than the psychiatrists at the Serbsky Institute. Kostoyev, at various times during the interrogation, had allowed him to see Chikatilo for a total of about forty hours. After that experience, Bukhanovsky agreed with Tkachenko on the judgment that Chikatilo suffered from organic brain abnormalities and a series of childhood traumas. But Bukhanovsky thought the Serbsky Institute opinion had been unduly influenced by Kostoyev, who selected the material from the investigation files that was sent to the psychiatrists for review. He differed with Tkachenko on the question whether Chikatilo was really capable of controlling his compulsions. "You can't get away from genetics," he said in an interview during the trial.

The trial, in the end, obscured more about the *lesopolosa* case than it clarified. On May 13, Chikatilo denied several murders that he had earlier confessed to.

"Of the fifty-three, how many do you acknowledge?" Akubzhanov demanded.

"Grushevsky Bridge, that didn't happen. [Grushevsky Bridge was the little bridge from which he had confessed to throwing the body of Yelena Zakotnova in 1978.] Also the one at Collective Farm No. 6, Stalmachenok. [Olga Stalmachenok was killed in Novoshakhtinsk in December 1982.] And the girl Tsana from Riga, I don't remember her. [Sarmite Tsana, a homeless woman originally from Latvia, was killed in July 1984 in Aviators' Park in Rostov.] I don't know whether you should count her or not. I doubt that I killed her. They used to talk to me from a list and I would remember things," Chikatilo said.

At a later session, Chikatilo added several other victims to the list of those he denied killing: Larisa Tkachenko, killed in 1981 in Rostov; Natalia Shalopinina, killed in 1984 in Rostov; and Ivan Bilovyetsky, killed in 1987 in Zaporozhe, a city in Ukraine.

At another session he said he had committed four additional murders that were not part of the accusation, although he could not give the names of three of the purported victims. They presumably were the three uncorroborated murders near Shakhty about which he had confessed to Kostoyev; the *militsia* had never been able to find any remains. The fourth was Irina Pogoryelova, the court secretary from Bataisk, killed in 1986. Chikatilo had denied killing her throughout his pre-trial interrogation. He gave no reason for choosing to admit her murder in court.

His denial of the six murders was spontaneous and surprised his lawyer. It made little sense from a legal point of view. The penalty for killing forty-seven people would be the same as the penalty for killing fifty-three.

To Viktor Burakov, who followed the trial from the *militsia* headquarters, Chikatilo's six denials and four new admissions were not surprising. Burakov had seen condemned men change their confessions before in an effort to delay the death penalty by requiring the *militsia* to investigate their new admissions. He assumed that Chikatilo had in mind the same thing.

The only denial that struck Burakov as plausible was that of the murder of Yelena Zakotnova. Burakov had gone over the record of the Zakotnova case carefully after Kostoyev elicited Chikatilo's confession. He still found it hard to believe that so many *syshchiki* and *sledovatyeli* could have erred in 1979, when they condemned and executed Aleksandr Kravchenko for that crime. He was not convinced that Chikatilo was guilty in the Zakotnova case. That, of course, did not change his certainty that Chikatilo had indeed committed the remaining fifty-two murders he was accused of.

The trial also failed to explain satisfactorily the discrepancy between Chikatilo's type A blood and the semen samples found on fourteen victims and analyzed as type AB. Judge Akubzhanov accepted a document from Dr. Gurtovaya's laboratory in Moscow attesting to the fact that Chikatilo's semen was type AB and stating that he was an example of an extremely rare, newly discovered phenomenon called "paradoxical secretion," in which an individual has blood of one type and secretions of another.

Dr. Gurtovaya's explanation would have been difficult or impossible to defend in a courtroom where the defense had the right to call its own expert witnesses. Special agent David Bigbee, chief of the FBI's DNA analysis laboratory in Washington, stated flatly in an interview for this book that "paradoxical secretion" does not exist.

So did one of the world's leading experts on blood and secretion analysis, Dr. Rafael Oriol of the French National Institute for Health and Medical Research in Paris. Dr. Oriol, after learning of Dr. Gurtovaya's theory, was convinced that the Soviet laboratory work on the killer's semen had been systematically flawed. He had, he said, helped organize an international conference on problems in blood typing in Lund, Sweden, in 1990. The Soviet delegation to the conference presented a newly developed laboratory reagent known as a monoclonal anti-B antibody. The Soviet antibody was found to work perfectly well in tests of blood. If it was applied to type B blood, it caused the cells to cluster under the microscope. But when it was used to type semen, the reagent caused a false B reading in some, but not all, type A semen. In other words, certain kinds of type A semen would be read, falsely, as AB. Until the international conference, the Soviet scientists had not been aware of the flaw in their reagent, Dr. Oriol said.

This monoclonal anti-B antibody was too new to have been in use in Rostov and Moscow in 1983 and 1984, when most of the semen analyses were done. Dr. Oriol speculated that some similar problem had caused a systematic error in typing Chikatilo's semen. That speculation was consistent with the article published by T. A. Stegnova in 1989 in the Russian journal *Forensic Medicine Expertise*, which found about a forty-percent error rate in semen samples initially judged to be type AB by Soviet forensic laboratories. But, due to Judge Akubzhanov's willingness to accept Dr. Gurtovaya's ''paradoxical secretion'' theory, there may never be a complete explanation of this critical aspect of the *lesopolosa* case.

On August 9, a warm and humid morning, the attorneys began their summations.

Andrei Chikatilo, wearing his Olympic souvenir sport shirt and baggy gray slacks, swayed gently on his bench, staring vacantly at the wall over Akubzhanov's dais, as he waited in his cage for the session to begin. His appearance had undergone another transformation since the start of the trial. The hair on his head had grown out somewhat, but it was completely gray, and his pate had gone bald. He had added a mustache, also gray, and resumed wearing glasses. He looked like neither the man who was arrested on November 20, 1990, nor the shaven-skulled demon who came to trial on

April 14, 1992. He looked like an old man, idle and used up.

Only a handful of spectators and journalists looked on as Judge Akubzhanov and the two jurors took their seats. Chikatilo rose to his feet and began declaiming in his loud monotone, talking about being exposed to radiation and still swaying back and forth. Suddenly, he let down his pants and exposed himself. The guards, quicker this time, were in his cage instantly, and they jerked Chikatilo down the staircase, pulling up his pants as they went. There was a crash and a shout from the cell block below, and then silence.

"We'll let him back in to have a final word if he wants it," Akubzhanov said.

Marat Khabibulin rose at his table, wearing an open white shirt, blue trousers, striped socks, and gray sandals. "I have no confidence that my voice will be heard above the general outcry to kill Chikatilo," he began.

He questioned the competence of Russian forensic psychiatry. "A healthy person couldn't have committed all these murders," he maintained. He again questioned Akubzhanov's objectivity and his decision not to allow the defense to obtain and present testimony from independent psychiatrists.

Khabibulin did not try to refute each charge against Chikatilo. He did raise four of the cases Chikatilo had denied, pointing out some flaws in the prosecution's evidence. A witness who came forward after the 1990 arrest and stated that she saw Chikatilo with Olga Stalmachenok had not come forward when police scoured Novoshakhtinsk for witnesses in 1982. There were no travel records to place Chikatilo in Ukraine when Ivan Bilovyetsky was killed. The sperm found on Larisa Tkachenko had initially been analyzed as type B, and was now being called undetermined. "Chikatilo was beaten down and indifferent when he was being interrogated," he said. "His confessions are dubious and senseless. How could he have given up his desire for self-preservation? It had to have been coerced. I don't know why he did it. But

I know it wasn't sincere. It was the fever of a sick man, reacting to prompting.''

He could not, of course, refute the two most convincing items of evidence against his client. The first was the way Chikatilo had led the investigators to murder scene after murder scene, especially the previously undiscovered grave of Aleksei Khobotov. The second was the fact that after Chikatilo's 1990 arrest, the *lesopolosa* killings stopped. Khabibulin mentioned neither. After an hour and forty minutes, he asked the judge and jurors to find Chikatilo not guilty, wiped his brow, and sat down. Akubzhanov declared a recess until the following day.

The next morning, Chikatilo was back in his cage, a slight smirk on his face. His guards had fashioned a belt from a length of rope and knotted it at his waist; he would need time to untie the knot if he decided to drop his trousers again. But this time, Chikatilo was in a mood to sing. As Akubzhanov took his seat, he broke into the ''Internationale,'' the anthem of the international Communist movement. When the song was over, he launched another monologue, rambling from the Assyrian Mafia to the nuclear disaster at Chernobyl to the independence movement in Ukraine.

Akubzhanov let Chikatilo go on for five minutes, then ordered him removed. After the guards had trundled him away, the judge turned toward the benches where journalists were sitting. ''I let him go on a little longer than I usually do for the benefit of the reporters here for the final arguments,'' he said.

Prosecutor Anatoly Zadorozhny began his summation by noting that 1990, the year of Chikatilo's arrest, was also the year of ''the two hundred and fiftieth birthday of the Marquis de Sade.''

Sadism, he said, ''is not a new phenomenon. But this is not a man who is sick or psychopathic. Leading experts have said he doesn't lack the ability to understand what he is doing or to control his actions.''

Zadorozhny went on to recount, drily and without emotion, the details of each of the crimes in the accusation. He asked for the death penalty, and sat down.

Judge Akubzhanov ordered Chikatilo returned to the courtroom. When the prisoner was again in his cage, he informed him that this was his final opportunity to say something in his own defense.

Chikatilo refused to speak or even to rise. He sat in his cage, mute, with his head bowed, and said nothing.

After glaring at the defendant for a few minutes, Akubzhanov declared a two-month recess to allow himself and the jurors to review the evidence and prepare their verdict. Then he walked down the center aisle and left the courtroom.

Chikatilo sat in his cage, waiting for his guards to take him away. Some spectators started to trickle out; others milled around, talking about the trial. A young man named Vladimir Kulyevatsky stepped out of the crowd and walked up to the cage. He took a small, heavy piece of metal from his pocket and hurled it through the bars of the cage. It hit Chikatilo in the chest and bounced to the floor. Chikatilo blinked, but said nothing. Kulyevatsky, an unemployed factory worker, was the half brother of Lyudmilla Alekseyeva, killed in 1984, and he had watched most of the trial. A sympathetic *militsioner* told him to get out of the courtroom before he got into trouble.

It would have been difficult to find many people in Rostov who did not sympathize with Vladimir Kulyevatsky. A random sampling of opinion on the streets found no one who thought that the court should spare Chikatilo's life, either on the grounds of insanity or because of general opposition to the death penalty. Russia is a country where millions of people have been unfairly put to death by their government, under both czars and commissars. But that has not, apparently, diminished public support for capital punishment. Even people who believed that Chikatilo was too insane to control his impulses tended to think that execution was the right way to deal with him. "Even if they sent him to jail for life, he might escape and kill someone again. Better to execute him," said a man named Volodya, whose view seemed to sum up that of many people.

On October 14, the courtroom was packed with people as Akubzhanov read the verdict. He took three hours to repeat the list of crimes and quote from Chikatilo's confessions regarding each. Some victims' relatives sobbed and wailed as the details of their children's deaths were read. Nurses stationed in the courtroom distributed valerian, a mild sedative sold over the counter in Russia.

Akubzhanov then pronounced Chikatilo guilty of five molestation charges and fifty-two of the fifty-three counts of murder. In one case, that of an Armenian girl named Laura Sarkisyan, who disappeared in 1983, Akubzhanov ruled that there was insufficient evidence to convict Chikatilo. He had confessed to killing an Armenian girl in that year, at about the same time as Sarkisyan had been reported missing. But the *militsia* had found only scattered remains that could not be precisely identified.

Whether the actual number of victims was fifty-two, fifty-three, or more, Chikatilo was the most savage serial killer to emerge from a modern society. The *Guinness Book of World Records* notes the case of Pedro Alonso Lopez, who confessed to the murder of three hundred girls, none over the age of ten, in Colombia, Ecuador, and Peru between 1973 and 1980. But after his confession, only fifty-three bodies were found. And Alonso Lopez did not disembowel his victims, as Chikatilo did.

Despite the number and nature of the crimes he found Chikatilo to have committed, Akubzhanov declared Chikatilo legally sane. "At every stage of his crimes, from the beginning to the end, Chikatilo was in complete control of all his actions," the judge pronounced.

"Why me? I demand the podium! Get me a lawyer!"

Chikatilo burst out as the verdict was read. "I didn't confess to anything! Show me the corpses!" He pressed his head against the bars of his cage before the guards led him down the stairs again.

In the spectator section, there were calls for blood. "They should rip him apart like a dog," said Lydia Khobotova, mother of Aleksei Khobotov. "I hope he dies the most horrible death, like my son did."

"Let me tear him apart with my own hands!" another woman shouted.

The next day, Akubzhanov gave the listeners the sentence that came closest, under law, to what they wanted. He condemned Chikatilo to be executed.

Marat Khabibulin prepared an appeal. In a Western legal system, given the case against him, Chikatilo might never have been convicted, at least not of fifty-two counts of aggravated murder. Independent psychiatrists would doubtless have testified that he was not legally responsible for his crimes. Independent forensic experts would have shredded the state's explanation of the discrepancy between Chikatilo's blood type and the semen found on the victims, which was the primary physical evidence in the case.

Most important, the case against Chikatilo depended largely on his confession. No Western defense lawyer would have permitted Chikatilo to talk freely to the investigators without first securing some kind of plea bargain, most likely lifetime confinement in a mental institution.

Khabibulin knew, he said, that all those factors would carry weight in a Western setting. He could not judge how they would be received in Moscow, where the Russian Supreme Court would review the trial and conviction. Under the old Soviet system, of course, an appeal would have had no chance to succeed. But these were new times. The Supreme Court was, as Chikatilo's trial ended, hearing a lawsuit over the abolition of the Communist Party. It might be willing to consider arguments that Kostoyev and Akubzhanov had violated Andrei Chikatilo's rights. Khabibulin could not guess, he said, how the appeal would end.

Andrei Chikatilo went back to his cell in the KGB building to await his fate.

Well before the trial ended, finger-pointing began among the investigators.

Procurator Isa Kostoyev, in a series of interviews in Moscow, told journalists that it was not his fault that it took so long to catch Chikatilo. He blamed the Rostov *militsia* for failing to follow up on his theory that the killer was someone who had already been under suspicion, as Chikatilo had been in 1984. In some interviews, he suggested that the *militsia* had all but hidden the file on Chikatilo from him.

That assertion was impossible to credit. In the booklet on the case that Viktor Burakov compiled and disseminated throughout the Soviet Union in 1987, Chikatilo was listed as the ninth suspect. That booklet was a basic primer on the case and available to anyone working on the investigation. If Kostoyev had not read it and did not become aware of Chikatilo until he surfaced at the Donleskhoz station in 1990, it could only be because Kostoyev had failed to do his homework.

Kostoyev also tried to denigrate the contributions of Dr. Aleksandr Bukhanovsky to the investigation. He told interviewers that Bukhanovsky's profile had been flawed, and hinted that Bukhanovsky was trying to profit financially from his involvement in the case. The latter insinuation angered Bukhanovsky, who wrote both of his profiles gratis, as a service to the investigation. Bukhanovsky countered by telling interviewers that if Kostoyev had only had the sense to use the profile he had written, by narrowing the search to heterosexuals with backgrounds in teaching and factory supply, Kostoyev could have wrapped the case up in 1987, saving more than a dozen victims' lives.

"Kostoyev kept looking for homosexuals. It was a reign of terror for them," Bukhanovsky said.

They were not the only ones. At least five people committed suicide as a result of the killings and the investigation: Vladimir Pecheritsa, the convicted rapist who fell under suspicion in Donskoi after the murder of Lyubov Biryuk in 1982; Viktor Chernyayev, Yevgeny Voluyev, and Anatoly Otryeznov, the three gay suspects in Rostov; and Vladimir Dyakonov, father of the victim Aleksandr Dyakonov. He slashed his wrists in 1990, a year after his son's death, apparently because of his remorse at having beaten his son the day before Chikatilo encountered him. And there was the matter of Aleksandr Kravchenko, executed in 1979 for the slaying of Yelena Zakotnova, a crime for which Chikatilo was convicted in 1992.

Burakov and Fetisov could say with justification that Chikatilo would have been caught far earlier but for the mistakes in the laboratory work. Both, though, were quick to acknowledge that the investigators had committed many mistakes, particularly in the early years of the case. There was the failure, in 1985, to find the travel records at NEVZ that would have established Chikatilo's presence in Moscow when Natalia Pokhlistova was killed. There was the failure, in 1984, to show Chikatilo to the witnesses who had seen a man walking away from the center of Novoshakhtinsk with Dmitri Ptashnikov. There was the failure to link Chikatilo to two victims whom he had known, Tatyana Petrosyan and Irina Dunenkova. But all those paled beside the decision made in 1984 that Chikatilo's blood type exonerated him.

The Ministry of the Interior opened two internal investigations into the *militsia*'s conduct during the case, one reviewing the Kravchenko conviction in 1979 and the other the treatment of Yuri Kalenik and other young men associated with the *internat* for the retarded in Gukovo, treatment that led to Kalenik's spending five years in jail.

But the latter investigation was apparently not very thorough. Kalenik, in an interview in the summer of 1992, said that no one had approached him to ask how he came to confess to several of the first murders in the *lesopolosa* series. If anyone had, he would have heard a frightening story.

During his first days of interrogation, Kalenik recounted, the *syshchik* Valery Beklemishchev "would give me hints. He said, 'We've been following you, we know everything. We know you killed.' He told me what I was accused of. He prompted me. He didn't give me all the details, but hints. They took me for a fool, because I'd been in the *internat*. But I'm not a fool. I realized it had to do with rape and killing and cutting eyes out.

"At the beginning I said I hadn't done anything, but he said, 'We know you did it,' and started to frighten me. He said they'd put me in a situation where I'd have no choice but to confess. Then they told me I was a retarded kid and that even if I confessed, I couldn't be convicted because of that. They took out a law book and showed me where it said that. Beklemishchev hit me on the head, not hard, and said, 'Think it over.' Then they took me back to my cell. The next day it started over again.

"They beat me," Kalenik said. This was not done by Beklemishchev, he went on, but by underlings. "It happened in the cell block. Then it happened when I was being put in a police van. A sergeant beat me."

Kalenik snorted when asked if the beatings had injured him. "Let me tell you, the *militsia* can beat you up scientifically," he replied. "They don't leave traces. They know where to hit you—around the kidneys, for instance. They cover their hands with towels so there's no blood. They're experienced at it. And you're simple and low. They tell you, 'You can't prove anything. We'll be right.' "

After a few days of this, Kalenik gave up. He relied in part on the assurance that, as a retarded person, he could not be convicted.

"I confessed," he would say nine years later. "I wanted

to save my health. I had no trouble making it up, fantasizing, because they'd told me a lot about the crimes already. As soon as I started to confess they stopped beating me. They started bringing me cigarettes.''

After his false confession, Kalenik found it easy to pass the next tests. The investigators showed him groups of three photographs, one of which would be a victim. ''At first I might point to an entirely different person. And then they'd say, 'Think hard.' You understand? They'd help me. So I'd point to another one.''

In much the same way, he said, he passed the test of finding the crime scenes. ''They'd prompt me,'' he recalled. ''Like at the music school in Novoshakhtinsk. They'd point it out. I knew that I was supposed to have met her at a school. I figured it out right away. They directed me with clever words. They wouldn't say, 'Go that way.' No. They're more clever than that. They'd do it with hints. I can't explain it exactly because it was so long ago, you know? If I went in the wrong direction, they'd say, 'Think better.' ''

Kalenik's story, had anyone listened to it, would have made a convincing argument for the wisdom of providing effective legal counsel to Russian suspects during interrogation.

Yuri Kalenik, like many of the individuals whose lives were disrupted by the *lesopolosa* case, wasted no energy following Andrei Chikatilo's trial. He was busy trying to survive in the battered Russian economy. After his release from prison in 1988, he did not return to the job he had trained for, laying floors. Instead, he found work as a boiler stoker at the *internat* in Gukovo, where he was paid the equivalent of a few dollars a month and felt somewhat secure. He tried, he said, to avoid the *militsia* whenever he saw them.

Valery Ivanenko, Viktor Burakov's informant in Rostov's gay community, suffered a stroke shortly after Chikatilo's arrest. He was paralyzed and unable to speak for six days, and then he died. His mother had died some years before, and he was alone and friendless. Viktor Burakov arranged for his funeral.

Boris Panfilov, swept up like more than a hundred other men in the investigation of gay suspects, tried to reassemble his life after getting out of prison. He returned to school and was taking economics courses, hoping to become a businessman in Russia's new, market economy.

Dr. Aleksandr Bukhanovsky took advantage of the changing economic system to become a medical entrepreneur. Though he maintained his position at the Rostov Institute of Medicine, he founded a private psychiatric clinic he called Phoenix. Some of the patients who came to him, he said, were men with conditions very similar to Andrei Chikatilo's in its earlier stages. He worried about whether Russia would be visited by a plague of serial killers.

Bukhanovsky continued to work with the *militsia*, writing profiles for use in murder investigations. And he began to organize what he hoped would be an international symposium on serial killers in Rostov in 1993, with the Chikatilo case as a focal point of study.

A few of the *militsionery* involved in the case went on to higher positions. Vladimir Kolyesnikov, who made the arrest of Chikatilo, received his general's star shortly afterward and transferred to Moscow. He became chief of the national division of criminal apprehension, in charge of monitoring searches for criminals throughout Russia.

Mikhail Fetisov preferred to remain in Rostov. After the aborted coup of August 1991, he dropped his membership in the banned Communist Party. Soon afterward, he hung a picture of Boris Yeltsin on the wall behind his desk. Fetisov tried to implement his plan to modernize the *militsia* with computers and new radio cars. In the summer of 1992, his office got its first personal computer.

Viktor Burakov was promoted to lieutenant colonel and remained in charge of the special unit that investigates sex murders in Rostov. He never bothered to remove the portrait of Feliks Dzerzhinski, founder of the KGB, from his office; it stands atop some of the file cabinets that hold the data compiled during the *lesopolosa* case. Burakov received no medals for his role in bringing Chikatilo to justice. This was not surprising, given the number of important people he had disagreed with during the investigation. He worried that he might reach the age of fifty in 1996 without making it to the rank of colonel. If that happens, he will have to retire, and he does not want to give up *militsia* work.

When he reflected upon the *lesopolosa* case, it seemed to him like a long nightmare. He remembered years when his head constantly ached and he could not get on a train without seeking on the face of every passenger the guilty eyes of a killer. He was not a religious man, but sometimes he thought he should be grateful to God, or to some natural force, for giving him the will to continue the pursuit for eight years.

He tried, after the Chikatilo interrogation was over, to spend more time with his younger son, Maksim. He knew that for the sake of the *militsia* and the *lesopolosa* investigation, he had left the rearing of his older son, Andrei, largely to his wife. Now he also spent more time on the tiny plot of land that he had been given, along with other *militsia* officers, on an old collective farm just outside Rostov. He put a fence around it, and his wife, Svetlana, planted grapes, cabbages, tomatoes, peppers, a pear tree, and an apple tree to supplement the family larder.

On weekends and during his summer vacation, while Svetlana tended the garden, Burakov began to build a brick cottage, with two rooms below and a single loft room above. The work went very slowly. Bricks and mortar were hard to find and increasingly expensive. But by the end of Chikatilo's trial, he had the walls built, topped by a tin roof. He thought that if he ever finished the interior, he and Svetlana might move there, leaving the apartment in Rostov for one of his sons.

One thing he did not have any qualms about was the prospect that Andrei Chikatilo would be executed. "As long as there have been civilized societies, there has always been a death penalty," he said, slightly puzzled that the question would even be raised. "It seems to me that for terrible, murderous crimes there must be a death penalty."

He thought, he said, that the best way to deal with Andrei Chikatilo would be to let the executioners do their job in the prescribed Russian manner: to arrive, unannounced, at his cell one morning; to take him from the cell down a dark corridor to the execution room; and there to put a pistol to his ear and a bullet through his misbegotten brain.

A Note on Sources and Names

The research for this book was done with the cooperation of Viktor Burakov and Mikhail Fetisov of the Rostov *militsia*. Both of them gave generously of their time in answering my questions. They helped arrange interviews with other law enforcement officials. And they provided access to investigative files, confession protocols, videotapes, and other records pertaining to the *lesopolosa* case. They spoke almost entirely on the record, even in response to sensitive questions. They neither asked for nor received any editorial control over the manuscript. All the interpretations and judgments—as well as any mistakes—are mine. I am deeply grateful to both of them for their help.

Dozens of other people graciously answered my questions, even when they touched on events that were still painful to them. Some went well out of their way to be helpful. Yuri Kalenik, for instance, rode an *elektrichka* for six hours to respond to my request for an interview. I am grateful to him and to all the others I interviewed both in Rostov and in Moscow. Their names are all cited in the text.

Dr. Aleksandr Bukhanovsky and Dr. Andrei Tkachenko, two psychiatrists who worked extensively with Andrei Chikatilo, were particularly generous with their recollections and time. Dr. Bukhanovsky showed me excerpts from his profile of the *lesopolosa* killer, and Dr. Tkachenko read at length from his files on Chikatilo's psychiatric evaluation. I wish to thank them both.

In a number of instances, I have changed the names of people involved in the case. Several gay men preferred that their real names not be published. So did Andrei Chikatilo's former son-in-law. The names of two *militsia* informants were changed at the request of Viktor Burakov. The names of several people who fell under suspicion during the investigation have been changed to respect their privacy.

My work was made much easier by the assistance of Olga Kolobova and Nikolai Sazhnev, who cheerfully transcribed hours of taped interviews, smoothing out my Russian grammar in the process.

My landlady in Rostov-on-Don, Valeria Ivanovna Krupenina, provided a spare room to sleep and work in and all the *baklazhan* I could eat. I am only sorry I didn't have room for more of her delicious cakes.

Robert Ressler, who pioneered in the FBI's study of serial killers and is now a private consultant, helped me understand some of the general features of these crimes. David Bigbee, the special agent in charge of the FBI's DNA analysis unit, patiently tutored me in the basics of blood and semen analysis. So did Dr. Rafael Oriol of the French National Institute for Health and Medical Research.

I would like to thank Rob and Web Stone for introducing me to the project, and Rafe Sagalyn and Kim Witherspoon for expediting it. Linda Healey, my editor at Pantheon, deftly saw the project through.

Finally, I must thank my wife, Ann, and my children, Peter and Catherine, for their abundant love and forbearance.

Chevy Chase, Maryland
January 1993